THE POETRY OF

Tennyson

THE POETRY OF

Tennyson

Alastair W. Thomson

ROUTLEDGE & KEGAN PAUL
London and New York

First published in 1986
by Routledge & Kegan Paul plc
11 New Fetter Lane, London EC4P 4EE

Published in the USA by
Routledge & Kegan Paul Inc.
in association with Methuen Inc.
29 West 35th Street, New York, NY 10001

Set in 11 point Garamond
by Inforum Ltd, Portsmouth
and printed in Great Britain
by St Edmundsbury Press Ltd
Bury St Edmunds, Suffolk

Library of Congress Cataloging in Publication Data
Thomson, Alastair W.

The poetry of Tennyson.

Bibliography: p.
Includes index.
1. Tennyson, Alfred Tennyson, Baron, 1809–1892—
Criticism and interpretation. I. Title.
PR5588.T56   1986   821'.8   86–3230
British Library CIP data available
ISBN 0–7102–0716–6

Contents

Preface

This study of Tennyson's poetry is intended to be of use to students of Tennyson, and of nineteenth-century English poetry generally. It is not, in any sense, a radical revision of generally accepted opinions about Tennyson. To examine the weaknesses of *Idylls of the King*, for example, or to limit the unity of *In Memoriam* to speculative processes, and the operation of the will, is hardly revision, if only since his contemporaries on the whole did not think *In Memoriam* a single poem, and did not think that the *Idylls* were Tennyson at his greatest. Later attempts to simplify him psychological-ly, or to think of him as a remarkable mystic, or to argue for the *Idylls* as the greatest poem of its age, are misleading, though useful in making us look closely again. A word about some modern criticism may be in order. Tennyson had long been out of favour when in 1948 Paull Baum published a hostile study, *Tennyson Sixty Years After*, which may have helped to cause a reaction. Baum is often rewarding, though capable of odd misreadings, but he writes, as someone once said, like a man performing a stern duty; the detail lavished on the poet's funeral by way of introduction leaves rather an unpleasant taste. Harold Nicolson's *Tennyson: Aspects of His Life, Character, and Poetry* of 1923 had established him as two Tennysons: the haunted private poet of the early years, and the serene official poet of the later; the division is perhaps typical of the period. He had always had his defenders, and Humbert Wolfe's brief *Tennyson* of 1930 put the case for him with considerable verve. But F.E.L. Priestley's influential paper of 1949 on *Idylls of the King*, together with E.D.H. Johnson's essay in *The Alien Vision of Victorian Poetry* of 1952, represented something of a new departure in Tennyson studies. One of the critics who did most to revise opinion was J.H. Buckley, whose *Tennyson: The Growth of a Poet* of 1960 made extended claims for him as a major poet, in particular the Tennyson of the *Idylls*, but also tended, as Donald Smalley said, to present a Tennyson larger than life-size. Smalley's review article of 1962, 'A New Look at Tennyson – and especially the Idylls', was properly cautious of large claims, the more so because he felt that Buckley's eloquent book might become the standard work. As to what the general opinion may be twenty-five years later, it is plain that although the standard two Tennysons view of the 1920s and later is outmoded, authoritative studies like those of Christopher Ricks and A. Dwight Culler have made it difficult to accept the major poet of Buckley, despite the enthusiasm in many quarters for the *Idylls*. Eliot's opinion is still the best: a great poet, and one who might have been a consummate master of minor forms, but who took to turning out large patterns on a machine.

As for the *Idylls*, which have been the focal point for several revisions, their effect of directly translated concept can probably best be understood in the context of that insistent Romantic idea of 'some work of glory', which Wordsworth despairs over at the beginning of *The Prelude*. In dealing with a late and brilliant idyll like *The Holy Grail* (which even for some unconvinced readers is Tennyson nearly at the height of his powers), we have to understand how and why he nudges the reader into acceptance. (Perhaps I have referred to Wordsworth too often in this study, but it is a comparison which is often forced on one.) One reason for the interest which the *Idylls* have aroused since the late 1940s may be the decline of Britain as a world power since 1945, and a consequent interest, particularly in North America, in a 'matter of Britain'; David Jones's experience of American interest and British lack of interest in these matters is probably significant. One's only quarrel with Eliot's remark is that the distinction he implies probably does less than justice to Tennyson's minor forms. Some of his finest work is in the exquisite friendship or social poems of his later years, and also in poetry like *To Virgil*, which is very much a poem of his maturity. In a way, this is appropriate, since we sometimes feel that he is not only a highly literary poet drawing extensively on his predecessors, but a man who felt himself to be nearly at the end of a tradition, in spite of the exhortations in *Merlin and the Gleam*. The lines about old Philip's 'weary daylong chirping' in *The Brook* are like a passing dilution of Homer's old men rejoicing like grasshoppers; *Morte d'Arthur* is like a distillation of the sense of loss and irresolution in the *Aeneid*. It is probably symptomatic that he showed few signs of thinking of his poetry as an exploration, or as anything other than personal support, again in spite of *Merlin and the Gleam*. *The Epic* of 1842 has been described as showing faith in poetry; one of its strongest effects for me is its sense of the homeless state of poetry in a new world. Arnold thought poetry might do more than that in his age. But even allowing for the difference in age, and for the younger poet's later rejection of his visions as hallucinations, few differences could be greater than that between the Tennyson of the later *Idylls*, and the sixteen-year-old Rimbaud who in 1871 spoke of the poet as *un voyant*, a stealer of celestial fire.

The other side of it, of course, is the Tennyson who may be moving in the direction of Symbolism, whose fluidity, and willingness to allow things to melt into each other, may not quite suggest synaesthesia, but look forward to much of what was to come. It is also fairly clear that some of what he looks forward to in twentieth-century English poetry is a refuge in religious or aesthetic experience. We are less conscious of this in Yeats, the greatest of his successors, who found strength elsewhere: in Ireland's history and aspirations, in the roles by which he met his age, and most of all in the passionate language, both heightened and direct, by which he made himself a part of past and present. There is a singleness in Yeats which casts a shadow on Tennyson, in spite of the great authority of the Victorian poet, and that variety in him which Eliot singled out for praise.

I wanted to indicate something of Tennyson's variety, and to pay some tribute to it, which is why so much attention has been given to so many poems. Perhaps to too many poems, and one effect of a survey like this could easily be to deaden rather than stimulate interest. My admiration for Tennyson began very early, but it was generally accompanied even at that age by a sense that distinctions had to be made. If some of the indications and distinctions that follow are found useful by readers of nineteenth-century English poetry, the study will have served its purpose. The recent critics to whom I owe a particular debt are F.E.L. Priestley, Jerome Buckley, Christopher Ricks, and A. Dwight Culler. I am grateful to J.M. Gray, A.N. Jeffares, George R. Kay, Stewart Sanderson, Walter Baumann, Hilda D. Spear, Alan Peacock, and Robert Ussher, from whose generously given advice I have benefited; the errors are my own. My thanks are also due to the Director and staff of the Tennyson Research Centre at Lincoln; to the Librarian of Trinity College, Cambridge; and to the librarians of the University of Ulster, in particular to Miss Margaret Vowles. Some of the material appeared in a paper, 'Tennyson and Some Doubts', which was published in the *English Association Annual* for 1982, and I am grateful to the English Association for permission to reprint it. I should like to thank the following for permission to reprint copyright material: Constable and Mary M. Martin for the quotation on page 253 from Helen Waddell's *Mediaeval Latin Lyrics*; A.P. Watt Ltd and Robert Graves for the quotation on page 89 from Robert Graves's 'Ogres and Pygmies'; Michael B. Yeats and Macmillan London Ltd for the quotation on page 218 from 'The Municipal Gallery Revisited' from *Collected Poems of W.B. Yeats*.

CHAPTER I

Early Experiments

Unlike Shelley and Keats, who were born only seventeen and fourteen years earlier, the Victorian Romantic Tennyson shows, on the whole, a disinclination to attempt high themes in long poems. He has no *Prometheus Unbound*, and no *Hyperion*. *The Princess* is an attempt at Shakespearian comedy in narrative form; *In Memoriam* is a sequence of elegiac and meditative pieces, whose mode is largely confessional; *Maud*, in which some of the frustrations of his youth may have found expression, can hardly be said to be planned on a grand scale. Tennyson's nearest attempt at a high theme in a long poem is probably the *Idylls of the King*, which on the whole is (or are) a failure. The age too late of nineteenth-century England and post-Revolutionary Europe undoubtedly had something to do with his avoidance of high themes, as did his tendency to retreat from ideas about the final authority of poetry, in spite of the large utterance of the early Cambridge piece *The Poet*. 'I thought that a small vessel, built on fine lines, is likely to float further down the steam of Time than a big raft.'[1] This was how he later explained his decision not to write an Arthurian epic, in twelve books. It was a well-turned description of his aspirations, and also an indication of the refusals that helped to define them.

Tennyson's tendency to avoid large constructions, unlike Shelley and Keats – although we cannot say that he drifted into *Idylls of the King*, there is little to suggest any initial

single idea of a poem 'in twelve books', to complete its title –
concurs, not surprisingly, with an apparent diffidence about
myth. Admittedly the concept of the older poets as men
reviving myth in an age of expansion will hardly do; *Prometheus Unbound*, and the acceptance of a great principle of
change in *Hyperion*, are also a comment on suffering and
oppression in post-war England and Europe. And though the
method of all-embracing myth or allegorising is commensurate with poets of the intellectual authority of Shelley and
Keats, it also has to do with a willingness to remove such
statements from identifiable public ground, which has sometimes been described – not always accurately – as an uncertainty about their public. But it cannot be denied that Tennyson had less need for myth, because he was a less intellectual
poet. There is a good deal of the confessional as well as the
elegiac in him, and his myths tend to be private, expressing
personal doubts and anxieties. He claimed that the confessional (and the triumph) of *In Memoriam* could be heard as
the cry of the whole human race rather than his own, but the
cry of *In Memoriam* is representative of type, rather than
representation. Keats's idea of the poet in *The Fall of Hyperion* is part of a larger structure, which it may have been
intended to inform. Tennyson's idea of the artist in *The Lady
of Shalott* is expressed in a haunting myth which is not so
much concerned with the choice between being an actor or a
dreaming thing, as with the impossibility for the artist of
continuing in either state. In *Tithonus* he uses a minor myth
to express the characteristic desolation of a state between life
and death, time and eternity. *The Kraken* presents a monster
whose shape can only be guessed, which sleeps on the ocean
bed, and will be known only when it rises on the day of the
latter fires. It is typical of Tennyson that the myth which most
haunted him seems to have been that of the dying king,
towards which the *Idylls* work: the king who does not quite
die, but who leaves the land desolate, and who may or may
not return. Significantly enough, one of the most poignant of
his short poems, *Break, break, break*, is a recognition of
meaninglessness in a world unshaped by metaphor, and so
not capable of myth. 'Without Neptune,' Lorca said, 'the sea
would be deaf, and the waves owe half of their fascination to

the human invention of Venus'; the world of *Break, break, break* is a world which gives neither metaphors nor reasons.[2] In the late dramatic monologue *Demeter and Persephone*, of 1889, he uses ancient myth to indicate the coming of kindlier gods than Dis and Zeus. Here, where it is less personal, the myth is very much under control and just a little distant. (Given the strength of Tennyson's faith, we can hardly speak of myth-making in *In Memoriam* VII, where the bitter 'He is not here,' with its dry reference to the angels before the empty tomb, is finally answered by so much in the closing sections.) *Merlin and the Gleam*, also of 1889, has something of the power of myth about it, expressing the magical powers of the artist, not as *The Lady of Shalott* had expressed them. But the gleam that Merlin has followed, the thing always seen and never grasped, suggests an idea of poetry which differs significantly from some at least of what can be inferred from the larger myth-making and allegorising of Tennyson's immediate predecessors.

The Tennysonian norm seems to be the Theocritean *English Idyls*, and their later development away from idyll, as in *Enoch Arden*; the elegies, and dark poems of loss; and the later poems of friendship. (The satire of the fine dramatic monologue *St Simeon Stylites* is not really part of his norm, which is a pity.) There are some high enough subjects, of a recognisable sort, in his first published collection, *Poems by Two Brothers* of 1827: *God's Denunciations against Pharaoh-Hophra*, *The Fall of Jerusalem*, *Lamentation of the Peruvians*. The 1827 poems are exercises in literature, in which he presents himself to himself as a poet of the age. The variety in stanza form is only superficially that of real exercise, or experiment; the stanzas are often like moulds into which the legitimate lamentations, farewells, and prophecies have been poured. One early piece in which he is willing to attempt a high theme is the unpublished *Armageddon*. Like the other early and unpublished pieces *The Coach of Death* and *The Devil and the Lady*, *Armageddon* is unfinished. That it breaks off before the last battle has been described as a kind of evasion of apocalypse, which may be partly explained by the nature of his faith, and his rejection of all forms, creeds, or definitions of the divine.[3] It has also been said to be characteristic of Tennyson's avoidance of definitive outcomes, as in *Ulysses*, where the speaker lingers on the shore, or in *St Simeon Stylites*, where the monologue ends with Simeon still thinking he has received the crown of sanctity. This is a feature of Tennyson's poetry which has interested several critics.[4] The idea is a little misleading so far as *Armageddon* is concerned. In fact, there may not be any common reason for the fact that the best of the early pieces were not completed, and to bring them all under the head of significantly non-definitive outcomes may be to see more than is there. In *The Devil and the Lady*, for example, it is not very difficult to understand how the widening gap between satiric farce and symbolism could not be bridged. The early *Perdidi Diem* has also been quoted, yet there is probably a simple enough reason for the fact that it remains a fragment. Two parts of the poem were written, and a third at least envisaged, since the MS has 'III' marked.[5] The despair of part I is uncompromising: 'I never *lived* a day, but daily die.' The second part of it is, on the face of it, a visionary reflux on this, with its 'sovran subtil influence' from God which broadens down through circles and files until it reaches the base of the great cone, the planets which, 'last of the link', wheel above man, and 'hear / The last beat of the thunder of God's heart.' But 'last' is at least as important as 'link', which is unexpectedly qualified: these suns and moons 'Are in their station cold'. The forty-six rather heavily orchestrated lines of part II, in fact, begin as his interlocutor's idea of a reassurance, which by the end, and in his hands, has begun to invite despair. 'You tell me that to me a Power is given', he says at the beginning of part II, in the tone of a man who has reservations, and although the lofty rhyme obscures the syntax slightly, the power he is told of is that 'sovran subtil influence' of fire and light which must fade as it descends. Probably the unwritten part III would have confirmed the mood of part I, with its 'I have lost / A life, perchance an immortality,' and the simile of the fallen fledgeling ravens. Unless there was to have been some revelation of nothingness, it could hardly have done more than that, and it is likely that this is why it was never written.

The sense of something to come on which *Armageddon* ends makes it almost as much induction as fragment. What it draws to, though not a close, is not simply a breaking off. (*The Coach of Death* also has something of the effect of a proem. A kind of ending is implicit in the roll-call of great deities out of Bryant on which, after some Miltonic preparation, this ballad experiment stops: in particular, the 'later brood / Of Saturn and of Jove' of the last lines.[6] 'But some have hearts that in them burn / With power and promise high, / To draw strange comfort from the earth, / Strange beauties from the sky': this, the last of the eight introductory stanzas, seems to look forward to some vision in despite of the sunless wastes of hell.) The subject of *Armageddon*, in fact, is not the last battle, but his own visionary power. Perhaps the formal statement about as well as of his visionary power is a sign of self-doubt, as well as a claim to rank with his peers. On one level the poem exemplifies, dramatically enough, both the young Tennyson's assurance, and his doubts: these doubts about himself, and about much besides, from which he drew so much subtle questioning, but which could also dull his mind and divert him into nerveless consolations. The only unmistakable sign of irresolution in it is its fragmentary state. The opening paragraph was at first to end with a classic appeal for illumination ('Pour on me now / The influence of thy nature, as shall throw / Bright light on what is darkest'), but quickly went beyond this to an acknowledgment of the light that had been given, by the power 'Whose wondrous emanation hath poured / Bright light on what was darkest, and removed / The cloud that from my mortal faculties / Barred out the knowledge of the Latter Times.'[7] Tennyson as visionary stands on the mountain overlooking the valley of Megiddo. Before him is a huge dreary plain. Horrible shapes flit by; the sun sets in a bloody haze; he hears the 'dissonance / Of jarring confused voices', some seeming hellish, some heavenly, and sees in the East silver tents beside the moon, and in the West a 'suite of dark pavilions', with a standard entwined by a mighty crested snake. A young seraph descends, to tell him what these things portend, and to order him to open his eyes (his sense being as yet 'clogged with dull Mortality'), and see.

. . . I felt my soul grow godlike, and my spirit
With supernatural excitation bound
Within me, and my mental eye grew large
With such a vast circumference of thought,
That, in my vanity, I seemed to stand
Upon the outward verge and bound alone
Of God's omniscience. Each failing sense,
As with a momentary flash of light,
Grew thrillingly distinct and keen. I saw
The smallest grain that dappled the dark Earth,
The indistinctest atom in deep air,
The Moon's white cities, and the opal width
Of her small, glowing lakes, her silver heights
Unvisited with dew of vagrant cloud,
And the unsounded, undescended depth
Of her black hollows. Nay – the hum of men
Or other things talking in unknown tongues,
And notes of busy Life in distant worlds,
Beat, like a far wave, on my anxious ear.

  I wondered with deep wonder at myself:
My mind seemed winged with knowledge and the strength
Of holy musings and immense Ideas,
Even to Infinitude. All sense of Time
And Being and Place was swallowed up and lost
Within a victory of boundless thought.
I was a part of the Unchangeable,
A scintillation of Eternal Mind,
Remixed and burning with its parent fire.
Yea! in that hour I could have fallen down
Before my own strong soul and worshipped it.

Tennyson was familiar with such moments of infinite or
Godlike perception, and described them as states of 'trans-
cendent wonder, associated with absolute clearness of mind'.[8]
What chiefly concerns him in *Armageddon* is the Everlasting
Man who seems, one way or another (the syntax is rather
confusing), to be 'capable / Of the extreme of knowledge'.
But the capacity is all, and the poem stops on the promise of
'some grand issue'. The pulsing and throbbing in the last lines
convey a sense of a vast and continuing life; the 'indefinable

chose what seemed to be the lesser of two evils, and Moxon's two volume edition of *Poems* duly appeared in May 1842.

Looking back on the poems of 1832 in a review of the 1842 volumes, Tennyson's friend James Spedding had this to say: 'The superiority of his second collection of poems lay not so much in the superior workmanship, (it contained perhaps fewer that were equally perfect in their kind,) as in the general aim and character . . . Not only was the aim generally larger, the subjects and interests more substantial, and the endeavour more sustained; but the original and distinctive character of the man appeared more plainly. His genius was manifestly shaping a peculiar course for itself, and finding out its proper business; the moral soul was beginning more and more to assume its due predominance – not in the way of formal preaching, (the proper vehicle of which is prose,) – but in the shape and colour which his creations unconsciously took, and the feelings which they were made insensibly to suggest.'[1]

Spedding's insistence on 'the moral soul' as it declared itself rather in 'the shape and colour which his creations unconsciously took' is applicable to the *Mariana* of 1830 as well as to *The Lady of Shalott* of 1832, but notably less applicable to poems like *The Palace of Art* (which Spedding admired) or the ambitious but imperfect *Oenone*. It is worth spending some time on these two poems, since their defects are not simply those of the immature Tennyson. *The Palace of Art* excited his friends because it attempted a major statement about social and intellectual principles of a kind which would appeal to thoughtful undergraduates conscious of their privileges. Unfortunately it is too much of a statement. The unfaltering delivery is that of a thesis, or sermon; the poetry itself often falters. The dangers of selfish withdrawal, whether by an individual or by a class of custodians, are shown in the punishment of a soul which tries to live in godlike isolation among the riches it seems to possess: 'Joying to feel herself alive, / Lord over Nature, Lord of the visible earth, / Lord of the senses five'. The image of the soul as still centre, or quiet king, is overtaken by the reality of stagnation and self-burial, exile from God, and the agony of inner fires. Obviously Tennyson is dealing with matters of deep concern to him; there is a striking mingling of attraction and repulsion in the poem. But whether social or intellectual, its force is not much more than that of a solemn warning that feeds on extended instance. In one sense it hardly gets beyond its first stanza.

> I built my soul a lordly pleasure-house,
>   Wherein at ease for aye to dwell.
> I said, 'O soul, make merry and carouse,
>   Dear soul, for all is well.'

This leaves little room for the exquisite irony some readers have found: we know well enough that all will not be well, and (broadly speaking) why. Tennyson said the poem was 'the embodiment of my own belief that the Godlike life is with man and for man', but it is more exposition than embodiment.[2] 'Perchance I may return with others there / When I have purged my guilt': this hint at the end that the palace may yet become a kind of college situate in a clearer air could hardly have made for a proper resolution. It returns us from the romantic splendours and miseries of the soul to the light of common day, but it also dissipates the effect of the single thesis.

The best things are probably the stanzas of despair near the end, and the arras landscapes of the first part, which are not merely 'gay, or grave, or sweet, or stern': there is a strange threat in the endless plain of line 74, in spite of the herds and river. But much of the poem is heavy embroidery of a different sort. It has been argued that the 1842 revisions made it more subtle, and that the glorious is everywhere inseparable from the sinister.[3] Perhaps the stained-glass windows of 49–52 ('Likewise the deep-set windows, stained and traced, / Would seem slow-flaming crimson fires / From shadowed grots of arches interlaced, / And tipt with frost-like spires') do indeed suggest the torments of hell, and their extremes of fire and frost. But unless we have to take as irony the lines about 'every legend fair / Which the supreme Caucasian mind / Carved out of Nature for itself', the vulgarisation in the religious pictures is merely vulgarisation. In making the poem more coherent, the revisions made the weakness of the conception more apparent. The improvements tend to be local, and stylistic.

Some were all dark and red, a glimmering land
    Lit with a low round moon,
Among brown rocks a man upon the sand
    Went weeping all alone . . .

One seemed all dark and red – a tract of sand,
    And some one pacing there alone,
Who paced for ever in a glimmering land,
    Lit with a low large moon.

Perhaps the sand and pacing figure of 1842 are more impress-
ive than the 1832 version, but since some of their authority
comes from Wordsworth's leech-gatherer ('In my mind's eye
I seemed to see him pace / About the weary moors continual-
ly, / Wandering about alone and silently . . .'), the revision is
more like a skilful working-up than anything else; it will not
for a moment stand comparison with the revision of *Mariana
in the South*. The poetry is always liable to fail, sometimes just
when the 'sort of allegory' (as the introductory poem
cautiously describes it) seems to begin to glow with convic-
tion.

Below was all mosaic choicely planned
    With cycles of the human tale
Of this wide world, the times of every land
    So wrought, they will not fail.

The people here, a beast of burden slow,
    Toiled onward, pricked with goads and stings;
Here played, a tiger, rolling to and fro
    The heads and crowns of kings;

Here rose, an athlete, strong to break or bind
    All force in bonds that might endure,
And here once more like some sick man declined,
    And trusted any cure.

The rhythm and tone of 'Below was all mosaic choicely
planned' perhaps invites comparison with another heedlessly
trodden picture-bearing floor, in *Hero and Leander*. But

even without the advantage Marlowe's warning floor has at the beginning of his narrative, it would be a damaging comparison, given the bathos of 'So wrought, they will not fail', with its empty future; the spun-out 'pricked with goads and stings' and 'heads and crowns of kings', all the worse for rhyming; and the indifferent wordplay of 'break or bind / All force in bonds'. Spedding's distinction between formal preaching and the real business of Tennyson's poetry is sound, but *The Palace of Art* is as near sermonising as anything he ever wrote. That he could spend so much time revising it for the 1842 volumes is significant; its weaknesses are in some respects comparable to the long work of his maturity, *Idylls of the King*.

Oenone is perhaps more complex, and certainly more confused. It restages within the lamentation of the deserted nymph the famous Judgment of Paris, by which man is judged, and by which generations of painters have made their own claim for judgment by their peers. Pastoral love lament mingles with the great issues of the choice – wisdom, or earthly power, or sensual pleasure – and the destruction that is to come. *Oenone* belongs to that tradition of Alexandrian poetry in which major themes are interpreted by minor actors. (She is a minor actor in another sense. One classical scholar has observed that 'with the exception of *Heroides* 5 and the tenth book of Quintus Smyrnaeus (259–489) no literary treatment of the myth of Paris and Oenone has survived', and expresses surprise that she is hardly mentioned in Latin poetry.)[4] She is touchingly human in her desire to have it out with Eris, the Abominable, who cast on the board the golden apple of Discord, and so 'bred this change'. This passage (216–24) was added for the 1842 publication. Tennyson probably wanted to bring Oenone nearer to us, for though not coldly distant in legend, she is sometimes muffled by the formalities of her complaint. The long melodious lament contains the narrative of the Judgment, and also creates some of the effects of monologue. With so much attempted, it is not surprising that there is unevenness. 'O happy tears, and how unlike to these! / O happy Heaven, how canst thou see my face? / O happy earth, how canst thou bear my weight?': it is like a re-creation of Elizabethan verse at its thinnest. Thirty lines or so earlier, on the other hand, occurs the following.

> Most loving is she?
> Ah me, my mountain shepherd, that my arms
> Were wound about thee, and my hot lips prest
> Close, close to thine in that quick-falling dew
> Of fruitful kisses, thick as Autumn rains
> Flash in the pools of whirling Simois.

This follows the wondering 'Fairest – why fairest wife? am I not fair?' The workings of pride and destructive sensuality are beyond her, but passion is something she does understand, and these are perhaps the loveliest lines in the poem, with the consonance of 'fruitful' and 'Autumn rains' held within the strong sense of transience, in Simois falling to the plains of Troy.

The difference between the thinness and the intensity confirms an uncertain purpose. The debate in the Judgment episode is conducted at the level of 'divinity disrobed', and the desire for an appropriately pregnant style produced some stiff Miltonising. Whatever his concern for the question of how to live, and the need for 'Self-reverence, self-knowledge, self-control', much of *Oenone* is poetry almost explicitly at the service of legend, as distinct from that high artifice by which legend seems to create itself, as in *Ulysses* and *Tithonus*. Herè stands forth to offer earthly power, Pallas the ideal of conduct that alone leads life to sovereign power. Language of relentless opulence, full of the liquid consonants Tennyson can draw about him like a cloak ('ample rule / Unquestioned, overflowing revenue / Wherewith to embellish state'), is countered by a near parody of sententious reasoning: 'to follow right / Were wisdom in the scorn of consequence'. Even though the opposing orations are meant to be demolished by the half-whispered promise of Aphrodite, the price is too great. Indeed, in her own way Aphrodite is as heavy as the others, because it is so much her own way. All we see of Herè is her angry eyes as she withdraws, and Pallas remains a statue except for her earnest eyes and angry cheek, unsexed at the outset by the very 'clearness' of her 'bared limbs.' Aphrodite draws her hair backward 'from her warm brows and bosom'; 'from the violets her light foot / Shone rosy-white, and o'er her rounded form / Between the shadows of the vine-bunches / Floated the glowing sunlights, as she moved.' That is, she assumes the characteristic pose we know from statues of Venus, and she moves. It is skilfully done, with 'as she moved' held back to the end of the stanza, but the skill is a little studied.

Tennyson's Oenone is more appealing than Ovid's, who is characterised not only as naive and *rustica*, but as foolish. But although there is a strong sense of real loss, as well as that of the catastrophe to come, close enquiries into her mental processes are not really justifiable. She is in a sense a spirit of the fruitful earth which Paris has rejected, singing to 'many-fountained Ida' as her mother, and announcing herself formally as 'the daughter of a River-God', who will 'build up all / My sorrow with my song, as yonder walls / Rose slowly to a music slowly breathed'. Her father was the river-god Cebren, but the only river she names here is Simois, which with Scamander (said to be sacred to Apollo) flows 'from the heart of piny Ida' to water the plains of Troy, and whose melody in *Ilion, Ilion* is associated with that of the building of Troy by music. Paris's desertion of her is marked by the despoiling of her tall dark pines. But the mists and vapours that move through the poem are a better indication of what this daughter of a river-god (as distinct from Ovid's) may represent, and perhaps her reference to the dry thickets where she wishes she could meet Eris is in keeping with this. (If she is anything of an earth-spirit, it probably was not this that made Tennyson slip for a moment into yet another key. In 'fiery thoughts / Do shape themselves within me, more and more, / Whereof I catch the issue, as I hear / Dead sounds at night come from the inmost hills, / Like footsteps upon wool', the dead sounds are like something from *The Prelude*, ominous natural sounds haunting a troubled child, here joined with the destructive element of fire she now invokes, and with which the poem ends: 'wheresoe'er I am by night and day, / All earth and air seem only burning fire'.)[5] The shape of the song she builds up is little more than that of the eventual turn from the incantatory 'until I die' to the threat of 'I will not die alone'.

Whatever unity the poem has is in the origin of lament and boding in Paris's rejection, but it is weakened by the mingling of styles. Perhaps some coherence can be discerned within the cycles of the two days, that of the Judgment, and that of her lament. She begins her song at noon, the quiet and evil hour associated with the sleeping Pan, and it was at noon that the three goddesses came to the bower, their arrival marked by a strange wind. Noon alternates with morning; after the morning view of Troy, we hear the noonday song which recalls the meeting with Paris at dawn, and the other noon of the Judgment, and which ends in the evening with Oenone's decision to go down to Troy and talk with Cassandra, 'ere the stars come forth'. Noon and afternoon of one day, morning and noon of another, the whole framed by 'the crown of Troas' in the morning, and the foreboding of the destruction by night that will come. But perhaps all that is discernible is the long afternoon and its lament, sung 'till the mountain-shade / Sloped downward to her seat from the upper cliff'.

Oenone and *The Palace of Art* still have their advocates, but a distinction must be made between them and a poem like *The Lady of Shalott*, which is poetry sure of its object. Except in the fourth and final part, which has its longueurs, its impulse is unflagging. Part I presents the world's idea of the fairy Lady, an unseen presence whose island towers draw the gaze of those who pass to and from Camelot, but whose song is heard only by the reapers. 'And up and down the people go, / Gazing where the lilies blow': this, which replaces the tremulous waterlily and daffodilly of 1832, is the shape and colour unconsciously taken by creation.

> There she weaves by night and day
> A magic web with colours gay.
> She has heard a whisper say,
> A curse is on her if she stay
>   To look down to Camelot.
> She knows not what the curse may be,
> And so she weaveth steadily,
> And little other care hath she,
>   The Lady of Shalott.

The first stanza of II carries over the gazing and listening and whispering of I into a strange actuality: 'a magic web with colours gay' is the voice of the peasant, for whom magic and colours would be almost equally marvellous. With the human reality of 'And so she weaveth steadily, / And little other care hath she', we are in the Lady's world, which is that of a mysterious duress. We know as little about the curse as she does; the whisper is that of an inner compulsion. The emphasis in II is not on the magic web, but on the mirror's 'shadows of the world', the transmuted richness which she delights to weave, and is also by moments half sick of. The lovers are the essence of the world she receives by reflection, and as such indicate a crisis in this life of the imagination, which is marked by tranquil pleasure, and sudden revulsion. Event, anticipated at the end of II by the poem's first preterites, breaks into her world of reflection with the sight and sound of Lancelot, the sun flaming on his armour and accoutrements. With 'A bow-shot from her bower-eaves, / He rode between the barley-sheaves', and 'The helmet and the helmet-feather / Burned like one burning flame together', the issues seem clear. But although the Italian novella which was Tennyson's source told how 'la Damigella di Scalot morì per amore di Lancialotto de Lac', his grasp of the real issues is firm. 'I met the story first in some Italian *novelle*: but the web, mirror, island, etc., were my own. Indeed, I doubt whether I should ever have put it in that shape if I had been then aware of the Maid of Astolat in *Mort Arthur*.'[6] Whatever might seem self-evident in the context of knight and embowered lady, there is no meeting or changing of eyes, in the old romance phrase. Later, in *Lancelot and Elaine*, Tennyson would tell how the maid of Astolat loved Lancelot, 'with that love which was her doom'. As for the Lady of Shalott, 'She saw the water-lily bloom / She saw the helmet and the plume, / She looked down to Camelot.' Lily, helmet, Camelot: it would be untrue to say that the poem has nothing to do with love, but it carries us past Lancelot, reducing him to the occasion.[7]

The visual effects are method, not self-indulgence, as initially comparable effects are likely to be with the Pre-Raphaelites. The images that pass in sequence, like those that

pass in the mirror, have the intimacy and clarity of paintings.
The Palace of Art deals in framed images. But 'On either side
the river lie / Long fields of barley and of rye' presents a living
picture, with '*the* river', and the sudden present of 'lie'.
Within the world of the poem, the device of Lancelot shows
the movement and stasis of painting: 'A red-cross knight for
ever kneeled / To a lady in his shield.' But in 'Willows whiten,
aspens quiver, / Little breezes dusk and shiver / Through the
wave that runs for ever', the wave which follows the delicate
crowding movements of leaves and water is living, pictured,
and returned to life. The least pictorial section is the dying fall
of IV; it is also the weakest, and, though shorter by one stanza
in 1842, the longest. The structure of the poem is that of an
alternation of the four parts between the outer world and the
Lady's world, and a division between the reflective present
tenses of I and II, and the active past tenses of III and IV. In
III the outer world breaks in on her, and in IV she imposes her-
self on it, turning everything to decay. Most of our attention is
concentrated on her in IV, but with the fulfilment of the curse
the poem loses something of its urgency. The simile 'Like
some bold seër in a trance, / Seeing all his own mischance' is
close enough to the event to dissipate rather than concentrate
attention. There is some diffuseness and blurring, and some
rhetorical insistence (the mournful carol 'chanted lowly, / Till
her blood was frozen slowly' steps forward to command our
blood to freeze) before the last word on this strange action.

> But Lancelot mused a little space;
> He said, 'She has a lovely face;
> God in his mercy lend her grace,
>   The Lady of Shalott.'

The 1832 parchment on the Lady's breast ('*The web was
woven curiously / The charm is broken utterly*') attempted
(with some success) the enigmatic. But like the 'He prayeth
best who loveth best / All things both great and small' of *The
Ancient Mariner*, Lancelot's musing and brief prayer express
the limits of our understanding. It is a perfect ending for this
most human of mysteries: the sinner praying for grace for
another, the man of action wondering before the defeat of the

unknown worker in images. *The Lady of Shalott* presents a conflict between fantasy and reality, but by its terms of mysterious curse, magic web, and mirror – the mirror by which she must gaze on herself by moments, as well as on the tapestry and the world – it also represents the dilemma of the introspective artist, condemned to a life of shadows, and risking destruction if he turns to reality.

The Lotos-Eaters sings so seductively of a retreat from action into dreams that despite the speciousness of the mariners' arguments, and although we know how the episode in the *Odyssey* ends, the impetus of the desire to escape from responsibility can still carry us with it. The beguiling beauty of the verse which sings of turning from a human to a vegetable state is such that it suggests withdrawal into poetry, and with that a hardly conscious reservation about the use of poetry. The appeal is for a paradisal life without toil (or even gardening), on the old analogy, specious but nearly irresistible, of the flower that 'ripens and fades, and falls, and hath no toil'. The latent burden of the song of the sailors is the fall towards the night of fruitful earth. *The Two Voices* has the insistent 'were it not better not to be?'; *In Memoriam*, whose oscillations sometimes create the effect of dialogue, at one point suggests ' 'Twere best at once to sink to peace, / Like birds the charming serpent draws, / To drop head-foremost in the jaws / Of vacant darkness and to cease' (XXXIV). But the mariners of *The Lotos-Eaters*, far from being stricken with loss of belief 'that life shall live for evermore', have simply found in Lotos-land a way of dropping out of the struggle. After the exhortation to courage of the first two lines, the Spenserians of the narrative passage are marked by the slowest of pulses. The wondering observation, half delighted, half fearful, of this 'land where all things always seemed the same', is delicately conveyed by the recurring 'seem', and by such living archaisms as the periphrastic 'did seem', 'did swoon', 'did go', most of which end lines, and two of which end stanzas. The Choric Song, which follows the eating of the lotos fruit, is a lyrical affirmation of passivity, of 'we will not', and 'let us alone'.

Lo! in the middle of the wood,
The folded leaf is wooed from out the bud
With winds upon the branch, and there
Grows green and broad, and takes no care,
Sun-steeped at noon, and in the moon
Nightly dew-fed; and turning yellow
Falls, and floats adown the air.
Lo! sweetened with the summer light,
The full-juiced apple, waxing over mellow,
Drops in a silent autumn night.
All its allotted length of days,
The flower ripens in its place,
Ripens and fades, and falls, and hath no toil,
Fast-rooted in the fruitful soil.

'Ripens and fades, and falls, and hath no toil' recapitulates the
slow 'ands' of the third stanza, and its underlying insistence
on decay and death. Reasoned abdication from will is by way
of II's classic complaint, 'We only toil, who are the first of
things', and 'Nor harken what the inner spirit sings, / "There
is no joy but calm!" ', which is as equivocal as the analogy of
the flowers: it is the drug which sings, not the inner spirit, of
which in this state they can know nothing. Lament and
reasoning alike are classic responses to the human lot, which
have the consoling finality of adage, given collective voice
under the influence of the lotos, and rendered in a grave and
beautifully irregular verse.

We know from Homer that the voice which exhorted to
courage at the beginning will prevail; the consequences of the
rejection of 'the sense of human will . . . By which we dare to
live or die' (*In Memoriam* LXXXV) are that they are brought
back weeping to the ships. But since only Ulysses will survive
these wanderings ('my mariners' in *Ulysses* is from Dante, not
Homer), it is arguable that his men would have been better off
if they had remained in this state of heightened senses and
dulled sensitivity, rapt from the world of perilous seas and
unpredictable divine tempers. To some extent this qualifies
the argument, that we learn from the *Odyssey* that *The
Lotos-Eaters* means that the common lot of toil must be
accepted. Of course this in turn is qualified by the fact that

Homer was more concerned with his hero than with his hero's companions. But perhaps Tennyson was not, and indeed there is a limit to how far his sources can enlighten us. The beauty of the Choric Song should not blind us to the fact that it is choric, and collective: in this instance, not a Shelleyan chorus of spirit voices, but the voice of the ordinary man confirmed in his desire by his fellows. The chorus or *Song* of *The Hesperides* – published in 1832, and placed just before *The Lotos-Eaters*, probably as a companion poem, but not reprinted by Tennyson – is very different in purpose. The enigmatic song of the daughters of Hesperus is the sacred garden expressed in song, and the complex rhetoric of symbolic opposition (Himala and Caucasus, Hesper and Phosphor, dragon and demigod, wasted world and magic apple) grows until it seems to fill the world. But there is no mysterious wisdom in *The Lotos-Eaters*; the lotos is the ordinary man's golden apple, which sinks him into dreaming. How far the original conclusion of 1832 differed in approving of the retreat from life is debatable. At all events Tennyson put it beyond doubt in the 1842 conclusion, where the occasionally chirping ecstasies of 1832 ('And no more roam, / On the loud hoar foam, / To the melancholy home / At the limit of the brine') are replaced by the irony of these half-alive creatures seeing themselves as gods. This is rendered in long sweeping rhythms and clanging triplets:

> Let us swear an oath, and keep it with an equal mind,
> In the hollow Lotos-land to live and lie reclined
> On the hills like Gods together, careless of mankind

rising to the chant of

> For they lie beside their nectar, and the bolts are hurled
> Far below them in the valleys, and the clouds are lightly
> curled
> Round their golden houses, girdled with the gleaming
> world . . .

Perhaps inevitably, the chant passes into a descant, at once resigned and credulously detached, on the miseries of the human state.

But they smile, they find a music centred in a doleful song
Steaming up, a lamentation and an ancient tale of wrong,
Like a tale of little meaning though the words are strong . . .

Several of the lighter poems of the late 1830s are charming,
although sometimes their charm is too earnest. The virtue of
'an idle rhyme' is stated in the unpublished poem of that title,
dating probably from about 1837. Its moral, the need to
accommodate oneself to life by taking a larger view of it, by
taking the day while hearing 'the deep pulsations of the
world', is one which at any time Tennyson would have reason
to feel. The extremes are extreme enough, even for an idle
rhyme. There is the muse conceived as 'the leading article in
verse', and there is 'I cool my face in flowers, and hear / The
deep pulsations of the world', the second line of which would
reappear at a supreme moment in *In Memoriam*, as the
fortieth line of section XCV.[8] The relative brevity of the
poem helps to carry it. But the soul of the 1842 poems *The
Talking Oak* and *Amphion* is garrulity. 'I found him garru-
lously given, / A babbler in the land', Tennyson says of his
sprightly Tory oak, and pleasant though the poem is, one
groans assent. *Amphion* is more firmly based – the legendary
poet who made the trees dance, and these latter days when
one can only dream of 'fiddling in the timber' – but it loses
itself in jolly longueurs.

> Whenever in a lonely grove
>   He set up his forlorn pipes,
> The gouty oak began to move,
>   And flounder into hornpipes.

A dozen or more variations follow: gallopading willows,
poplars promenading with cypresses, yews poussetting with
sloe-trees. The lumbering dance of the poem, with its predict-
able figures ('And wasn't it a sight to see'), ends with a few
jeers at the expense of the Botanic Treatise-reading modern
muses, and some cheerful insistence on the virtue of unaided

toil on one's 'proper patch'.

Amphion uses the stanza of Burns's *The Holy Fair; Will Waterproof's Lyrical Monologue* ('Made at the Cock') uses the same stanza, except that there are no feminine rhymes in the first quatrain. The defensive jauntiness that sometimes characterises these lighter poems is at the heart of this one. The speaker, his burst of self-confidence over ('Half fearful that, with self at strife, / I take myself to task'), ruefully admits time lost – 'How goes the time?' is almost his first word in the poem – and wasted talent, and perhaps the absence of any talent to waste. 'Lyrical' is ironic rather than playful: this is not the prattling of a soak, but the musings of a man whose slightly drunken fancies are a substitute for what he cannot write. The Archpoet of Cologne flashes into poetry with wine ('Dum in arce cerebri / Bachus dominatur, / in me Phebus irruit, / et miranda fatur'), Waterproof drinks that he may sentimentalise.[9] It is the liquor, not the Muse, whose 'gradual fingers steal / And touch upon the master-chord / Of all I felt and feel', and by whose influence 'that child's heart within the man's / Begins to move and tremble'. From this comes a vinous confidence in self and world, rising to a parody of vision.

> This earth is rich in man and maid;
>   With fair horizons bound:
> This whole wide earth of light and shade
>   Comes out a perfect round.
> High over roaring Temple-bar,
>   And set in Heaven's third story,
> I look at all things as they are,
>   But through a kind of glory.

('Kings may be blest, but Tam was glorious, / O'er a' the ills o' life victorious.') All that comes out of it is the decorative fancy about the fat head-waiter as Ganymede, and the cock of the tavern as Jove's eagle, followed by some uncomfortable thoughts about himself. It may sound ungrateful, but the question is whether this is a fancy portioned to his imagination (the violet of a legend blowing among the chops and steaks), or self-indulgence on Tennyson's part. But perhaps it is answered by the cosy self-indulgence of lines like 'A something-pottle-bodied boy / That knuckled at the taw', or by our sense that the poem is, simply, too long. It contains one unforgettable image, in a passage where the earlier fancy about the head-waiter is followed by something less classical, and nearer home.

> But thou wilt never move from hence,
>   The sphere thy fate allots:
> Thy latter days increased with pence
>   Go down among the pots:
> Thou battenest by the greasy gleam
>   In haunts of hungry sinners,
> Old boxes, larded with the steam
>   Of thirty thousand dinners.
>
> We fret, we fume, would shift our skins,
>   Would quarrel with our lot;
> Thy care is, under polished tins,
>   To serve the hot-and-hot;
> To come and go, and come again,
>   Returning like the pewit,
> And watched by silent gentlemen,
>   That trifle with the cruet.

The language of the phrase about the head-waiter's latter days is traditional: Byron, writing of Petrarch in a passage Tennyson may have had in mind, says:

> They keep his dust in Arqua, where he died;
>   The mountain-village where his latter days
> Went down the vale of years . . .
>   (*Childe Harold*, Canto IV, xxxi)

For illustrious retirement, Tennyson substitutes a gross continuance, the dull chink of 'pence', and the duller finality of 'pots'. Perhaps the greasy gleam or highlight hints at a mocking contrast with the light the poet seeks, as in Wordsworth's *Elegiac Stanzas Suggested by a Picture of Peele Castle*, and in Tennyson's late poem, *Merlin and the Gleam*.

Whatever the truth of this, the last two lines are among his most felicitous. Elsewhere he is less happy with 'gentleman': Arthur coming again in *The Epic* 'like a modern gentleman / Of stateliest port', or the struggle to justify the word in section CXI of *In Memoriam*, with its 'grand old name of gentleman, / Defamed by every charlatan'. Here the vacancy of 'silent gentleman' is sardonic, the vacant trifling eye and hand a haunting image of *ennui*.[10]

There have been various opinions about the 'English Idyls', with which the second of the 1842 volumes begins. (The common form 'idyll' will be used throughout, except when reference is made to the English Idyls.) Many critics, from E. C. Stedman onwards, have dwelt on Tennyson's debt to Theocritus.[11] The Alexandrian qualities of Tennyson's poetry are generally recognised: its literariness and allusiveness, its high finish, its frequent insistence on modernity, its tendency to approach myth or legend from an unfamiliar angle. It is partly as a result of this that some of these poems have been admired too much; there is a point at which this recognition ceases to be a criterion.

'In me there dwells / No greatness, save it be some far-off touch / Of greatness to know well I am not great: / There is the man.' So Lancelot of Arthur and himself in *Lancelot and Elaine*, and Tennyson commented 'When I wrote that, I was thinking of Wordsworth and myself.'[12] In *Dora* he attempts something comparable with *Michael*, and fails. The action is hardly comparable: there is nothing in *Dora* like the fall of Luke, quietly stated at the end of a paragraph like something that had to be: 'Meantime Luke began / To slacken in his duty; and, at length, / He in the dissolute city gave himself / To evil courses: ignominy and shame / Fell on him, so that he was driven at last / To seek a hiding-place beyond the seas.' The power of Wordsworth's 'Meantime' is great, and the repetitions that follow the catastrophe, directed by the musing 'There is a comfort in the strength of love', are those of heroic resolution. The repetitions of *Dora* are superficial, and its simplicity is staged. 'She bowed down / And wept in secret; and the reapers reaped, / And the sun fell, and all the land was dark': Dora's anguish is set formally against the same harvest scene as in the previous episode, a scene staked down and held flat, as it were, by many 'ands'. No English poet better understood the use of 'and' than Tennyson, but its use here resembles that of the participle in 'and Dora promised, being meek' – a participle which has been abused as a short-cut to *gravitas* by poets as unlike each other as Yeats and Coventry Patmore. *The Gardener's Daughter*, from roughly the same period (the early to the middle 1830s), is as studiedly rich as *Dora* is bare. The poem is idyllic in the commonest sense of the word. Tennyson pointed out that the lover was an artist, but it seems excuse rather than reason.[13] Of course the richness of much of the monologue, which only gradually declares its mild dramatic purposes, is also that of age's cherished memories of youth. 'Mine age', on which it ends, accomplishes the fullness of the tale told before the painting to whose unveiling it has been a prelude. The original of the central word-painting is Milton: 'she, a Rose / In roses, mingled with her fragrant toil'. Our recognition that it lacks the shadow which makes the passage in the ninth book of *Paradise Lost* so moving does not mean that we are confusing modes; if anything, the reference is overt enough to make the confusion Tennyson's, whose Eden is altogether too charming, like a happy dream, or a sublimation of one kind of Englishness. The only shadow is the slight English melancholy in

> sitting muffled in dark leaves, you hear
> The windy clanging of the minster clock.

Behind the lovely ease of the verse (' "Eustace," I said, "this wonder keeps the house" ' . . . 'Love's white star / Beamed through the thickened cedar in the dusk') a solemnity waits its hour: 'that veiled picture – veiled, for what it holds / May not be dwelt on by the common day. / This prelude has prepared thee. Raise thy soul; / Make thine heart ready with thine eyes . . . ' The perfect marriage of the artist and the gardener's daughter probably does mean the marriage of the creative spirit and the created world, as Robert Pattison suggests.[14] There are several marriages between high and low in Tennyson. This one is unusual in being happy, and the fact is probably significant: the poem embodies a thesis.

Walking to the Mail, Audley Court, and *The Golden Year* (the last not published until 1846) are among the most interesting of the English Idyls. *Walking to the Mail* derives something from the Fourth Idyll of Theocritus. The casual 'walking' – probably for exercise, along a by-way leading to the turn-pike – is a contrast to the bustling communication of 'mail'. The dialogue takes news as its starting-point, and 'mail' has its connotations of 'daily life' and 'the sense that handles it'. But the news we get is of a jaundiced sort. John, who takes a pleasure in the world, asks the questions. James gives the answers, and it is an odd pretty sort of world that they reveal, as far from that of *The Gardener's Daughter* as could be imagined: our morbid devils, our household ghosts; love fading as beauty fades; social barriers; how to mend uneven law by taking things into your own hands; the fear of revolutionary pikes that drives Sir Edward Head abroad; unquestioning acceptance by James of the two Englands of the haves and the have-nots; the need for charity ('What know we of the secret of a man?'), but the likelihood, if James is anything to go by, of getting something less than charity. It is James who speaks of 'the sense that handles daily life – / That keeps us all in order more or less'. He responds with satisfaction to this limiting 'sense', defined by its application to daily life, which is probably the only life he can conceive of. He is of harder stuff than Sir Edward Head, who fled from the Reform Bill and the Chartist violence to come, leaving behind his soured and loveless wife, a cottager's daughter who had married out of her class. This is what happens if one loses this sense: the morbid devil will not be shaken off, any more than the poltergeist of Jocky Dawes. 'Let him go; his devil goes with him' is his sour dismissal of a man not strong enough to stand his ground. As for Chartist violence, he himself was destructive when a boy, and did not get what he wanted; it is likely that he would be so still, in spite of the sense that handles daily life. The schoolboy thieving, culminating in the farrowing sow dragged to the top of the college tower, is something he recalls with particular satisfaction: after all, there are 'those that want, and those that have'. He remarks sardonically of the grieving sow, 'What lot is pure?', and his last words, in reply to John's 'They found you out?', are the satisfied 'not they': the message of this child's heart within the man's is, simply, we paid them out. 'A Tory to the quick', he understands the Chartists well enough; in their place he might have acted in the same way, only he is in his place.

Except for John's praise of Sir Edward's wife as he knew her ten years ago, the verse is plain and dry. Most of it consists of James's answers, made up of assertively clipped or bony phrases, unless when he expands sardonically on the theme of Sir Edward, 'Vexed with a morbid devil in his blood / That veiled the world with jaundice', whose 'nice eyes / Should see the raw mechanic's bloody thumbs / Sweat on his blazoned chairs' (like a transference of the old Raw Head and Bloody Bones to modern fears of revolt), or on the sow, 'alone / Upon her tower, the Niobe of swine'. But unless we are willing to lose ourselves in admiration of speech rhythms, before which many critics tend to genuflect, the poem must be recognised as an astute performance. In the end the careful direction of meaning beneath casual talk becomes a little obtrusive.

> But put your best foot forward, or I fear
> That we shall miss the mail: and here it comes
> With five at top: as quaint a four-in-hand
> As you shall see – three pyebalds and a roan.

After his pointed remarks about why people with sound nerves should not mimic this raw and ignorant world, John's attempt at conversation reaffirms a delight in the shapes and colours of things, on which the idyll begins and ends. But the image in the quaint four-in-hand of working to a common end is touched with a hint of mystery (five, four, three) which is rather easily bought.

As for the two young men who sing in the orchard at Audley Court – Francis Hale, the farmer's son who sings of living as he pleases, and the narrator, who has some means, and lives as he pleases – there is little point in casting up the differences between them, for the similarities are much more important: they are young. On the one hand there is the careless ease of youth; on the other, change, and some decay. Though Audley feast hums like a hive, Audley Court is deserted; the song the narrator sings is from a volume of old Sir Robert's library, which was knocked down to him at auction. As in *Walking to the Mail*, there is the shadow of another whose place knows him no longer, although Sir Robert is hardly mentioned, except for his beloved books which came under the hammer: 'the more the pity, so I said'. Their talk is a gossiping conversation appropriate to an age when (as Scott Fitzgerald somewhere says) one has seen enough of life to know one will never be older. It deals with the 'old matters' of who is dead, or married, or likely to be married, and passes by the scarcity of game to 'the farm, / The four-field system, and the price of grain', until they strike and split on the corn-laws, then agree on William IV, about whom there could be much agreement. Like the Seventh Idyll of Theocritus on which Tennyson based it, the poem breathes the richness of the earth, and a strong appetite for life. It is a modern pastoral, with the picnic, the pasty and cider, and the songs. (Paul Turner points out the strange figure originally included in the crowd on the quay: 'over hollowed tubes / Purse-lipt the swarthy piper moved his beard', which suggests a shepherd's pipe, and a figure out of earlier pastoral to play on it.)[15] The picnic is at the centre of it, and Tennyson gives three lines to the pasty: 'half-cut-down, a pasty costly-made, / Where quail and pigeon, lark and leveret lay, / Like fossils of the rock, with golden yolks / Imbedded and injellied' – a geological pasty, but in nothing else resembling Pecksniff's geological cake. The end of it, after the songs, is the sleeping port, the classically oily sea, the simple 'and we were glad at heart'. The 'were' informs the poem, turning it to a quiet backward glance at an age when (in spite of 'old matters') the laws of time and chance were suspended, and 'let me live my life' was a simple statement of intent.

Perhaps the best of these Theocritean idylls is *The Golden Year*, which derives as much from Virgil's Fourth Eclogue as from Theocritus. In *Audley Court* the glad present of the two friends is sealed in by the past tenses of the conclusion. ('So sang we to each other, Francis Hale, / The farmer's son, who lived across the bay, / My friend': the phrases muse, the pauses prolong themselves, 'my friend' becomes a memory of the past.) The Theocritean contest in *The Golden Year* has to do with the past, the present, and the future of mankind, and the debate is kept open by its conclusion, which is the blast from the slate quarry. A nineteenth-century contest could hardly be beween poet and poet. This contest is between a recognisably nineteenth-century poet, and a Carlylean figure who reproves him for his 'stuff'. The speaker tells how Leonard, halfway up the mountain, sang his song about the coming golden year; and how old James, for whom this is 'an age, when every hour / Must sweat her sixty minutes to the death', censured him, and prophet-like broke his staff on the rocks in the warmth of his feelings. (At least one of Carlyle's rare ventures into poetry has to do with the unforgiving minute, or day: 'So here hath been dawning / Another blue Day: / Think, wilt thou let it / Slip useless away?') Leonard is troubled by the age, and by his own place in it. In answer to the banter about how 'he lived shut up within himself, / A tongue-tied Poet in the feverous days' of greed and arrogance, he claims to have been born too late. His song has more substance than the songs in *Audley Court*, which are not much more than a gentle rendering of youth that dreams of freedom and love. It starts with an evocation of cosmic and human cycles, and passes to a vision of human progress, which at first resembles the great year of Virgil's Fourth Eclogue: 'The Sun flies forward to his brother Sun; / The dark Earth follows wheeled in her ellipse; / And human things returning on themselves / Move onward, leading up the golden year.' The hope for modern man within these cycles is factually stated.

> 'Fly, happy happy sails, and bear the Press;
> Fly happy with the mission of the Cross;
> Knit land to land, and blowing havenward
> With silks, and fruits, and spices, clear of toll,
> Enrich the markets of the golden year.'

Twentieth-century sentimentality, forgetful of all that 'the Press' means – Tennyson did not mean the *Daily Telegraph* – may mock a vanished ideal by which Christianity is bracketed by printing and the heaven-haven of free trade. If we still find Leonard's words prosaic rather than firmly grounded, it is possible that this is because he meant to show that he does not live 'shut up within himself'. Or perhaps they are the words of a poet who is only halfway up the mountain, nearer the everyday than the blushing fleece of the ram which marks the returning age of gold in Virgil.

The weaknesses in Leonard's 'measured words' sound like self-parody. 'Shall eagles not be eagles? wrens be wrens? / If all the world were falcons, what of that? / The wonder of the eagle were the less, / But he not less the eagle': life in the golden age will not be dull for lack of a hierarchy, but it has something of the puffiness of uninspired riddling. The preceding stanza conceals some clumsiness under many liquid consonants. 'When wealth no more shall rest in mounded heaps, / But smit with freër light shall slowly melt / In many streams to fatten lower lands, / And light shall spread . . .' It resembles a poeticised version of Bacon's *Of Sedition and Troubles:* 'Above all things, good policy is to be used, that the treasure and money in a state be not gathered into few hands. And money is like muck, not good except it be spread.' Leonard's mounds of snow will melt and water the valleys, but the old analogy of money and dung peers through his decorous imagery, not to its advantage. (It may be significant that the first line of the idyll promises us the song which he 'wrote', not 'made'.) The song ends on a mournful question: 'But we grow old. Ah! when shall all men's good / Be each man's rule . . . ?' And James, roughly dismissing dreamers of golden ages past and to come, breaks in with what amounts to 'the time is now': 'well I know / That unto him who works, and feels he works, / This same grand year is ever at the doors'. (Tennyson originally had twenty-two lines in which Leonard, troubled by James's mockery of his 'Ah! when', begins to doubt in earnest, and seems to comment obliquely on his cycles and rolling years by tracing widening circles with a pair of shadowy compasses.) The blast from the quarry is a third voice.

> He spoke; and, high above, I heard them blast
> The steep slate-quarry, and the great echo flap
> And buffet round the hills, from bluff to bluff.

This follows James's outburst, and the voice from high above, following the formal 'He spoke', is like an approbatory peal of thunder for the prophet who broke his staff and condemned false witnessing. It is also the voice of the present; the ancient hills, the former haunt of gods and poets, are now quarried for industrial man. Perhaps the truth is that it returns ironically on both speech and song. A Marxist might say that Tennyson spoke more truth than he knew, and of course the quarrymen are not called in evidence, either on the golden year, or the dignity of labour. But whatever its origins, the third voice and its echoes are not easily enlisted, being sound made purer by the hills, and with a momentary effect of passing beyond its context.

On the whole, the English Idyls should not be dismissed as Douglas Bush dismisses them. Bush refers, rather wearily, to those who have pointed to the Theocritean analogues, and comments that 'apart from occasional lines, [they] are for us what sham-philosophical novels (and Ben Jonson) were for Tennyson, "like wading through glue" '.[16] (Bush has just described the line from *The Princess* 'Now lies the Earth all Danaë to the stars' as little better than a forced conceit, and before that has singled out for praise a line from *The Death of Oenone*, 'Thin as the batlike shrillings of the Dead', which is remarkable only for its repetitions.) But although revaluations of Tennyson have made us pay these poems more attention, they should not be overestimated. Anyone who says they are not Tennyson at his best invites various charges, the most serious of which is that there is no sense in stern demands that the man we admire must always be at his best. But they are inferior to his finest poetry, and references to a common purpose with Theocritus and Virgil will carry us only so far. The great poems of the 1830s are the dramatic monologues *St Simeon Stylites, Ulysses*, and *Tithonus* (in its 1860 form), and the *Morte d'Arthur* and its modern frame of *The Epic*. As to why these poems are greater than *Audley Court* or *The Golden Year*, the most obvious reply is that they engage more of us, which need not be taken either for a disregard of mode, or the unacceptable face of Romanticism. A monologue like *Ulysses* is recognisably the product of internal debate. In *The Two Voices*, on the other hand, the workings of the mind are presented in the actual form of an inner debate, in which the 'still small voice' which argues for self-destruction is defeated, and falls silent. The poem was originally called *Thoughts of a Suicide*. It was begun in 1833, some months before Hallam's death, but was probably not finished before 1837 or 1838, Tennyson having been uncertain for some time about how to end it. In the final version the debate is pushed beyond the triumphant reply to the still small voice, 'With thine own weapon art thou slain' (311), and a coda added in which a second (or third) and even smaller voice ('A little whisper silver-clear') confirms the knowledge of a hidden hope, in the context of a celebration of unity with man and nature. The poem has affinities with the *Supposed Confessions of a Second-Rate Sensitive Mind* of 1830, but the close argument from point to point shows how far Tennyson has travelled. The triplet form sustained through the 460-odd lines of the poem represents an intense concentration on the question of being or non-being. The effective response to the argument for suicide is 'A deeper tale my heart divines', as in section CXXIV of *In Memoriam*: 'A warmth within the breast would melt / The freezing reason's colder part, / And like a man in wrath the heart / Stood up and answered "I have felt." ' The faith in man and nature would be restated with greater authority in *In Memoriam*. Yet *The Two Voices* is not dry abstraction. It has the flesh and blood of a long night of anguish, nowhere more than when the voice that counselled suicide falls silent as the light increases. Although it has been defeated in argument, there will be no victory until the other and smaller voice has combined with man and nature to restore him to an acceptance of life. The 'I' has argued from instincts too deep to be rationalised: 'Of something felt, like something here; / Of something done, I know not where; / Such as no language may declare.' The effort drains him ('I ceased, and sat as one forlorn'), but also leaves him like a vessel ready to be filled.

The argument for non-being, as argument and feeling, seems to touch Tennyson more closely. The despairing, 'For I go, weak from suffering here: / Naked I go, and void of cheer: / What is it that I may not fear?' survives the vacuity of 'void of cheer' as a statement of intense anguish. Many readers have thought that the still small voice gets the best of it from the beginning: the dry still irony of 'Were it not better not to be?', the lines about the dragon-fly ('A living flash of light he flew') – a favourite image of rebirth in Tennyson, here an argument for death which invokes the miracle of life, and plainly the voice of a subtle tempter. (A sarcastic declaration by the voice, in an unadopted manuscript passage, about Spenserian 'Intelligences fair, / That range above thy state' reappears as part of a strong affirmation in *In Memoriam* LXXXV.)[17] The economy of the bitter comment on the desire to recover lost hopes is characteristic of the early and best part of the poem.

> 'Yea!' said the voice, 'thy dream was good,
> While thou abodest in the bud.
> It was the stirring of the blood.

> 'If Nature put not forth her power
> About the opening of the flower,
> Who is it that could live an hour?'

The cynicism of the assent echoes in the dull clipped rhyming of 'bud' and 'blood' against 'good', and the second triplet has something of the finality of epigram. Such sour reduction is what the voice is best at; its most characteristic statement is the twice-repeated 'There is one remedy for all.' This is probably why it is usually happier than 'I' in the triplet form, an effect of which (particularly with octosyllabics) is the force of the couplet driven further home by the third rhyme. It suffers its first check after the reiteration of its one remedy in line 201. The human example of Stephen is incontrovertible, although with the sneering reminder of the human condition the 'I' yields to despair. (The language of affirmation is confused as well as ecstatic, as in the risky 'He prayed, and from a happy place / God's glory smote him on the face.' This is hardly the true voice of feeling, which earlier could not speak: 'I would have said, "Thou canst not know," / But my full heart, that worked below, / Rained through my sight its overflow.' The third line of this is congested, and 'from a happy place' in the later passage is Leigh Huntian slipslop.)

But it is not long before the voice over-reaches itself, and its arguments about the comfort of darkness, and the death of the senses, are turned against it when the powerful Tennysonian doubt (sometimes hardly distinguishable from 'I have felt') rises from the darkness: 'With thine own weapon art thou slain.' The voice essays a reply, insisting on non-being, only to be met squarely on its own ground by argument about re-birth (we remember the dragon-fly): 'But if I grant, thou mightst defend / The thesis which thy words intend . . .' The reference to metempsychosis which follows is a rhetorical use of a great image of continuing life; as in *In Memoriam*, the conclusion is reached as much by will as faith.

On the whole, the voice does not get the best of it, despite its singleness of purpose. (At the same time, and though it ceases as the light grows, it is far from fading like a spirit fading on the crowing of the cock. Nor does Tennyson qualify in any way the manner of its last comment: 'Then said the voice, in quiet scorn, / "Behold, it is the Sabbath morn." ' 'Quiet scorn' does not sound like defeat.)[18] Some of its arguments – it throws in a good many – are less than skilful. In lines 64–72, although the form of its strictures neatly inverts that of what it opposes – the human striving and life of nature of 67–69 and 70–73 against the life of nature and human striving of 58–60 and 61–63 – its reasoning is specious, not to say muddled: the introductory 'yet' is meaningless, and the wordplay in 64–66 (' "Yet," said the secret voice, "some time, / Sooner or later, will gray prime / Make thy grass hoar with early rime" ') is unconvincing; 'early' exists only for the dull play against 'gray'. It is about here that the verse begins to falter and slacken, although the arguments on the whole remain close; such a sustained use of the triplet form obviously put Tennyson under a strain. Even in simile, where weakness would be least expected, the triplets can fail.

> As when a billow, blown against,
> Falls back, the voice with which I fenced
> A little ceased, but recommenced.

The voice has been given a crusher ('With thine own weapon art thou slain'), but it will try again: its last attempt, as it happens. But 'fenced', which suggests an opponent held in play, hardly accords either with the urgency of the debate, or with the imagery of wind and sea.

Nor does the conclusion of the poem satisfy. It owes something to the tradition of the dream poem from which the dreamer wakes restored to a renewed world. But the night-long debate ends not with the affirmation of life without beginning or end, and the cry for 'more life, and fuller', but with the speaker's emptiness: 'I ceased, and sat as one forlorn.' Will has done all that it could, and the effort has exhausted him. What follows is supposedly an influx of strength from man and nature, as immediate proof of life, with the second and smaller voice as guide. But its simplicity is coy, whether in the vignette of the triune family group, or in such neat Wordsworthian as 'And Nature's living motion lent / The pulse of hope to discontent' which seems confused as well as coy. 'You scarce could see the grass for flowers' is like a case rested on *Lyrical Ballads*. And yet the second voice is

> Like an Aeolian harp that wakes
> No certain air, but overtakes
> Far thought with music that it makes

In spite of the slight tremolo in 'music that it makes', this classic Romantic image might help to reassure us about more voices than one.

Nothing that Tennyson had published could have prepared his readers for the voice of *St Simeon Stylites*. The savage comedy of this dramatic monologue is necessarily more complex than that of such an invective poem as, say, *Holy Willie's Prayer*. Burns's Holy Willie is of the Elect, and accommodates himself to sin by speculating that fornication may be God's way of keeping him from the great sin of pride. ('If sae, Thy han' maun e'en be borne / Until Thou lift it.') Simeon's sins, or rather the self-inflicted punishment for them, are his path to glory.

On the coals I lay,
A vessel full of sin: all hell beneath
Made me boil over. Devils plucked my sleeve,
Abaddon and Asmodeus caught at me.
I smote them with the cross; they swarmed again.
In bed like monstrous apes they crushed my chest:
They flapped my light out as I read: I saw
Their faces grow between me and my book;
With colt-like whinny and with hoggish whine
They burst my prayer.

(This fear of sexuality would again be expressed thirty-five years later in *Lucretius*, with its vision of the Oread and the satyr, and such lines as 'and worst disease of all, / These prodigies of myriad nakednesses, / And twisted shapes of lust, unspeakable, / Abominable . . .') Carlyle remarked that no man became a saint in his sleep, and Simeon is at least sleepless in his quest for sanctity.[19] Since he will be canonised, he is a great type of human error. 'A sign betwixt the meadow and the cloud, / Patient on this tall pillar I have borne / Rain, wind, frost, heat, hail, damp, and sleet, and snow': the sign is that of suffering. Much of Tennyson's poetry has to do with passive suffering: *Mariana*, *Tithonus*, *Locksley Hall*, above all the passion or the passivity of *Maud*, and the passion that is slowly transformed by will of *In Memoriam*. Simeon's passive suffering is defended by furious mental action, an exploration and justification of suffering as meticulously documented as a squalling claim for promotion. The posture is, among other things, a caricature of withdrawal, for the watcher on the column is visible at a great distance, and surrounded by worshippers. Gibbon, on whom Tennyson drew, commenting on 'this *celestial* life', and the unlikelihood that 'the fanatics who torment themselves are susceptible of any lively affection for the rest of mankind', speaks of Simeon's repeated attempts at 'pious suicide'.[20] Tennyson conceals the final withdrawal by Simeon's noisy insistence on being gathered to the saints. Death for him will be new life: 'This dull chrysalis / Cracks into shining wings.' Gibbon's stance is that of the aloof observer of human folly, of 'the singular invention of an aërial penance'. Tennyson had little regard for such forms of asceticism, but his monologue deals with matters which are part of him: conviction of sin, and the desire for death.

From the 'grasp' on the hope of saintdom in the fifth line, to the 'clutch' at the crown sixteen lines from the end, Simeon is defined by his appetite for sanctity.

> Although I be the basest of mankind,
> From scalp to sole one slough and crust of sin,
> Unfit for earth, unfit for heaven, scarce meet
> For troops of devils, mad with blasphemy,
> I will not cease to grasp the hope I hold
> Of saintdom . . .

The obliquity is fairly clear: Simeon is far from believing himself to be the basest of mankind, and 'although' is rather close to 'because'. Consciousness of sin buys sanctity, and is most readily made apparent by its punishment. In 'From scalp to sole one slough and crust of sin', an image of the self-inflicted filth and sickness of his state, the two are indistinguishable. William Hone, on whose *Every-Day Book* of 1825 Tennyson drew extensively, remarked that 'One of [Simeon's] thighs rotted a whole year, during which time he stood on one leg only.'[21] Tennyson's 'And both my thighs are rotted with the dew' does more than double Simeon's pains, or the hint of sexuality in 'thigh'; with 'dew', a recurring image in the poem, the line fuses death in life, and blessing, or fertility. Simeon's 'A sign betwixt the meadow and the cloud' is accurate enough; in his isolation between two images of fertility he is a sign of barrenness, whose life of death is all his witnessing. The fervent enumeration of his sufferings which supports this high image of himself is grotesque: 'In coughs, aches, stitches, ulcerous throes and cramps.' The anxiety that God should understand he is not complaining about what he inflicts on himself; the remembered triumph over the owl in the days when his lungs could stand it; the direction of God's attention to the convent down there and the mountain up yonder, as things God might overlook if not directed; the envious whine of the flat 'while thou and all the saints / Enjoy themselves in heaven', as if bliss were a party to which he had not been invited; the preposterous 'saint me' of 'lower voices saint me from above'; the sudden incongruity of 'my high nest of penance': it is almost like caricature. But 'high *nest* of penance' goes beyond caricature, and reveals the complex hypocrisy in a single word.

As his declaration of act and merit begins with lies, so does the process by which he achieves confirmation of sanctity. His effective proof of fitness is the cry of the people round the column: ' 'Tis their own doing: this is none of mine; / Lay it not to me.' Of course their worship is very much his doing, and from the lying disclaimers ('They think that I am somewhat. What am I?') he turns again to grasp eagerly at sainthood bought by suffering: 'thou wilt bear witness here'. He has one eye on God, and one on the people, to whom ('you do ill to kneel to me') his attitude resembles Mark Antony's in the forum: his good friends, sweet friends, must not let him stir them up to such a sudden flood of canonisation.

> Yet do not rise; for you may look on me,
> And in your looking you may kneel to God.

The healing, the going forth of power, the acclamations duly follow, and are followed by the proclamation from the high nest of penance. The time that 'may come', of worship without reproach, turns in the utterance to 'now, now, now', and the crown is fiercely clutched. The triumphant prophecy of his death 'tonight' may confirm our suspicion, that all this has happened before. But once at least something of pathos touches us.

> I think that I have borne as much as this –
> Or else I dream – and for so long a time,
> If I may measure time by yon slow light,
> And this high dial, which my sorrow crowns –
> So much – even so.

The pathos of this survives the whining voice. The image focuses the sense throughout of a creature imprisoned in time and self, from the enumeration of the ages of penance, to the climax of the promised translation for 'A quarter before twelve'. ' "Simeon Stylites" is said by the prophane, that is the mathematicians Spring Rice and Heath, to be not "the watcher on the pillar to the end," but to the nth . . . O Alfred! could you only have made the height of the pillar a geometrical progression!'[22] So Tennyson's friend John Kemble. The assurance of the monologue is such that crazed asceticism raised to the nth power commends itself to us as being not much more than the truth.

The two other great monologues of this period, *Ulysses* and *Tithonus*, were written during the period of activity that followed the death of Arthur Hallam in September 1833. All three have to do with frustration, a lingering between life and death. But whereas Simeon imagines his chrysalis cracking into shining wings, Tithonus and Ulysses look for death: Tithonus openly, as a release, Ulysses covertly, and with nobility, as the last adventure. *Tithonus* (originally *Tithon*, and first published in 1860, in its revised and slightly longer form) is the lament of the endlessly ageing lover of Aurora, goddess of the dawn, who granted him eternal life, but not eternal youth, and now cannot grant him death. It was conceived as a pendant or companion to *Ulysses*. On the face of it, there is a strong contrast between the withering Tithonus who asks for death, and the old hero who declares 'Though much is taken, much abides', and exhorts his companions to strive, and not to yield. But the will in *Ulysses* also has a defensive role, and the mood, as is generally agreed, is as much that of *ennui* as of heroic endeavour. Behind their classical mask of age, *Ulysses* and *Tithonus* are deeply personal. They are much shorter than *St Simeon Stylites*: *Ulysses* has 70 lines, *Tithonus* 76, whereas *St Simeon Stylites* has 220. It has the expansiveness of satiric comedy, extended through instance after instance, whereas the slower-paced *Ulysses* and *Tithonus* have the concentration of carefully weighed personal statements. As is the way of such statements, they expand in our minds, and set up many echoes. *Tithonus* wheels continually between past and present; its pace reflects the oppression of the eternity from which Tithonus speaks. And much combines to make *Ulysses* seem longer than its 70 lines: the variations in pace and contrasting paragraphs, the evocation of the past, the complexity of reason and motive.

Perhaps the most revealing phrase in *Ulysses* is its last four words: 'strong in will / To strive, to seek, to find, and not to yield.' It has been said that the resoluteness is undercut by irony, since Satan's 'And courage never to submit or yield' in *Paradise Lost* is not far away.[23] More important than the literary allusion is the fact that 'not to yield' seems less a condition of striving, seeking, and finding than a separate statement. Speaking to James Knowles about *In Memoriam*, and admitting that it was 'too hopeful . . . more so than I am myself', Tennyson said, 'There is more about myself in *Ulysses*, which was written under the sense of loss and that all had gone by, but that still life must be fought out to the end.'[24] If 'more about myself' means anything at all, the will in *Ulysses* has probably less to do with seeking and finding than with the loss of purpose against which it fights. In fact the loss of purpose, the 'sense . . . that all had gone by', is a condition of the expression of will from beginning to end. Tennyson drew on Dante's Ulysses, whose last voyage (in Canto XXVI of the *Inferno*) ended in death, and who suffers for his guile in the eighth circle of Hell. Tennyson's Ulysses, like Dante's, speaks of following knowledge, but his voyage purposes mainly death. In the last paragraph, sturdy exhortation ('Though much is taken, much abides') mingles with mournful cadences: 'The long day wanes: the slow moon climbs: the deep / Moans round with many voices.' Like the lines about the untravelled world in the second paragraph, this moves so slowly as to seem hardly to move at all. Both passages are centrally placed within the confident affirmations of their paragraphs. The first undermines the claim that follows: 'Life piled on life / Were all too little.' The voices of the deep in the second are those of the past, and the dead. 'There gloom the dark broad seas' holds out its promise, but 'gloom' has swallowed the earlier 'gleams' of 'gleams that untravelled world'. Even at its most subtly exhortative (and its most sharply Dantean, in 'And see the great Achilles, whom we knew'), *Ulysses* broods over what has been: a lost companionship, the days of greatness. No doubt the mariners he exhorts would not be troubled by any gap between striving and not yielding, and would agree that without the courage not to yield there is no other virtue. But for us who have listened to the voice from the dry 'It little profits' of the first line, it sounds more like the stubbornness born of despair. And perhaps the echo in 'To strive, to seek, to find, and not to yield' of the movement of the fifth line ('That hoard, and sleep, and feed, and know not me') is less a matter of contrast, than of a curious affinity between what disgusts him, and the escape from it proposed.

The frustration is harshly and egotistically expressed in the short opening paragraph. Even here, however, there is some ambivalence. 'It little profits' has an ominous biblical echo, but it is also a dry version of the idea of right conduct given in several of the poems which he wrote in the 1830s.[25] The curt negations and rejections (including that of Penelope: the still hearth has less to do with fire than with children) are followed in the second paragraph by a rush of passionate affirmations: 'I cannot rest from travel: I will drink / Life to the lees: all times I have enjoyed / Greatly, have suffered greatly . . .' The reiterated 'I', the short phrases and strong enjambment, with the appeal to the known opposites of experience (enjoyed/ suffered, loved/alone, shore/sea), slows to 'I am become a name', the loss of identity in legend. The *recueillement* which follows is undoubtedly noble in tone, when he speaks of the past: 'And drunk delight of battle with my peers, / Far on the ringing plains of windy Troy.' But the yearning to follow knowledge, the *virtute e conoscenza* to which Dante's Ulysses exhorted his men, fails to convince us.

> . . . but every hour is saved
> From that eternal silence, something more,
> A bringer of new things; and vile it were
> For some three suns to store and hoard myself,
> And this gray spirit yearning in desire
> To follow knowledge like a sinking star,
> Beyond the utmost bound of human thought.

Earlier 'I cannot rest from travel' did not quite carry us with it, even if we ignore the connotations of 'travel' that hardly suggest heroic voyaging. Now 'a bringer of new things' seems trifling, even if it is meant only to offer a human challenge to the eternal silence. As for the last three lines, it is not really a matter of whether Tennyson should have written 'wisdom' rather than 'knowledge', or that 'gray spirit' and 'sinking star' suggest the dark. The lines are like a dream of what it might be to have such yearnings.

This being so, the question – it is one of several which are often asked – is whether Tennyson wanted Ulysses to speak like that, or whether he is intruding a 'far-far-away' into a dramatic poem which would be better without it. The answer almost certainly is that he is not intruding anything. Ulysses may not be his mouthpiece for heroic voyaging, but he can well speak from 'the sense of loss and that all had gone by', and also from the spurious excitement by which age persuades itself that there is more to come. The emptiness, the consolatory fine words and dreaming images, are consonant with the event, or non-event. Mentally Ulysses turns back and remembers much, and perhaps this voyage is as real as the other. The only effective futures envisaged are the being washed down by the gulfs, or touching the Happy Isles – these are the Isles of the Blest, and 'touch' is wonderfully apt, somewhere between the tentative, and the idiom and actuality of voyaging – where they would see the great Achilles, 'whom we knew'. The last phrase may return on the 'newer world' to be sought seven lines before. At all events, it is with the evocation of a great past before them that the poem moves to its conclusion.

If the lines about following knowledge seem too poetic, the language of the short third paragraph has seemed to many readers prosaic. 'This is my son, mine own Telemachus . . .' The movement is unlike anything else in *Ulysses*. In particular, its soft even pace is markedly different from the curtness of the first paragraph, with which it has obvious structural affinities. If taken as speech rather than interior monologue, a presentation of the inheritor of the sceptre and the isle, the language may seem appropriate. But it is probably interior monologue; it is with line 45 ('My mariners') that *Ulysses* becomes speech. The deliberate movement of the paragraph suggests a detachment from his son, as from all else on Ithaca, except his men. Not that there is contempt for Telemachus, although Ulysses turns from him to his old companions with relief. What separates them is very clear in 'My mariners, /

Souls that have toiled, and wrought, and thought with me', where the rhyming 'thought' follows 'toiled, and wrought' with the force of a truth suddenly grasped. Few sons think with their fathers in that sense. But 'prudent', 'common', 'decent' are not slighting. As has been shown, the terms used are traditional, and honourable.[26] The intricacies of duty to men and gods in a heroic age meant that 'decent' and 'blameless' were high attributes. 'Most blameless is he', which may seem most open to charges of irony and condescension, is probably least open; 'blameless' is the attribute of Arthur in the *Idylls of the King*. The unusually regular verse is that of a detached appraisal. (The first three lines of the paragraph are all 4.6, the only passage in the poem where there is a sequence of more than two lines with the same pause, and the eleven lines contain four of the thirteen 5.5 lines in the seventy lines of the poem.) There is a sense of detachment even in 'This is my son, mine own Telemachus', in spite of – or in part because of? – the repeated possessives. Perhaps this is hindsight, from the force of 'souls' and 'thought' thirteen lines later. But it is like a musing appraisal not only of Telemachus's qualities, but of the common phenomenon of an adult son: his, yet another. ('Mine own Telemachus' takes up and particularises 'my son', and in doing so begins to lose identity and waver, as words sometimes do when written, and names when spoken.)

Most of the last paragraph, except for the lines about the waning day and the moaning deep, is not only fine poetry, but fine rhetoric, by a leader of men who was traditionally a master of persuasion.[27] The identification with his men, and the praise of their firmness, by which they opposed 'free hearts, free foreheads', is followed by the sudden challenging drop which always commands attention: 'you and I are old'. 'Old age hath yet his honour and his toil' is the immediate and reasoned reflux, strengthened by the intimate 'his'; 'Death closes all' is merely the ineluctable fact to which tribute must be paid, and by which all are strong in paying it; in 'but something ere the end, / Some work of noble note', the deed is mainly specified in the praise of his hearers, to which (and to his identification with them) he now returns: 'Not unbecoming men that strove with Gods'. The dramatic achievement of the last paragraph is one of the finest things in *Ulysses*. Perhaps the heroic words will always tend to have their way with us. Even as we hear them again, the rejoicing in the past, and the need for a noble end, tip the balance towards the 'more life, and fuller', and away from the 'better not to be', of *The Two Voices*.

There is less of this human complexity in *Tithonus*, which presents an aberration, a state out of nature. This is concealed at first by what looks like such a response to decay as *A spirit haunts*. But the first four lines present the natural cycle at the point where Tithonus may not return to it: that is, death.

> The woods decay, the woods decay and fall,
> The vapours weep their burthen to the ground,
> Man comes and tills the field and lies beneath,
> And after many a summer dies the swan.

The insistence on the ground he cannot enter, present in one form or another at the end of each of the first three lines, ends only with the swan, long-lived, but mortal. As in the other great poems of this period – indeed, as in all great poetry – much of the authority of *Tithonus* is in the working of contraries: the dark earth and the natural cycle; the 'spaces of the East', cold inhuman light, and 'cruel immortality'. (*Tithon* had 'fatal immortality'; there is no finality in 'cruel', which is the voice of the weakened spirit.) Of the world of men beyond which he tried to pass, Tithonus must linger as a dried thing beyond its movements, at its quiet limits. The most pervasive opposition in the poem is that of light and dark, and their reasons are reversed: warmth is in the 'dark earth' and its weeping exhalations, so different from Aurora's 'far-folded mists'. The monologue is spoken at the moment of her mystic change – the soft air before dawn, the light growing from and around her, the rising of her team – and the 'dark world where I was born' is dark under night as well as distant in time and place. But it is also darkly fruitful, the world of growth and decay.

The embrace of the goddess and the withering human is so far beyond a grotesque January and May that we hardly think of it: Tithonus lies in her arms like a child. Their closeness, in spite of the fate against which neither can appeal, is strangely moving. It is easy to see how apt the legend was to Tennyson's purposes: as easy, perhaps, to overlook the difficulties he faced. The fragment *Semele*, probably written in the same year, also had to do with mortal love for a god, and a thoughtless request. Semele is consumed by fire, not immortality, and the rhetorical frenzy of her death passes (not very convincingly) into the characteristic frenzy of Bacchus, her son to be. This, like the transitions of the verse itself, is perhaps something of an evasion. But the slow even pace of *Tithonus* evades nothing. The wasting body is still in Aurora's arms, her tears are on its cheek.

> Can thy love,
> Thy beauty, make amends, though even now,
> Close over us, the silver star, thy guide,
> Shines in those tremulous eyes that fill with tears
> To hear me?

This indication of another power is one of Tennyson's subtlest effects. Tithonus's question trembles between knowledge of his fate, and a refusal to accept it, and the final ominous answer is not in Aurora's tears, but in the star which they reflect. In *The Lover's Tale* the star is 'silver-smiling Venus'; here she is named only in Tennyson's gloss. She is more than Aurora's guide, the planet visible as a morning or evening star. The tiny silver star is the 'alma Venus' or nurturing Venus of Lucretius, 'quae terras frugiferentis / concelebras': 'who fillest with thyself the earth with her kindly fruits'; the goddess of nature, so presented in *Lucretius*, as in the *De Rerum Natura* which it echoes, who will not forgive the mortal who slipped out of the cycle of death and rebirth.[28] Her power is contained by the periphrasis of 'the silver star,' and by the tiny brilliant reflection itself: at once near and far, and ominously near in meaning. Its containment, and its radiation – by the containment itself, as well as by the nature of the image, and its exactly central position in the passage – gives it something of the effect of a jewel in its setting.

This is one kind of achievement; the pathos of the

conclusion is another. Tithonus, trying to look forward to death, can still recall what was.

> Yet hold me not for ever in thine East:
> How can my nature longer mix with thine?
> Coldly thy rosy shadows bathe me, cold
> Are all thy lights, and cold my wrinkled feet
> Upon thy glimmering thresholds, when the steam
> Floats up from those dim fields about the homes
> Of happy men that have the power to die,
> And grassy barrows of the happier dead.
> Release me, and restore me to the ground;
> Thou seëst all things, thou wilt see my grave:
> Thou wilt renew thy beauty morn by morn;
> I earth in earth forget these empty courts,
> And thee returning on thy silver wheels.

(The recurring 'ever' of the poem is feebly challenged in 'Yet hold me not for ever'; the 'longer' of the second line is delusion.) The conclusion of the monologue turns back to the natural cycle with which it began. But in place of the distance of 'Man comes and tills the field and lies beneath', there is the immediacy of 'grassy barrows of the happier dead' – another addition to *Tithon*, evoking with exquisite fitness the lost human community whose tribal dead remain a part of it. Tennyson's art is at its finest in the last line. Earlier Tithonus remembered how ('with what another heart') he 'lay, / Mouth, forehead, eyelids, growing dewy-warm / With kisses balmier than half-opening buds / Of April'. His present is now the empty courts, but 'thee returning on thy silver wheels' is past as well as present, a yearning for what was which lingers even as he asks for death.

In *Tithonus* and *Ulysses* Tennyson makes superb fiction out of his life-weariness, and his anguish over Hallam's death. In the lyric *Break, break, break*, also inspired by Hallam's death, there is no such translation. Cleanth Brooks thought it thin, in comparison with *Tears, idle tears*, and there have been attempts to discover and defend its denseness.[29] Yet although 'thin' is the wrong word, it is the failure or refusal to make one kind of fiction which is the lyric's strength.

> Break, break, break,
>   On thy cold gray stones, O sea!
> And I would that my tongue could utter
>   The thoughts that arise in me.
>
> O well for the fisherman's boy,
>   That he shouts with his sister at play!
> O well for the sailor lad,
>   That he sings in his boat on the bay!
>
> And the stately ships go on
>   To their haven under the hill;
> But O for the touch of a vanished hand,
>   And the sound of a voice that is still!
>
> Break, break, break,
>   At the foot of thy crags, O Sea!
> But the tender grace of a day that is dead
>   Will never come back to me.

The essence of the poem is the regularity of the 'Break, break, break' of the first and last stanzas; the feeling that such regularity must have meaning; and, in the slow anapaestic lines deriving from and questioning the movement, the inability to find meaning. Within the dull breaking is the sight of little and larger victims, at play and at work: the fisherman's boy and his sister; farther out, the sailor lad, and the stately vulnerable ships. The climax of the anguish, and of the attempt to utter what cannot be uttered, is in the third stanza, with its suggestion of a completed voyage, and so perhaps of the voyage of the one who remains. But it is only a hopeless reaching out at meaning, and even the attempted apprehension of 'thy cold gray stones' turns at the end to the dry 'at the foot of thy crags'. What the lyric perfectly expresses is the fact of loss in a world which gives neither metaphors nor reasons.

It is the fact of loss that is at the heart of the *Morte d'Arthur*, which unlike *Ulysses* says plainly that the past will not be recovered. The *Morte* is narrative, not monologue, and the archaic heroic mode removes its actors still farther from us. Though not bare, the style has a certain austerity, aided by the contrast with the sword Excalibur's 'subtlest jewellery', by the ritual repetitions that accompany Bedivere's three attempts to throw away Excalibur, and by the bleakness of the setting. In a sense, whatever courage there is in the poem is in its language, not in its actors or their speeches. Arthur speaks nobly, but is almost beyond the human. Bedivere, who fails him, can only lament his loss. It is the heroic style, after all, which makes the proper response, in heightening the loss.

'So all day long the noise of battle rolled / Among the mountains by the winter sea; / Until King Arthur's table, man by man, / Had fallen in Lyonesse about their Lord, / King Arthur . . .' 'On one side lay the Ocean, and on one / Lay a great water, and the moon was full.' The opening lines pause before all that has gone by, and what is to come; the expectation in 'and the moon was full' makes it sound almost like a present tense. (Tennyson used the phrase again, more picturesquely, in Lancelot's adventure at Carbonek in *The Holy Grail*, line 815.) But there is no great action to come, and the only magic is the arm raised from the lake to catch Excalibur, and whatever may be inferred from the three Queens on the barge. After the initial narrative impulse, there is in fact a continuing reduction to something less than action.

> So saying, from the ruined shrine he stept
> And in the moon athwart the place of tombs,
> Where lay the mighty bones of ancient men,
> Old knights, and over them the sea-wind sang
> Shrill, chill, with flakes of foam.

> . . . He gazed so long
> That both his eyes were dazzled, as he stood,
> This way and that dividing the swift mind,
> In act to throw: but at the last it seemed
> Better to leave Excalibur concealed
> There in the many-knotted waterflags
> That whistled dry and stiff about the marge.

The real voice of the poem is in 'Where lay the mighty bones of ancient men, / Old knights', where the musingly reductive parenthesis 'Old knights' works by the reversal of the vowels of 'mighty bones'. And in the second passage it is less the Virgilian introspection of 'This way and that dividing the swift mind' that matters, than the ironic turn from it to the impersonal observation of moral defeat in 'but at the last it seemed / Better to leave Excalibur concealed . . .' (Virgil's 'atque animum nunc huc celerem, nunc dividit illuc' (*Aeneid* IV. 285) derives from Homer ('and within his shaggy breast his heart was divided in counsel', *Iliad* I. 188), and perhaps the faint reference to an even older heroic poem than the *Aeneid* is not accidental.) The mighty ancient men are only old knights, and the living Bedivere fails. The heroic style takes its own account of it, knowing more than we do, and bearing the agony for us.

In the end, the narrative action of the poem turns to yielding, and passivity: the King's passing, his last knight's submission and despair. Before this, of course, there is the temptation of Bedivere. It is easy to misunderstand this, and to suppose that Tennyson is attempting, without much success, a psychological study. To throw away the sword is to accept the end of a great age, and this Bedivere can hardly bring himself to do. But it was no part of Tennyson's deeper purpose to show any trial other than that of loss. 'Long stood Sir Bedivere / Revolving many memories' means much more than Bedivere standing and dividing the swift mind. The dying King's words about the changing of the old order, and the mystery of God's fulfilment of Himself, are remote. Prayer is the only consolation, and the chill contraction of Malory in Arthur's 'Comfort thyself: what comfort is in me?' is uncompromising.[30] The promise of the seasonal cycle in this midwinter death is hardly for Bedivere; the *Morte d'Arthur*, obviously enough, is a statement of a void which will not be filled in our time.

There are some lapses, like the 'knightly growth that fringed his lips', or the posing of the dying King 'looking wistfully with wide blue eyes / As in a picture'. 'He heard the deep behind him, and a cry / Before. His own thought drove him, like a goad': the first sentence is a little too intent on its spareness, and the simile of the second, with or without the reassurance of 'own', seems commonplace. But the heroic style is one of Tennyson's greatest achievements of the 1830s. In the 270-odd lines, there are only three 'epic' similes, which is one of the differences between the *Morte d'Arthur*, and Arnold's *Sohrab and Rustum*. Two describe actions: the casting away of Excalibur (136–42), and the departure of the barge (265–69). Not surprisingly, the most powerful of the three has to do with grief rather than action.

> . . . and from them rose
> A cry that shivered to the tingling stars,
> And, as it were one voice, an agony
> Of lamentation, like a wind, that shrills
> All night in a waste land, where no one comes,
> Or hath come, since the making of the world.

This is the least formally epic of the three similes, and its categories are much closer than those of the others. Excalibur 'Shot like a streamer of the northern morn'; the barge 'Moved from the brink, like some full-breasted swan'. But the equivalence here is of shivering cry and shrilling wind, of wind in an eternally waste land and the voice of agony in the winter waste of Lyonesse. A few lines before, Bedivere, carrying the wounded King, 'swiftly strode from ridge to ridge, / Clothed with his breath, and looking, as he walked, / Larger than human on the frozen hills'. This is hardly reductive, though 'looking' is cautious enough, but perhaps Tennyson is guilty of some sleight of hand with 'strode from ridge to ridge', which implies giant steps without quite saying it. But there is no sleight of hand in the simile of the cry; the one voice is like a lamentation of the earth, which is appropriate, since Arthur has something of the attributes of a dying god. What lapses there are hardly disturb the poem, as it proceeds, with a grave composure which is like the voice of fortitude, to its desolate conclusion. 'Revolving many memories' . . . 'This way and that dividing the swift mind': for whatever reason, these two phrases stay in our minds as long as anything else in the *Morte d'Arthur*, and it is not accidental that they should have a common origin, in the epic of Tennyson's loved 'Roman

Virgil'. It has been said of the *Aeneid* that it enlists our
sympathy on the side of loneliness, suffering, and defeat, and
that Virgil's hero has nothing to which to look forward, and
only too much to which to look back.[31] Tennyson's poem is
like a distillation of this. The elegiac *On a Mourner*, written
when he first heard of Hallam's death, ends with a direct
evocation of the *Aeneid*, of the comfort given in the third
book to 'Troy's wandering prince' by the voices at night that
promised empire. But the nineteenth-century poem has no
deeper directing voices from within, and even Arthur's mind
is clouded with a doubt.

When Tennyson published the *Morte d'Arthur* in 1842, he
framed it within the modern introduction and conclusion of
The Epic, and put it at the head of the English Idyls. The
frame is not (as is sometimes supposed) apologetics designed
to forestall criticism of 'faint Homeric echoes'. It is a skilful
mediation between poetry and audience which approves the
Morte, but which also – and in part involuntarily – leaves
room for doubt about the place of poetry in the modern age.
The setting is 'Francis Allen's on the Christmas-eve', with the
host, 'the parson Holmes, the poet Everard Hall', and the
narrator, talking late at night after the usual Christmas games
are over, and the women have gone to bed. Talk of how the
old honour has gone from Christmas leaves the field free for
Holmes, who is a bore, and he 'settles down' on 'the general
decay of faith / Right through the world', and the lack of any
anchor to hold by. Allen presents the diffident Hall as his
anchor. Hall, it appears, holds by the wassail-bowl; he
burned his Arthurian epic, but the eleventh book that Allen
saved from the hearth is brought for him to read, when

> the poet little urged,
> But with some prelude of disparagement,
> Read, mouthing out his hollow oes and aes,
> Deep-chested music, and to this result.

This is not Hall and his wassail-bowl, but 'the poet', and
'deep-chested music' brings him before us a second before the
deep-chested music of the *Morte d'Arthur* itself.

Whereas the introduction is separate from the *Morte*, the

conclusion is line-numbered consecutively from it. The epic style of 'Here ended Hall', eight lines after the 'So said he' on which the barge moves out, confirms the man we have not known till now. Holmes has slept, and wakes only to grunt 'Good!'; the age's lateness lives in this decent parsonical bore, 'sent to sleep with sound, / And waked with silence'.

>   ... but we
> Sat rapt: it was the tone with which he read –
> Perhaps some modern touches here and there
> Redeemed it from the charge of nothingness –
> Or else we loved the man, and prized his work;
> I know not: but we sitting, as I said,
> The cock crew loud; as at that time of year
> The lusty bird takes every hour for dawn ...

Nothing in the reservations after 'rapt' lessens its force. The crowing of the cock is part of the response, and is so presented: 'but we sat ... but we sitting, as I said ...' The reference is to Shakespeare's bird of dawning in *Hamlet* (I. i. 157–64), and though it is not a sign to dispel any doubts in the hearers about whether they did well to be rapt, it is such a sign for us. Nothing more is said, except Allen's muttered 'There now – that's nothing!' as he drives the smouldering log home with more force than usual. But an authentic word has been spoken, by which a change has been wrought. 'And so to bed', where the narrator passes into a dream of Arthur, which towards morning turns to a vision of his return, confirmed by the early Christmas bells.

It is nevertheless difficult to believe that *The Epic* offers unqualified reassurance about poetry in this age, partly because at one moment Tennyson seems to become uncertain of his purpose. Although Hall insists on modernity, that 'a truth / Looks freshest in the fashion of the day', and although his burning of his epic may mean other things to come, there is an air of defeat about him, and his 'gift' for drinking, that remains with us in spite of the deep-chested music, the sitting rapt, and the dream and waking. Of course the self-disparagement and understatement are all very English, and Hall's talent for drinking may mean little one way or the other. (Tennyson had something of a gift for port, and frequently exuded an air of defeat, or worse.)[32] But we have a feeling that it is not only the old honour of Christmas that has dwindled down to odd nooks like Francis Allen's on the Christmas-eve. What emerges clearly is the homeless state of poetry in this age, and the poet's uncertainty. Allen and the narrator own the effect of poetry: it momentarily changes the world for them, and Tennyson handles this with great skill. But although the dream of Arthur's return is obviously intended to approve this, it fails exactly where it should not, with that part of it which is visionary, and occurs at dawn, when dreams, in a Shakespearian way, 'begin to feel the truth and stir of day'. 'To me, methought, who waited with a crowd, / There came a bark that, blowing forward, bore / King Arthur, like a modern gentleman / Of stateliest port; and all the people cried, / "Arthur is come again: he cannot die." ' 'Methought' is visionary, and the closing lines of *The Epic* remind us of others who have dreamed visions, and waked to Christmas morn and its abiding hope. But the weakness of 'modern gentleman / Of stateliest port' is unmistakable. 'Modern' offers only stiff support to the blank 'gentleman', and 'Of stateliest port' is like a screen hastily trundled forward to cover a mistake. For this reason alone – the failure at one moment of the poetry – it is a lying dream, despite the truth and stir of day. It is not merely an aberration on Tennyson's part, offering clumsy proof of something which has already been subtly confirmed. Coming where it does, as a visionary conclusion to a mediation between poetry and audience which demonstrates poetry's enduring power over those who can hear, the orotundity suggests an unwillingness to trust his poetry, and with it a hesitancy about poetry itself, of the sort which sometimes comes to the surface in *In Memoriam*.

His youthful vision of himself in *Armageddon* had been that of a prophet endowed with extraordinary powers. *Timbuctoo*, with the speech of the Spirit of Fable, both yields to and counters doubts about the place and power of poetry. *The Poet* of 1830 makes grandiose claims: with his word, Freedom (like Johnson's 'steady Roman' in *The Vanity of Human Wishes*) 'shook the world'. In some respects, *The*

Hesperides of 1832, with its complex symbolism and daring technique, is Tennyson's most uncompromising and most enigmatic statement of the poet's function. It may or may not be significant that he did not republish it. But in *The Golden Year*, an English Idyl and a near contemporary of *The Epic*, Leonard believes he has been born too late among poets, and the weaknesses in his song may bear him out. (This is not really invalidated by the detachment Tennyson shows in the poem, the readiness to take account of other points of view, and even to make fun of himself.) The unpublished *What Thor Said to the Bard Before Dinner*, on the other hand, is merely a response to Croker's hostile *Quarterly* review of April 1833. Its title is the best of it; the language is resolutely cranky and old-mannered – 'Be not fairspoken neither stammer, / Nail her, knuckle her, thou swinge-buckler! / Spare not: ribroast gaffer and gammer' – and all it proposes is some cheery encouragement. The most obvious contemporary locus for Tennyson's doubts about poetry might seem to be the monologue *Tiresias*. This was partly written in 1833, though not published until 1885, and has obvious affinities with *Ulysses* and *Tithonus*. The occasion is the imminent destruction of Thebes, and Tiresias's urging of Menoeceus, son of Creon, to sacrifice himself and save the city. Its substance is the failure of poetry, and the need for deeds. Prophecy has helped no one; 'virtue must shape itself in deed'; there is no sound 'so potent to coerce, / And to conciliate' as the names of those who act and die nobly for their country: they are 'a song / Heard in the future'. Nothing could be farther from Spenser's classic claim, in *The Ruines of Time* (400–3): 'For deeds doe die, how euer noblie donne, / And thoughts of men do as themselues decay, / But wise wordes taught in numbers for to runne, / Recorded by the Muses, liue for ay.' But it may not seem very far from Wordsworth's observation, some thirty years before: 'However exalted a notion we would wish to cherish of the character of a Poet, it is obvious, that while he describes and imitates passion, his situation is altogether slavish and mechanical, compared with the freedom and power of real and substantial action and suffering.'[33]

But such a comparison would be inappropriate, for *Tiresias* is not Tennyson at his best, being heavily explicatory, and replete with the sense of a large message. 'Thou refusing this, / Unvenerable will thy memory be / While men shall move the lips' is typical of its classicising stiffness. It begins with 'I wish', and the closing movement (whose verse Tennyson admired) opens with 'I would': the heroic action implied is contained within a lament for the lost powers of sight and words. Before his blindness, Tiresias sought everywhere 'the meanings ambushed'; now, having moved Menoeceus to action, he would be where he may find 'the wise man's word, / Here trampled by the populace underfoot, / There crowned with worship'. Here 'Virtue must shape itself in deed, and those / Whom weakness or necessity have cramped / Within themselves, immerging, each, his urn / In his own well, draw solace as he may'. This is central to the poem, and imposes itself as central. Its eloquence is resolutely stayed on the legend of Pallas Athene, and its message is delivered as from a rostrum. Given the inferiority of the monologue, we cannot look here for Tennyson's deepest feelings about what poetry could or could not do. But in *The Lady of Shalott* (if we can for a moment limit the parabolic statement to what it certainly includes) the apparent self-sufficiency of the poetic imagination was shown to be treacherous; the fatality in the poem transcends any suggestion that the artist will do well enough if he sticks to his shadows. There can be no doubt about his need to write poetry: it was what he lived for. The rather unequal poems of the 1830s commonly called 'political poems' – *Hail Briton!, Of old sat Freedom on the heights, You ask me, why, though ill at ease, Love thou thy land, with love far-brought, I loving Freedom for herself* – and generally dating from the early 1830s, show a need to turn outward. But his deepest need seems to have been for what he could master, and make his own, by which he could make head against his *ennui* and depression. It probably brought its own uncertainties with it. Although he is fascinated by spiritual decay, and what moves him most will obviously produce his finest poetry, the exquisite lingering over decay and defeat in the Choric Song of *The Lotos-Eaters*, for example, is implicitly a criticism of poetry itself, which may indicate the real relationship between that poem and *The Hesperides*, with its celebration of the mystery of poetry.'My words are only words, and moved / Upon the topmost froth of thought': these lines from section LII of *In Memoriam* may not mean more than 'I would that my tongue could utter', or the despair over 'matter-moulded forms of speech' in XCV which other poets besides Tennyson have felt. Although the use V finds in 'measured language' is only that of 'The sad mechanic exercise, / Like dull narcotics, numbing pain', it is a measure of the pain, that poetry for the moment is no more than that. But again we are left with a feeling that the words have a wider application, and are not just a momentary reaction against what he had given his life to. Perhaps the last irony in *Tithonus*, one of the most perfect of his poems, is that of an unspoken comment on language: that this most melodious of laments will pass, according to the legend, into the dry chirping of the grasshopper which Tithonus will become. We must of course distinguish between any apparent hesitation about the value of poetry, and the recognition that the age was late. For that matter, what we may see as signs of a reservation about poetry may be nothing more than a lack of self-confidence in Tennyson. (Spedding said of him, 'He seeks for strength not within but without, accusing the baseness of his lot in life and looking to outward circumstances far more than a great man ought to want of them, and certainly more than they will ever bring.')[34] As for *The Epic* – graceful, modern, allusive – it is haunted by an equal sense of the power of poetry, and its homeless state.

The Poet's Song, the last piece in the 1842 volumes, seems to offer reassurance. In place of the puffing of *The Poet* of 1830, and the edgy scolding in *The Poet's Mind* of the same year ('So keep where you are: you are foul with sin; / It [the sacred fountain] would shrink to the earth if you came in'), there is a glad evocation of Orphic song.

> The rain had fallen, the Poet arose,
>   He passed by the town and out of the street,
> A light wind blew from the gates of the sun,
>   And waves of shadow went over the wheat,

And he sat him down in a lonely place,
   And chanted a melody loud and sweet,
That made the wild-swan pause in her cloud,
   And the lark drop down at his feet.

The swallow stopt as he hunted the fly,
   The snake slipt under a spray,
The wild hawk stood with the down on his beak,
   And stared, with his foot on the prey,
And the nightingale thought, 'I have sung many songs,
   But never a one so gay,
For he sings of what the world will be
   When the years have died away.'

Perhaps there is something of Shelley in it, the Shelley of the
Song of Pan, which also speaks of a magic song and a hushed
audience, of birds, insects, and lizards, and which incidentally
has a good deal to say about the nature and workings of
poetry. It may be the uncharacteristic optimism of its close
that makes us think of other poets. The movement, and the
mood, are more like Yeats than anyone else: the song the poet
sings is 'gay', and for once a Tennysonian swan is not dying,
but only pausing in her cloud. The anapaestic lightness is
slowed a little by the absence of rhyme in alternate lines, an
absence more marked in the second stanza, which continues
the alternation of unrhymed four-beat and rhyming three-
beat lines begun at the end of the first stanza. (In 1842 line 9
ended with 'bee'. The correspondence with the 'be' of line 15
is minimal, but Tennyson cared enough about it – or the
repeated vowel in 'beak' two lines later – to change it to 'fly' in
1888.)[35] The effect of the unrhymed lines is to take the edge
off the anapaests, and to leave something open; there is a sense
of wonder at what is evoked. But though the conclusion looks
forward to a perfected world – not that of the crowning race
of *The Princess* and *In Memoriam*: the lyric has no room for
meditation – the last line still keeps it at something of a tired
distance. It seems that Tennyson was in no doubt about what
should be sung, even in these later days. His poet's song is a
magic song, the essence of world-creating poetry. But the
evocation of what is to come is slightly muted, with the
lingering thought of the time that has yet to die.[36]

CHAPTER IV

The Princess

The Princess is an experiment in comedy, more particularly in Shakespearian comedy, in narrative form. Although often republished, it did not much please the more discriminating of Tennyson's contemporaries, and did not entirely please Tennyson himself. Twenty-two years after its appearance in 1847 he spoke of it 'with something of regret, of its fine blank verse, and the many good things in it', adding that 'though truly original, it is, after all, only a medley'.[1] The remark suggests that he understood well enough that some of the originality of his first long poem (if we except the early *The Lover's Tale*, not published until 1879, and then only because it had been pirated) was purchased on fairly easy terms. The stylistic achievement of *The Princess* is considerable, but one feels that Tennyson is working well within his powers. At its deepest level, the union of man and woman finally achieved in the poem is probably a reflection of the longing for concord within himself. On another level – the figure may be specious – Tennyson is addressing himself publicly to the contemporary problem of women's rights.

He had always been willing to show sympathy for the woman's cause. In *A Dream of Fair Women* of 1832, he had spoken of the selfishness of 'the stronger sterner nature', and had wondered whether 'the gentler mind / Might reassume its just and full degree / Of rule among mankind'. But there is little doubt what he had come to think that degree was, despite his prince's talk of men and women 'Yoked in all exercise of noble end'. Another contemporary question, that of the education of the people, is more than glanced at in the Prologue. At the same time *The Princess* is concerned with the education or enlightenment of the governing classes. It is by Arnold's barbarians that the debate between man and woman is given expression, and it leaves some of them thinking, sitting 'rapt' like the undergraduates who listened to the eleventh book of Everard Hall's epic.

> . . . we sat
> But spoke not, rapt in nameless reverie,
> Perchance upon the future man.

The form is that of a 'mouth to mouth' tale (an entertainment popular with the Victorians) in seven parts, within the framework of a Prologue and Conclusion. The setting is Vivian Place, seat of Sir Walter Vivian, who has given his park for the day to the local Mechanics' Institute. 'Strange was the sight and smacking of the time', says the narrator. Tennyson's description of the new age of educative experiment delights in contrasts: 'Somewhat lower down / A man with knobs and wires and vials fired / A cannon: Echo answered in her sleep / From hollow fields.' The house party gathers on the trim sward of the ruined Abbey, some of whose carved stones form part of the jumble of objects of 'every clime and age' in and around the house, a jumble which reflects the confusion of this age, heir to so many ages, and like the house itself not quite clear what should be done with them. (The Latinate inversion with which the description of the jumble begins – 'And me that morning Walter showed the house' – is both an ironic introduction to, and a necessary stay against, modern confusion.) The talk turns on the rights of women, and out of it arises the tale, to be 'drest up poetically' by the narrator, but given 'as wildly as it rose': a condition which has less to do with mere playfulness than we might think. (The working classes are 'taught . . . with facts' on Sir Walter's lawns, the governing classes will be amused by, perhaps instructed out of fantasy: the social comment of the division between the two sorts of instruction is less important than the recognition that art in the modern age is more than ever parenthetic.) An iron-willed feminist princess founds a women's university, which collapses when infiltrated by her rejected fiancé, a prince of a neighbouring country, and when the matter becomes an affair of state, and the occasion for armed intervention. The threatened war is resolved by a tournament, and the heroic princess yields to a prince who has all the charm of defeat and deathly wounds, and who believes passionately in his espousal (within reasonable bounds) of some parts of her cause. The Conclusion makes its guarded apologies, offers through the thoughtful narrator its hopes for progress, hints at thoughts of 'the future man', and closes, like the ending of a play, with Lilia, the young and passionate spokesman for women's rights, taking off the feminine silks in which she had laughingly robed the statue of Sir Ralph Vivian, her crusading ancestor.

The close is beautifully apt: 'our revels now are ended'. But there are several difficulties in the way of understanding, or realisation. The first, and most obvious, is that we sometimes fail to understand that *The Princess* is an attempt at comedy, and that the feminism is only the occasion for the comic action. Like the Shakespearian comedy which it echoes, the poem is concerned with continuity, and its convictions – man growing more like woman, and woman more like man – look forward in a way which has little to do with revolution. Princess Ida becomes woman, the Prince man, but neither was a hopeless case to begin with, despite her will, and his yellow ringlets. The parallel in the contemporary frame is that the feminist Lilia Vivian is left thinking – she has been described, significantly enough, as 'half child half woman' – and that the narrator is teased and puzzled into further thought, frustrated in his attempt to please both the mocking men and the supposedly realist women by writing up the tale, pleasing neither them nor himself, and succeeding only in moving 'as in a strange diagonal'. Tennyson's intentions are reasonably clear, and the diagonal in which he moves is not to be dismissed as apologetics. But the poem has serious weaknesses. One major difficulty with his revels has always been their disconcerting change of course. The Princess is heroic in her dedication to the future. Celibate, but looking forward to equal partnership in marriage for all women, her only errors the belief that women are 'sphered / Whole in ourselves', and that as 'living wills' they can match her dedication, she holds her enterprise together by force of will. The comedy begins to mingle more and more uneasily with the figure of the lonely and heroic founder of the women's university, and with the struggle against her. 'If women ever were to play such freaks,' Tennyson remarked, 'the burlesque and the tragic might go hand in hand.'[2] His comment is revealing, in more ways than one. The difficulty of accommodating heroic and burlesque in *The Princess* drives him to some rather obtrusive expedients. In the end the narrative stiffens into melodramatics, before dropping gently in the final section into the idea and prospect of a marriage which will type the highest marriages of the ages to come.

But the clash between heroic and burlesque – it makes little sense to pretend that there is no clash, or to try to resolve it by making wide gestures at comic principles – is the result of a limitation in Tennyson, which makes his failure in this kind of comedy perhaps inevitable. In spite of his prince's 'For woman is not undevelopt man, / But diverse', his own attitude to women, though overlaid by a good deal of sympathetic theorising in the last section, is less than sympathetic. Ida's project falls to pieces, not only because of the entry of the men, but because of the actions of Psyche and Blanche, and these complementary figures are a fair indication of Tennyson's reservations, or suspicions. (He was probably in control of his comedy when he presented Psyche as 'a quick brunette', and Melissa as 'a rosy blonde'; feminist cries of 'sex objects' should be aimed at the narrators here, not Tennyson.) Psyche is gentle in what many men believe is a womanly way, and lets the men in. Blanche, who is soured in what many men believe is a womanly way, completes the ruin by turning on Ida. The action is skilful enough, with Psyche concealing the men from pity, and the corrupt Blanche for advantage. But they remain rather vulgar stereotypes.

There is in fact a good deal of crudeness in *The Princess*, which has sometimes been mistaken for timidity, and which is to some extent concealed by the linguistic skill. The revealing division of the comedy into heroic and burlesque is evident almost from the beginning. Princess Ida is 'all beauty compassed in a female form', and her utterance is dignity itself: 'better not be at all / Than not be noble'. By contrast her assistant Psyche's lecture to the new students on the subjection and triumphs of women through the ages (the 'bird's-eye-view of all the ungracious past') is almost pure burlesque. The style is a wickedly accurate evocation of passionate doctrinaire oratory strained through feverish note-taking.

> Let them not fear: some said their heads were less:
> Some men's were small; not they the least of men;
> For often fineness compensated size:
> Besides the brain was like the hand, and grew
> With using; thence the man's, if more was more . . .

> . . . in arts of government
> Elizabeth and others; arts of war
> The peasant Joan and others; arts of grace
> Sappho and others vied with any man . . .

As F.E.L. Priestley remarks, the reported lecture combines 'suggestions of a tub-thumping party speech, a lecture in a survey course, and a reporter's mangled account of a public address'.[3] There is no mockery of the triumphant close, in which Psyche rises 'upon a wind of prophecy' to speak of the age of equality to come; by then, of course, none is needed. The stratagem by which Psyche is induced to break her vows, when she discovers the identity of the disguised Prince and his companions (one of whom is her brother), in this place where it is death for a man to enter, confirms her as a stereotype. Her resistance is easily broken down by the Prince's and Florian's repetition of the formula, at once appeal and condescension, 'Are you that Lady Psyche . . .? You were that Psyche, but what are you now?', to which Cyril gives the responses. (The rhetorical formality recalls *Love's Labours Lost*, with which there are obvious affinities.)[4] Masculine assurance has its way in this neatly orchestrated evocation of things as they have been and (despite the college) are – as it later will with Ida in her hour of victory – and danger dissolves in 'sweet household talk, and phrases of the hearth'. But the masculine assurance is Tennyson's as well. Psyche talks of the Spartan Mother and Lucius Junius Brutus, but her orders are that on pain of death they leave 'today, tomorrow, soon'.

On a more superficial level the comedy sometimes has a satisfying completeness. The description of the morning's lectures, for example, is a delightfully bland caricature of misguided purpose, with the quoted 'jewels five-words-long / That on the stretched forefinger of all Time / Sparkle for ever', and the 'scraps of thundrous Epic lilted out / By violet-hooded Doctors'. Like Robert Graves's 'The thundering text, the snivelling commentary', the last is a comment on the age, as well as on the women. The fact that Ida is real, and her university unreal, means, among other things, the difficulty of realising visions in an imperfect world. ('Why, Sirs, they do all this as well as we': it is not only Ida's college which is being mocked.) The description of the students in class ('like morning doves / That sun their milky bosoms on the thatch') is rather a long way even from the 'pretty, suggestive, pathetic sight' of the girls in the dormitory of the Melchester Training College in *Jude the Obscure*, with their 'tender feminine faces upturned to the flaring gas-jets'. And the peculiar unreality of the place suddenly becomes apparent in a passage which faintly recalls Boccaccio.

> . . . some hid and sought
> In the orange thickets: others tost a ball
> Above the fountain-jets, and back again
> With laughter: others lay about the lawns,
> Of the older sort, and murmured that their May
> Was passing: what was learning unto them?
> They wished to marry; they could rule a house;
> Men hated learned women . . .

These brief glum phrases of conformity ('could rule a house'), which merely ruffle the surface of the verse, mean more than Ida's solemn psalms and silver litanies, with which the devoted labours of the day will end. The tone and placing are exquisitely apt; we know what will rise up, and why.

When the visitors are discovered to be men, during the geological field-trip in IV, Tennyson has to abandon the advantage of observation by disguised (and erotically stimulated) intruders. What follows is handled with great skill, but it is at this moment that we begin to understand what limits his Shakespearian invention. The two songs *Tears, idle tears* and *O Swallow, Swallow* failing to satisfy the Princess, she asks for a song 'That gives the manners of your country-women', and turns 'eyes of shining expectation' on the Prince. And the unsentimental Cyril, drunkenly heedless, and perhaps suffering from the strain (he has had to sit through the Prince's attempt to sing his *O Swallow, Swallow* in a woman's voice, and no doubt 'country-women' tipped the balance) responds with 'a careless, careless tavern-catch / Of Moll and Meg, and strange experiences / Unmeet for ladies'. The Prince's 'Forbear, Sir' and angry blow complete the ruin. (The Prince himself is suffering from the strain, giggling as he runs away from two female proctors who have surprised him during a priggish defence of Cyril to Florian: 'at mine ear / Bubbled the nightingale and heeded not, / And secret laughter tickled all my soul.') Perhaps the song about Kate in *The Tempest* was somewhere in Tennyson's mind (for what it is worth, there is more than one Kate in his early poetry): 'She loved not the flavour of tar nor of pitch, / But a sailor might scratch her where'er she did itch.' It is Tennyson's revenge on these women, as well as Cyril's, and he will not let the song alone: the Prince returns to it, in his earnest analysis of Cyril just before the proctors arrive, with 'the song / Might have been worse and sinned in grosser lips / Beyond all pardon – as it is, I hold / These flashes on the surface are not he. / He has a solid base of temperament . . . ,' continuing, ludicrously enough, with a dainty simile about a starting and sliding water-lily. It may or may not be a flash on Cyril's surface; more to the point, it is not a flash on Tennyson's. Appropriately enough, mockery by (and of) linguistic skill takes over.

> . . . and then another shriek,
> 'The Head, the Head, the Princess, O the Head!'
> For blind with rage she missed the plank, and rolled
> In the river. Out I sprang from glow to gloom:

> There whirled her white robe like a blossomed branch
> Rapt to the horrible fall: a glance I gave,
> No more; but woman-vested as I was
> Plunged; and the flood drew; yet I caught her; then
> Oaring one arm, and bearing in my left
> The weight of all the hopes of half the world,
> Strove to buffet to land in vain.

The dramatics of 'Out I sprang from glow to gloom' respond
to the farce of 'the Head, the Princess, O the Head!' rolling in
the river, and excited metrics interpret the rescue: 'woman-
vested as I was / Plunged; and the flood drew; yet I caught
her; then / Oaring one arm . . .' The heavy iambics of 'The
weíght of áll the hópes of hálf the wórld' (a confused weight,
with the dull opposition of 'áll' and 'hálf', and a mockery of
Psyche's 'the secular emancipation . . . of half this world')
turns, like a parody of metrical skill, to the abrupt trochaics of
'Stróve to búffet'. There is a comparable effect in the next
passage, where the Prince, returning by 'beelike instinct
hiveward', climbs over Ida's portals.

> Two great statues, Art
> And Science, Caryatids, lifted up
> A weight of emblem, and betwixt were valves
> Of open-work in which the hunter rued
> His rash intrusion, manlike, but his brows
> Had sprouted, and the branches thereupon
> Spread out at top, and grimly spiked the gates.

> A little space was left between the horns,
> Through which I clambered o'er at top with pain . . .

The metrical flatness of the last two lines is like a weary
response to the complex imagery of valves (which the trium-
phant Ida will 'burst' from within in VI, and which reappear
in the 'dark gates' the Prince speaks of at the end (VII.341)),
manlike intrusion, and sprouting brows which suggest not
only Actaeon but the cuckold, ancient symbol of man's
laziness or indifference.

What more than anything else reveals Tennyson's attitude,

and the weakness at the heart of his comedy, is a brief phrase in the description of the tumult which breaks out in Ida's hall, on the arrival of the Prince's father with an army, carrying Ida's father as hostage. The Prince has publicly declared his love. His declaration, though eloquent ('With Ida, Ida, Ida, rang the woods ... The mellow breaker murmured Ida'), ends with a remarkable stroke of tactlessness when to prove that he comes 'not all unauthorized', he offers Ida a letter from Gama, her weak and devious father. Ida is about to speak, but

>   ... there rose
> A hubbub in the court of half the maids
> Gathered together: from the illumined hall
> Long lanes of splendour slanted o'er a press
> Of snowy shoulders, thick as herded ewes,
> And rainbow robes, and gems and gemlike eyes,
> And gold and golden heads; they to and fro
> Fluctuated, as flowers in storm, some red, some pale,
> All open-mouthed, all gazing to the light,
> Some crying there was an army in the land,
> And some that men were in the very walls,
> And some they cared not; till a clamour grew
> As of a new-world Babel, woman-built,
> And worse-confounded: high above them stood
> The placid marble Muses, looking peace.

The nearly parenthetical 'And some they cared not' recalls yesterday's murmurers, now in open revolt. The snowy shoulders and open mouths, with the imagery of sheep and flowers, make Tennyson's meaning plain enough. But 'a new-world Babel, woman-built, / And worse-confounded' is uncompromising, even brutal. The Princess, rejecting the 'fancies hatched / In silken-folded idleness' of *Tears, idle tears,* had said 'let the past be past; let be / Their cancelled Babels'. The returned contempt of 'woman-built, / And worse-confounded' is overt, leaving us under no illusions about the reason for Cyril's song before the expectant Ida, or the feeling behind the old king's expression of masculine empire: 'We hunt them for the beauty of their skins; / They love us for it, and we ride them down.' (The difference between what the age would accept in verse, and could hardly bear to think of in prose, is often surprising.)

The problem of how to end the fourth section must have been a severe test of Tennyson's skill. His use of one of those cataleptic seizures which periodically overtake the Prince (perhaps suggested to Tennyson by his own fears about epilepsy) looks like an escape. The seizures had been added to the fourth edition of 1851, as a mediation between dreams and reality within the fantasy, which would give it more substance. The verse is impressive. 'The Princess with her monstrous woman-guard, / The jest and earnest working side by side, / The cataract and the tumult and the kings / Were shadows; and the long fantastic night / With all its doings had and had not been, / And all things were and were not': some of this reminds us of *A Midsummer Night's Dream*, but the gathering up of aspects of one reality, the tumult and cataract and shadows, and the turn on 'were' recall the great Simplon Pass passage in *The Prelude*, which Tennyson admired. This derivation suggests that he is pulling all the stops out, which is consistent with the awkwardness of the device. Despite the fact of narrative, 'The jest and earnest working side by side' is one of those explanations of what has been done that lessen one's trust, like an apology for the balancing act of the long fantastic night. And the simile with which IV ends promises more than it can perform.

> . . . for spite of doubts
> And sudden ghostly shadowings I was one
> To whom the touch of all mischance but came
> As night to him that sitting on a hill
> Sees the midsummer, midnight, Norway sun
> Set into sunrise . . .

Like the men themselves, the fourth section sidles out rather guiltily. Something of the staginess that will overtake the tale is already present in the mourning Psyche of V: 'wrapped in a soldier's cloak, / Like some sweet sculpture draped from head to foot, / And pushed by rude hands from its pedestal, / All her fair length upon the ground she lay.' In the Prologue, Lilia robed Sir Ralph's statue in feminine silk. But the reference, which is part of a wider context of such reference, cannot help this passage. As for Psyche's lament for her child, it is the first time in the poem that a false note has been held for so long. It is more than ever a mouth to mouth tale, since with the threat of war Tennyson seems to have got himself into a nearly impossible position. But the trial of arms is turned into a tournament, in which no one is killed, and in which the wounded (to judge by the last thirty lines or so of VI) seem to be voiceless, their cries replaced by groaning doors, shuddering echoes, and marble shrieking under iron heels. The tournament itself is muffled by a dream; like IV, section V has its weird seizure near the end, and though the Prince recovers before the tournament, 'Yet it seemed a dream, I dreamed / Of fighting', a dream which is urged on us four times in the sixty-odd lines describing the combat. It might have become stern reality for the Prince when he is struck down, but he is spirited into a state described in some of the weakest lines in the poem.

> My dream had never died or lived again.
> As in some mystic middle state I lay;
> Seeing I saw not, hearing not I heard:
> Though, if I saw not, yet they told me all
> So often that I speak as having seen.

'For so it seemed, or so they said to me, / That all things grew more tragic and more strange.' It is with the 'tragic' of VI, as most readers have understood, that the medley finally fails. In spite of the reference to *The Winter's Tale* in the Prologue, such 'tragic' cannot really be defended by referring it to the medley of romance, if only because this narrative can hardly hope to emulate the pace of drama. The breaking of Ida's will in her hour of triumph, bayed about as she is by the men of both sides, and by the vindictive Blanche, has its impressive moments, but it is intolerably stagy. Ida and the King over the wounded Prince ('So those two foes above my fallen life, / With brow to brow like night and evening mixt / Their dark and gray'); the return of the child ('and so / Laid the soft babe in his hard-mailèd hands'); Cyril's all too

powerful speech demanding the child's return ('beware /
Lest, where you seek the common love of these, / The
common hate with the revolving wheel / Should drag you
down'): there is nothing which will give this substance.
Tennyson did well to drop the 1847–48 reading of VI. 138,
'Bruised, where he fell, not far off, much in pain', with its
heavily Miltonic pauses, but the whole passage is over-
wrought. The epic 'so said' or its equivalent occurs five times
during the episode, ludicrously enough with Gama's speech:
'So said the small king moved beyond his wont.' His scolding
heroics – 'was it then for this, / Was it for this we gave our
palace up . . .' – are comical enough, but they are as heavy in
their own way as the ponderous confrontation of Ida and
Cyril. When Ida rises 'once more through all her height' over
the fallen Cyril ('remembering his ill-omened song' is a
disastrous phrase), and Cyril rouses himself to kiss her robe
and denounce her cruelty, it is rather difficult not to think of
them as a couple of actors trying to keep their faces straight.
Ida, not surprisingly, is reduced to begging the Prince's father
to allow her to nurse him. 'Passionate tears followed':
perhaps the impersonality is that of a natural reaction, and has
nothing of contempt in it. But 'the king replied not', like
'woman-built, / And worse-confounded', obviously has
Tennyson's approval; it is like a sulky revenge.

  The failure is radical. And although there is a much firmer
grasp in VII than we would have expected from the staginess
of VI, it is partly because male authority has been recovered.
The tale ends, fittingly enough, on the promise of marriage.
Ida's concern has been to liberate women so that they will be
fit for marriage on equal terms, and will play their part in
evolving that crowning race towards which Tennyson
thought mankind was progressing.[5] It would be a mistake to
suppose that the serious and often very beautiful discussion
of ideal union, with its recognition of likeness in difference,
and the hope of more sweetness for the man and greater
mental breadth for the woman, is merely discussion. For one
thing, mere discussion has its part to play in that it represents
a return to order. But the description of the ministering
women moving among the wounded 'like creatures native
unto gracious act, / And in their own clear element' has more

to tell us than all the Prince's raptures about the woman's cause being the man's. Although Ida has had her women learn nursing, 'foreseeing casualty', and although initially at least their care is freely offered, the verse rejoices quietly in the restoration of women to their place. 'It was ill counsel had misled the girl', the narrative version of the penitent Ida speaking of herself to the Prince, is revealing in a different way; the reversal of roles ('you cannot love me') seems dangerously complete, despite the terms of the discussion. Although the Prince does not woo Ida merely by saying what will please her, he seems to be seeking his own manhood in her, which perhaps confirms him as a man. His Diotima has been his mother, and his description of her affirms the necessarily subordinated higher being.

> '. . . one
> Not learnèd, save in gracious household ways,
> Not perfect, nay, but full of tender wants,
> No Angel, but a dearer being, all dipt
> In Angel instincts, breathing Paradise,
> Interpreter between the Gods and men,
> Who looked all native to her place, and yet
> On tiptoe seemed to touch upon a sphere
> Too gross to tread, and all male minds perforce
> Swayed to her from their orbits as they moved,
> And girdled her with music.'

Loving women through her, he learned to look to the dream that Ida now disclaims: 'The single pure and perfect animal, / The two-celled heart beating, with one full stroke, / Life.' Perhaps Ida understands the situation well enough: 'It seems you love to cheat yourself with words.' Thinking now only of love, she is yielding to an unequal partnership: the Prince has in effect appropriated the future from her.

> 'Then comes the statelier Eden back to men:
> Then reign the world's great bridals, chaste and calm:
> Then springs the crowning race of humankind.
> May these things be!'

(Her unexpected 'I fear / They will not' is truth itself.) And
the last words of the tale are his.

> 'Accomplish thou my manhood and thyself;
> Lay thy sweet hands in mine and trust to me.'

He has longed for Ida as boys long for manhood, and her
'truthful change' has cured him of his seizures. But the
penultimate line suggests another kind of truth, that Ida will
accomplish herself in accomplishing his manhood.

It is Ida, not the Prince, who has awakened from a dream,
and nothing has changed. It will not do to argue that this is
appropriate, since nothing does change in comedy. Although
this comedy, or Long Vacation pastoral, is concerned with
continuity, the sense of process that we associate with the
kind or kinds of comedy that Tennyson draws on is present
only in a limited sense, and this cannot be blamed on the
narrative mode. The Conclusion has something to tell us
about what has been completed. The tale is to be 'drest up
poetically' by the narrator, but the men insist on bantering
'mock-heroic gigantesque,' and the women ask that Ida
should be 'true-heroic – true-sublime' . . . 'Or all . . . as
earnest as the close.'

> Then rose a little feud betwixt the two,
> Betwixt the mockers and the realists:
> And I, betwixt them both, to please them both,
> And yet to give the story as it rose,
> I moved as in a strange diagonal,
> And maybe neither pleased myself nor them.

It may reflect uneasiness, but it need not be apologetics.
Tennyson gives 'the random scheme as wildly as it rose', and
the story as it rose among them – the men telling the tale, the
women influencing it by their songs or by their presence –
reflects an order that he is glad to accept: man as actor,
woman aiding him in action. (The women become more
involved as the poem proceeds: the last three intercalary
songs, in particular *Ask me no more*, comment directly
enough, and *Thy voice is heard* has its effect on the tale.) In

this, if in nothing else, the medley finds its own form. In his anxiety for the public to understand *The Princess*, or not to condemn it, he may have exaggerated the importance of the intercalary songs. His comment that 'the child is the link through the parts, as shown in the Songs (inserted 1850), which are the best interpreters of the poem' seems defensive.[6] There is something of the same uneasiness in the way in which Psyche's star-like child is kept in the foreground. The idea of the child is constant: Ida's unambiguous wish that children 'grew / Like field-flowers everywhere' (perhaps recalling the babies that 'rolled about / Like tumbled fruit in grass' of the Prologue), her call to women to lose the child and assume the woman, and the Prince's belief that the woman of the future will not 'lose the childlike in the larger mind'. Four of the six intercalary songs have to do directly with children and parents. The undying human echoes of *The splendour falls* may be future generations, or undying ideals, or both, and though the last of these songs (*Ask me no more*) has no child, it is a rendering of a woman yielding to love, and particularly apt to Ida's yielding, with its 'I strove against the stream and all in vain: / Let the great river take me to the main.' (The idea of death or loss of personality in this image of fulfilment in the third and last stanza is of a different order from the conventional sickness unto death of the rejected lover in the second.) They interpret the poem in that, despite the rights of women, these seem to be the only themes the women know or care about.[7] Of course, the songs accompany a romantic tale of love. But even when disapproving of the 'raillery, or grotesque, or false sublime', and calling for 'some grand fight to kill and make an end', Lilia, the Ida of the frame, sings a song of a soldier inspired in battle by wife and 'brood'.

In the 1847 and 1848 editions, Lilia's thoughtful silence after the tale was followed by the elevation of Sir Walter Vivian, with whom the poem begins: 'And there we saw Sir Walter where he stood . . . / No little lily-handed Baronet he, / A great broad-shouldered genial Englishman.' Race and sex share nearly equal honours in that last line. Sir Walter is the modern enlightened landowner, to whom the land is lent, not given, and who makes two blades of grass grow where one grew before. 'A pamphleteer on guano and on grain, / A

quarter-sessions chairman, abler none': these two small cy-
cles say what has to be said. They also omit such virtues as
imagination. Part of the emphasis is on kind, and Sir Walter
comes before us like a reassurance which was there from the
beginning, among the strange jumble on his broad lawns.
Does the celebration of this 'patron of some thirty charities'
and 'raiser of huge melons and of pine' also indicate the
qualities which the ruling classes lack, and which the Prince
and Princess of the tale possessed? It is a measure of the
poem's weakness, that one has to speculate. In 1850, troubled
by the political events of 1848 in Europe, and anxious to be
understood, Tennyson added forty lines before the
apotheosis of Sir Walter, so separating him from Lilia, and
avoiding some of the implications of this contrast. The garden
of England is set against the tumult of revolutionary France,
'the red fool-fury of the Seine', as he called it in *In Memor-
iam*, and the contrast is sanctioned by a heart-felt speech by
one of the guests. 'Some sense of duty, something of a faith, /
Some reverence for the laws ourselves have made, / Some
patient force to change them when we will, / Some civic
manhood firm against the crowd': the anaphoric 'some'
rejoices in English practice against French theory, the human
against the abstract. Some of the national feelings were Ten-
nyson's own, but they are given, not to the narrator – or to
young Walter Vivian, Lilia's Arac, whose response to the tale
was the unexpected 'I wish she had not yielded!' – but to 'the
Tory member's elder son'. But it can hardly prepare us for
what Sir Walter lacks, or confirm what is needed if we are to
get beyond prize oxen and charities. Perhaps the hope for the
future is in Walter Vivian's generous impulse, as in Lilia's
thoughtfulness. On his side the narrator counsels patience,
and a wider view drawn from this 'genial day': 'there is a hand
that guides'. 'Maybe wildest dreams / Are but the needful
preludes of the truth,' he says, taking up the other's references
both to the political dreams across the Channel, and their
own fantasies that afternoon. For an hour or so imagination
has had its way with Arnold's barbarians, and now we are
more or less left with Sir Walter and the happy English
valleys. It is not to discount Tennyson's hopes for the distant
future, to feel that the real failure is perhaps that the deeper

processes of comedy have been transferred to an idea of social history.

If anything in this addition was meant to offer reassurance about the guiding hand in the poem itself, we would have to reject it. One way in which the medley of the mouth to mouth tale found its form has been suggested, and it is of course true that the collective fancy ends in the restoration of order, the rejection of extremes, and a willingness to discuss common problems. But whatever formal order can be found, the invocation of Shakespearian comedy fails, because Tennyson's opinion of women is not that of Shakespearian comedy. We can quote till things fall apart his statements about Christ as 'that union of man and woman, sweetness and strength', without altering this in the least.[8] What more than anything else could persuade us of some form at work in *The Princess* is the beauty of its ending: the sitting rapt in nameless reverie while night falls, Lilia's quiet disrobing of Sir Ralph's statue.

> . . . the walls
> Blackened about us, bats wheeled, and owls whooped,
> And gradually the powers of the night,
> That range above the region of the wind,
> Deepening the courts of twilight broke them up
> Through all the silent spaces of the worlds,
> Beyond all thought into the Heaven of Heavens.

Our revels now are ended, and, in further Shakespearian phrase, the deep of night is crept upon our talk. Speech becomes silence, and what is invoked for this conclusion moves 'beyond all thought'. But for all except the most resolute theorist, *The Princess* must sometimes come close to exemplifying the view of Tennyson as a master of language with not very much to say. Not that it is faultless: one or two weak passages have been instanced, and there are others, like such a dragging tautology as 'well-nigh close to death / For weakness'. But nowhere in Tennyson is the language more subtly worked. Some of it, like the 'fancies hatched / In silken-folded idleness', has a Shakespearian felicity.

> ... transient in a trice
> From what was left of faded woman-slough
> To sheathing splendours and the golden scale
> Of harness, issued in the sun, that now
> Leapt from the dewy shoulders of the Earth,
> And hit the Northern hills.

This is like a conflation of memories of *Hamlet* I. i. 166–67 ('But look, the morn, in russet mantle clad, / Walks o'er the dew of yon high eastern hill'), and the passage in *Henry IV*, Part I (IV. i. 97–103) about young Harry with his beaver and cuisses on, rising 'from the ground like feathered Mercury', glittering with his comrades 'in golden coats, like images'. Sometimes there is a recognisably Shakespearian movement, without any particular origin, or notable felicity.

> 'For woman is not undevelopt man,
> But diverse: could we make her as the man,
> Sweet Love were slain: his dearest bond is this,
> Not like to like, but like in difference.'

Sometimes the resemblance seems thrust on us.

> '. . . many a famous man and woman, town
> And landskip, have I heard of, after seen
> The dwarfs of presage . . .'

But this, and more notably lines like

> . . . and loose
> A flying charm of blushes o'er this cheek,
> Where they like swallows coming out of time
> Will wonder why they came . . .'

– with their rapid grace, and the play on 'charms', are more than a borrowed apprehension. Although mockery (it is Cyril who is speaking of himself dressed as a woman) they make a claim on the Shakespearian comedy which Tennyson is adapting. The most imitative of his writing is *The Devil and the Lady*, which is unashamed pastiche. *The Lover's Tale*, of which the first three parts may have been written as early as his seventeenth year (and five lines of which were incorporated into the Conclusion of *The Princess*), is also full of Shakespearian sounds.[9] 'The flow / And hourly visitation of the blood'; 'Be cabined up in words and syllables'; 'Her words did of their meaning borrow sound'; 'Or had my fancy / So lethargised discernment in the sense, / That she did act the stepdame to mine eyes, / Warping their nature, till they ministered / Unto her swift conceits?': these are all from the first part of *The Lover's Tale*. Tennyson spoke of it as 'very rich and full', and its Elizabethan moments contribute notably to the richness and fullness.

The imitation or recreation of Shakespearian language in *The Princess* is one of its greatest successes; it is probably a substitution for the comedy which he could not re-create. Sometimes he turns elsewhere, as in the virtuoso simile describing Ida's putting off her 'falser self'.

> . . . lovelier in her mood
> Than in her mould that other, when she came
> From barren deeps to conquer all with love;
> And down the streaming crystal dropt; and she
> Far-fleeted by the purple island-sides,
> Naked, a double light in air and wave,
> To meet her Graces, where they decked her out
> For worship without end.

'A double light in air and wave' takes this far beyond imitation, but the provenance is unmistakable. The Miltonising in *The Princess* has mostly been used for mock (or false) heroics; here it is a reassurance. (Ida's description of Diotima and Socrates, incidentally – 'She rapt upon her subject, he on her' – suggests a characteristic reversal of Milton's 'He for God only, she for God in him' (*Paradise Lost* IV. 299).) This, on the other hand, is Tennyson's own.

> And twilight gloomed; and broader-grown the bowers
> Drew the great night into themselves, and Heaven,
> Star after star, arose and fell.

'Laborious orient ivory sphere in sphere' recalls, perhaps reverses, the music of Virgil's 'tendebantque manus ripae ulterioris amore'; 'Cyril, with whom the bell-mouthed glass had wrought,' has more than the charm of studied periphrasis. But the suppleness of these lines, the quiet movements in them that render the 'moving Universe' from which the wounded Prince is divided, are a different achievement. The passage is again from the seventh section, which is either rich in borrowing, or has its share of contrivance, depending on one's point of view: the Aphrodite simile, the Prince's rapid eloquence, with such a line as 'Yoked in all exercise of noble end'. This section also contains the songs *Now sleeps the crimson petal, now the white*, and *Come down, O maid, from yonder mountain height*. Both are love songs, and seem to urge Ida to yield to love. (She reads them 'to herself, all in low tones' from 'a volume of the Poets of her land': Psyche's excited description of the 'double growth' of poets who would sanction the new age is very much in the past. As is Ida's song *Our enemies have fallen, have fallen*, where the lack of rhyme, common to the integral poems, works with the riddling imagery ('The little seed they laughed at in the dark' . . . 'There dwelt an iron nature in the grain') to give something of the effect of a translation, and an alien ethos; the song has all the savage rejoicing of a chosen and persecuted people who have asked for judgment, and received it.) In *Now sleeps the crimson petal*, the quiet 'now' seems to will the woman's yielding, like an opening within the enclosing or enfolding peace of the spaces of garden, earth, and sky. Whereas nature here is invoked so tranquilly as to seem to participate in the union, its invocation in *Come down, O maid, from yonder mountain height* belongs to a traditional mode of courtship. On the one hand there is virginity ('height and cold, the splendour of the hills'); on the other, fulfilment of nature's purposes, with the valley's 'happy threshold' and its calling children; the last suggesting perhaps the unborn calling for life, and so a hint of what the woman's duty is. Aided by late caesurae and strong enjambment, the shepherd's song seems to descend throughout its course, drawing the maiden down from the cold heights to the sheltered peace of the valley, and the sounds of swarming life in which the song comes to rest, and where it rests its argument. The suggestion that whether she knows it or not the maiden on the heights is looking for love belongs to this formula of courtship.

> Nor wilt thou snare him in the white ravine,
> Nor find him dropt upon the firths of ice,
> That huddling slant in furrow-cloven falls
> To roll the torrent out of dusky doors:
> But follow; let the torrent dance thee down
> To find him in the valley . . .

The strong deliberate movement of the last line and a half argues a yielding to nature, to the downward moving torrent which will make the valley fruitful.

> . . . let the wild
> Lean-headed Eagles yelp alone, and leave
> The monstrous ledges there to slope, and spill
> Their thousand wreaths of dangling water-smoke,
> That like a broken purpose waste in air:
> So waste not thou; but come . . .

With the grave 'So waste not thou', followed by the final imperative, the song turns to the expectant present tenses of its final phase – 'await', 'arise', 'call', 'pipe' – and its culmination in an evocation of sound:

> Myriads of rivulets hurrying through the lawn,
> The moan of doves in immemorial elms,
> And murmuring of innumerable bees.

So much, in this exquisitely melodious poem, depends on sound and silence – the silence of the frozen wastes, broken only by the eagles and the torrent; the voices of the children, the voice and music of the shepherd rising from the murmuring populous valley – that its ending in this rich luxuriance of sound is entirely appropriate. Though its arguments are potent, in the last resort its mode is that of lyric song.

It is probably this kind of assurance that one remembers longest about *The Princess*. The apparent turn from the darker poems in the 1842 volumes to the comedy of *The Princess* surprised some readers, though it need not have surprised anyone who had read the English Idyls attentively. It disappointed as well as surprised; with the 1842 volumes Tennyson had seemed poised for something greater. But a reader's view of successive volumes can be misleading, and though there will always be a tendency to think of the more troubled poetry of the 1830s as the only norm, we have to take *The Princess* on its own terms. Perhaps the mouth to mouth tale does create or justify its form; perhaps 'medley' means more than it does at first sight, or than Tennyson was willing to allow in talking about the poem afterwards. The adaptation of Shakespearian comedy to nineteenth-century narrative, with the necessary fantasy both contained and liberated by the frame, was an interesting experiment. (The Elizabethanising belongs to that nineteenth-century verbal expansion which sometimes declares itself in attempts to recover earlier styles, apparent in poems as different as *Endymion* and *Sordello*, and (on a different level) in some of the cadences of Carlyle.) But the comparison is one which Tennyson, if only for the reasons suggested, is unable to sustain. The poem's timidity before the rights of women is much less important than its crudeness as comedy, despite its wit, and its linguistic achievement. Paul Valéry said that the first business of criticism is the study of a work in terms of whatever problem the author has set himself, and the degree of his success in solving it.[10] It is perhaps enough to say that the quality of the problem Tennyson set himself in *The Princess*, as distinct from that of adapting Shakespearian comedy or romance, remains in doubt.

CHAPTER V

In Memoriam

Arthur Henry Hallam died in 1833; *In Memoriam A.H.H.*, a series of 131 elegiac sections or 'cantos', was published in 1850. Tennyson began writing the elegies soon after Hallam's death, which seems to have been the worst emotional shock he ever experienced. The friendship was an equal one, but after Hallam's death it became a dependence of lower on higher, in which 'the man, that with me trod / This planet' is revealed as a noble type or forerunner of the crowning race. The effect of Tennyson's comment that the poem was meant to be a kind of *Divine Comedy*, and that he had no idea of weaving the short sections into a whole 'until I found that I had written so many', is a little unfortunate.[1] It suggests that he did not quite know what he was doing, but thought that it might, with a little luck, be something fine. *In Memoriam* is more of a unity than most sequences of poems, and in its later stages the themes are drawn together with great skill. But this is not to say much more than that at some stage it becomes an unusually coherent sequence, which can be called a single poem only in a general sense. Bradley's suggestions about structure (based on the internal chronology, and the Christmas sections, to which Tennyson had drawn attention) are more diffident than those of later critics, for whom this sometimes seems to be the greatest problem about *In Memoriam*. Turning from the internal chronology to 'the structure of this whole', he looks for a turning point like the 'Peace, peace! he is not dead, he doth not sleep' of *Adonais*, seems to find it only in LXXVIII (the second Christmas section), then, dismissing this as unlikely to strike anyone who is not looking for transitions, goes back to Tennyson's divisions as they appear in the *Memoir*. 'Falling back, then, on the divisions pointed out by the author': the phrase does not suggest much confidence in these divisions. Tennyson suggested another grouping to James Knowles, but the two are so different that there is no reason to suppose that he thought either of the groupings more than an indication of how not to lose oneself in *In Memoriam*.[2] The near singleness of mood passes into singleness of purpose, but although there is some temptation to think of it as a work whose structure only becomes apparent as it gets to its final stages, the evidence is against this. And although dreams are important in Tennyson's poetry, arguments about structure based on the direction and coherence given by the dream-lyrics are misleading. Sometimes the waking and struggling human will relaxes, and something is achieved or foreshadowed in sleep. But claims like 'But in my spirit will I dwell, / And dream my dream, and hold it true' (CXXIII), or 'Behold, I dream a dream of good, / And mingle all the world with thee' (CXXIX), have relatively little to do with actual dream sections like LXIX or LXX, and though part of the conclusion, do not really conclude anything that is structurally important. Arguments that CIII is a significant conclusion to the dream sections are almost enough to discredit such a structure, whether imposed by Tennyson or his critics. CIII ends the eighth of the nine groups recorded by Knowles, for what that is worth, but it is an unequal poem, a complacently shiny dream allegory, with an air of being too well-fed. The only criterion, after all, is the poetry.

The working of Tennyson's sequence, unlike that of *The Prelude*, where there is the sense of a continual stirring, and sometimes of a labouring to bring forth, is a slow and diffuse process of eddying and circling, from a partial to a more complete vision. There is no refinement of the self on easy terms; he merely speaks of himself in the Epilogue as having 'grown / To something greater than before'. Nor is there a great single vision at the end. Aubrey de Vere admired the elegies, but wanted a *Paradiso*. He received instead Tennyson's blunt statement that he had written what he had felt and known, and would never write anything else. 'Chè la mia vista, venendo sincera, / e più e più entrava per lo raggio / dell' alta luce, che da sè è vera': his sight becomes more pure, notably in the two closing sections CXXX and CXXXI, but the near superlative of 'sincera' is another matter.[3] De Vere's query about a *Paradiso* shows that he had not understood what happens in the closing stages of *In Memoriam*, where Hallam, after all the yearning, has become a diffusive power, both near and distant in God and Nature. That, and the marriage in the Epilogue as a type of greater growth, are probably as near as it could have come to a closing vision. Sometimes the poem seems meant to convince Tennyson himself, to 'show / That life is not as idle ore, // But iron dug from central gloom, / And heated hot with burning fears, / And dipt in baths of hissing tears, / And battered with the shocks of doom // To shape and use'. This is a rhetorical insistence on a main action: the working of the will, from the merely angry human will of IV, to the invocation in CXXXI of a human will that participates in the divine. But the strongest impressions that the long sequence leaves us with have probably more to do with process than conclusion; not so much the final affirmation, as the struggle with despair.

The most powerful expression of despair in the early sections is VII: 'Dark house, by which once more I stand'. The section is one of those added after the trial edition of 1850. Placed where it is, it counters with the one certainty of loss the wavering movement of the opening sections, and their attempts at understanding or accommodation. With the loss of the object, and belief that 'men may rise on stepping-stones / Of their dead selves to higher things', identity seems lost, and nothing remains but the drunkenness of grief, or the confession that time has triumphed over love and the man who identified himself with love. 'Let Love clasp Grief lest both be drowned' is the cry of the first section, and he turns from this to another extreme in II: from the drunkenness, the dance with death, to something outside the confused self: 'Old Yew . . . Who changest not'. It is an attempt to identify himself with the endurance of an alien growth which is rooted in the dead, and keeps its own seasons. The remoteness in the sudden Latinism of the close – 'grow incorporate into thee', against 'stubborn hardihood' – is arresting, in more than one sense. I and II, each in its own way, reach out to an escape from the threatened self. But if the drunkenness of grief, and the yearning for the hardihood of the yew, are like charms against the knowledge of loss, VII is the starkness of loss itself. Its authority is in the bleakness of the statement, from the bitter 'Behold me' to the vision of things as they are, and the taking up of another day.

> He is not here; but far away
> The noise of life begins again,
> And ghastly through the drizzling rain
> On the bald street breaks the blank day.

From this knowledge of meaninglessness, the sequence takes momentary refuge in one of its few events: the return to England of Hallam's body. It is like someone stricken by grief, but able to keep up because there is still something to be done, and some fancies which can be indulged, while the body is above ground. There are few parts of *In Memoriam* where Tennyson's stylistic skill, and skill in self-analysis, are more apparent than in the ship lyrics of IX to XVII. Harsh truth is fended off by fancy; fancy and speculation are recognised for what they are. The Horatian calm of IX and XVII is traditional, like a drawing on the strength of imagination of others who have known.[4]

> All night no ruder air perplex
> Thy sliding keel, till Phosphor, bright
> As our pure love, through early light
> Shall glimmer on the dewy decks.

The bird-like ship of IX (which may have been the first section to be written), the planets, men, the elements, are bound in one society. Even the dewy decks suggest a mingling of the great freshness of the land with the 'placid ocean-plains'. But characteristically the statement is no sooner made than qualified. In X the idealised ship becomes actual: 'I hear the noise about thy keel; / I hear the bell struck in the night: / I see the cabin-window bright; / I see the sailor at the wheel.' The bell and wheel mean human resolution, and the dangers faced; 'thy dark freight, a vanished life' denies the use of what is being done. 'So bring him: we have idle dreams', with its echo of the 'So draw him home to those that mourn / In vain' of IX, epitomises the reaction. We are the fools of habit, and the prayer of IX is now like the consolation of fancy. The vision in the last stanza of X of a Hallam engulfed with the ship means that for all the good such fancy does, he might as well visit the bottom of the monstrous world as be brought back to Clevedon church.

Within this phase, XI and XV act as pendants or companion poems, of 'calm despair' and 'wild unrest'. In XI eye and ear are at work, the conscious mind hardly at all. The chestnut patters, the eye falls on the twinkling gossamers, and sweeps from the high wold to where the crowded plain meets the sea. What an earlier generation of English poets called the goings-on of nature are at work; everywhere there is fruition, except in the observer. 'Calm is the morn without a sound, / Calm as to suit a calmer grief': the full meaning of the second line is not apparent until the fourth stanza – 'Calm and deep peace in this wide air, / These leaves that redden to the fall; / And in my heart, if calm at all, / If any calm, a calm despair.' The quiet observation, the unhurried beat of the verse, has allowed us to believe nearly to the end that there is help and comfort in nature. 'And dead calm in that noble breast / Which heaves but with the heaving deep.' 'Dead calm': the phrase is exact, the irony final. The more rapid XV ('Tonight the winds begin to rise') is simpler: the confusion of the storm is matched by confusion within, by a struggle between fears for Hallam's ship, and sympathy with the storm. The balance is precarious enough, with mere fancies which 'aver' the peace of the sea that returns Hallam, over against the fear that it is not so, and the fascination with that labouring breast of cloud which might as well be his own. The reality of this confused state is faced in XVI, with its urgent despairing questions, where the movement between calm and storm as aspects of sorrow leads to a figure of sorrow as uncompromising as the vision of the street in VII.

What words are these have fallen from me?
  Can calm despair and wild unrest
  Be tenants of a single breast,
Or sorrow such a changeling be?

Or doth she only seem to take
  The touch of change in calm or storm;
  But knows no more of transient form
In her deep self, than some dead lake

That holds the shadow of a lark
  Hung in the shadow of a heaven?

This is as far as may be from the figure of the blind priestess in
the vaults of death of III. The negation is the more complete
from being unexpected: the apparent comfort in permanence
that brings us to sorrow's 'deep self' vanishes with the dead
lake and its shadows. Sorrow's self is unknowable, and what
we know and love is mocked by it. Tennyson has been
playing with fancies, finding consolation or achieving a spe-
culative balance where and as he can. Here it is as if he were
overtaken by this figure of negation, and the virtual confes-
sion which ends XVI (am I 'that delirious man / Whose fancy
fuses old and new, / And flashes into false and true, / And
mingles all without a plan?') is in its way as conclusive as VII's
'Behold me', which helps to bring to an end a similar process
of figuring and fancying. XVII ('Thou comest, much wept
for') returns us to the style and mood of IX. Once again the
limpid Augustan style requires our acquiescence, and our
trust.

So may whatever tempest mars
  Mid-ocean, spare thee, sacred bark;
  And balmy drops in summer dark
Slide from the bosom of the stars.

But in its context in the sequence, the lovely stylisation which
begins and ends this phase is like a celebration of the event
that can only defer despair.
  What will meet despair is, of course, love and the will to

live, leading in the end to the feeling of Hallam as a diffusive power, mixed with God and nature, and everywhere known by Tennyson. Since it is feeling, not received truth or reason, the process by which he reaches it is diffuse, and includes hopes and fears that may mean little to us, like the fear that in evolution beyond death he will always be a stage behind Hallam. Sometimes its expression is not very memorable. 'Still onward winds the dreary way; / I with it; for I long to prove / No lapse of moons can canker Love, / Whatever fickle tongues may say': even though the context (XXVI) is that of a rejection of suicide, this seems trivial. The actual working of the will is another matter. The Christmas Eve section XXIX is dry, and shrunken.

> Make one wreath more for Use and Wont,
>   That guard the portals of the house;
>
> Old sisters of a day gone by,
>   Gray nurses, loving nothing new;
>   Why should they miss their yearly due
> Before their time? They too will die.

'One wreath more' is perhaps more negative than Use and Wont, but the contemplation of their death (unlike the mere 'dying use' or 'ancient form' of CV) is like the drying up of the spirit. But the use and wont of XXX, in spite of the 'vain pretence / Of gladness', achieve something: not only the Christian hope with which the section ends, but the natural human bond against the outer cold.

> We paused: the winds were in the beech:
>   We heard them sweep the winter land;
>   And in a circle hand-in-hand
> Sat silent, looking each at each . . .
>
> Our voices took a higher range;
>   Once more we sang: 'They do not die
>   Nor lose their mortal sympathy,
> Nor change to us, although they change . . .'

And in what follows, the will which in IV had cried 'Thou shalt not be the fool of loss' begins to act. XXXIV ('My own dim life should teach me this') and XXXV ('Yet if some voice that man could trust') form a sequence of argument, and the first part of it shows a stubborn disposition to reason for something while in the grip of what opposes it. In XXXIV and XXXV Tennyson is reasoning for immortality, without which life is meaningless, although almost everything he knows or feels points to death's supremacy. The reasoning is at first cautious enough; his own 'dim life', though very different from the type of faith honoured in XXXIII, should teach him the truth of immortality. ('Should' replaced the 'can' of the trial edition: the hesitation in 'My own dim life should teach me this' is not accidental.) If not, 'earth is darkness at the core, / And dust and ashes all that is . . .'

> This round of green, this orb of flame,
>   Fantastic beauty; such as lurks
>   In some wild Poet, when he works
> Without a conscience or an aim.

But the second stanza, which starts like a paean to all that is, quickly qualifies the already hesitant argument for immortality by the analogy of the purposeless artist and the merely fantastic beauty he sometimes achieves. It is a dazzling stanza, and designed to dazzle, since it presents illusion. 'What then were God to such as I?' he asks, and with that yields to the seduction of mortality: 'To drop head-foremost in the jaws / Of vacant darkness and to cease.' In XXXV the argument can only narrow to the idea of a momentary stay by love against mortality, and the answer comes before the stanza is over.

> Might I not say? 'Yet even here,
>   But for one hour, O Love, I strive
>   To keep so sweet a thing alive:'
> But I should turn mine ears and hear
>
> The moanings of the homeless sea,
>   The sound of streams that swift or slow
>   Draw down Aeonian hills, and sow
> The dust of continents to be.

After such a statement of geological time, we hardly need the last accents of love telling us on a dying fall that love itself cannot survive the thought of mortality: 'Half-dead to know that I shall die'. The sudden reaction in the fifth stanza takes the form of a passionate argument for the reality of human experience – that love has been – which rejects the drift of thought and feeling since the cautious opening of XXXIV.

> O me, what profits it to put
> An idle case? If Death were seen
> At first as Death, Love had not been,
> Or been in narrowest working shut,
>
> Mere fellowship of sluggish moods,
> Or in his coarsest Satyr-shape
> Had bruised the herb and crushed the grape,
> And basked and battened in the woods.

Yet (it is typical of the to-fro movements in *In Memoriam*, and the way in which a statement so often contains its opposite) 'O me' sounds almost like a cry of despair. And the last stanza betrays a fascination with mortality in the lingering over love's coarsest satyr-shape. Though reasoning for love and immortality, Tennyson is still ready – as he always was – to give way to thoughts of death. It is more will, perhaps, than reason which is at work: the beginnings of that stubborn human will which in the end will have its way.

The sequence of short poems, with its continuity and its interruptions, its local intensities and its effect of wandering at will, is an apt form for embodying this kind of working, and also for that mingling of opposing elements, which sometimes leaves us in a state of puzzled suspense, not sure if we have been foxed by some elegant periphrasis intended only to slide away from a problem. Some readers have been put off by what looks like deprecating comment within the elegies on their purpose and form, as in XXXVII, and more notably in XLVIII. XXXVII ('Urania speaks with darkened brow') suggests self-criticism, and a modest defence. The question seems to be what these low-powered elegies can speak of, and what they should abstain from. XXXVI, after the hardly resolved struggle over mortality in the two preceding sections, spoke of the perfection of the Word made flesh, that wrought 'in loveliness of perfect deeds, / More strong than all poetic thought'. In XXXVII Urania frowns on his presumption, and dismisses him to his native rill and proper place. And Tennyson's muse ('my Melpomene') replies. As Bradley points out, Urania as the goddess of heavenly poetry is a Miltonic conception, and Wordsworth had called on her, or on a greater, in the Prospectus to *The Recluse*.[5] Tennyson's 'earthly Muse' mingles humility and proper pride. The 'little art' that she owns is dedicated to giving human love its dues, and characteristically she no sooner speaks of love than her elegiacs gather strength, before fading on a duly politic conclusion.

> 'But brooding on the dear one dead,
>   And all he said of things divine,
>   (And dear to me as sacred wine
> To dying lips is all he said),
>
> 'I murmured, as I came along,
>   Of comfort clasped in truth revealed;
>   And loitered in the master's field,
> And darkened sanctities with song.'

Hallam, the 'dear one dead', becomes a Christ-like figure. The confession of the last line is like an apology for having seemed to usurp the function of the goddess of strictly heavenly poetry. Of course in the nineteenth century it could hardly be otherwise; the Spenserian 'great Intelligences fair' of LXXXV are purely figurative, and their function at that stage is to abstract the experience. And the will to love is paramount in *In Memoriam*; in the end it will create the strong sense of a continuing presence which is neither figurative nor forced.

But the question of what the elegies can or cannot handle, of how far Tennyson thinks he can go, may still seem to have been left open here, so that we feel he is trying to have it both ways. XLVIII ('If these brief lays, of Sorrow born') is openly apologetic about them. They resolve no deep problems; Sorrow

> sports with words,
> But better serves a wholesome law,
> And holds it sin and shame to draw
> The deepest measure from the chords:
>
> Nor dare she trust a larger lay,
> But rather loosens from the lip
> Short swallow-flights of song, that dip
> Their wings in tears, and skim away.

The unwillingness to trust a larger lay has made many readers suspicious. There is nothing of the confidence in humility of Milton's 'But now my oat proceeds', against the strain of Phoebus. Even if to draw the deepest measure from sorrow's chords would be to injure mental health (Bradley's reading), the idea of short swallow-flights, in a sequence which plainly is attempting more, may grate on us. But something is due to the section's place in the sequence. XLVII ('That each, who seems a separate whole') is the culmination of a series of elegies which speculate about the state of the soul after death; XLIX ('From art, from nature, from the schools') acknowledges that there is no comfort in thought, or fancy, or song; between them this section seems in itself a sporting with words, a moment's stay between incomprehension and despair.

As for the comments on the elegies in the Prologue and Epilogue ('wild and wandering cries', 'half but idle brawling rhymes'), the first deals with the source of life, the second with the end of a process. In the matter of what poetry can or cannot do, XLVII is of some interest.

> That each, who seems a separate whole,
> Should move his rounds, and fusing all
> The skirts of self again, should fall
> Remerging in the general Soul,
>
> Is faith as vague as all unsweet:
> Eternal form shall still divide
> The eternal soul from all beside;
> And I shall know him when we meet:

And we shall sit at endless feast,
   Enjoying each the other's good:
   What vaster dream can hit the mood
Of Love on earth? He seeks at least

Upon the last and sharpest height,
   Before the spirits fade away,
   Some landing-place, to clasp and say,
'Farewell! We lose ourselves in light.'

Harry Puckett argues that 'the rejection of extravagant despair and images of loss is counterpointed in *In Memoriam* by the concurrent rejection of extravagant hopes and the imagination that gives them form', and suggests that this section 'illustrates the process of rejected hope in a particularly extreme form'. Puckett points to the leaving open by the last stanza of that possibility of 'remerging in the general Soul' which was rejected earlier in the poem, and says that the question 'What vaster dream can hit the mood / Of Love on earth' indicates the main problem of *In Memoriam* in its dealings with images of hope. 'What imaginative construct – what "myth", we might say today – can embody the human condition and human fate in such a way as to equal our actual experience of "Love on earth"?'[6] It is an acute comment on a section which has puzzled many readers. Tennyson observed: 'The individuality lasts after death, and we are not utterly absorbed into the Godhead. If we are to be finally merged in the Universal Soul, Love asks to have at least one more parting before we lose ourselves.'[7] The belief in absorption into 'the general Soul' which he speaks of in the first stanza is rejected in the second, where he affirms the eternal individuality of the soul. The tone of this affirmation in the third stanza is perhaps more puzzling than Puckett allows for. The MS first reading of 'vaster' was 'dimmer', and since Tennyson told Knowles that by 'vaster' he meant 'less defined', 'vaster dream' resembles the dismissal as vague faith of the doctrine of the first stanza.[8] Given the tone of 'hit the mood', it seems reductive, and although what precedes it is consonant with much of *In Memoriam*, the trumpeting couplet of 'Eternal form shall still divide / The eternal soul from all beside' seems to be subverted by the lingering ('And . . . And . . .') over what begins to sound like a childish vision of felicity. The section seems to call in question our right to have any firm beliefs at all about what happens to the soul after death. And 'some landing-place' (the phrase has been much discussed, at times without proper attention to 'some') may imply a comment on our attempts to embody or find a local habitation for ideas about immortality, of which this section is one. He seems at the same time to accept and reject: accepting the soul's eternal form on the level of human understanding, dismissing it on a level which is beyond faith, or poetry.

Not all the speculation has this urgency. XLIII ('If Sleep and Death be truly one') takes the belief that the soul sleeps until the day of judgment as the starting point for what looks like fancy. The neo-classicism of 'the sliding hour', or evocation of earlier modes like 'intervital', gives it the kind of gravity which makes it less a retreat from deeply troubling questions, than a glimpse of a possibility which he is willing for a moment to entertain. It is a very beautiful poem, with its play of tense and mood: 'So then were nothing lost to man; / So that still garden of the souls / In many a figured leaf enrolls / The total world since life began.' But the still garden of the souls is only a figure. The force of the rejection of speculation or fancy, when it comes, is all the greater.

> From art, from nature, from the schools,
>   Let random influences glance,
>   Like light in many a shivered lance
> That breaks about the dappled pools . . .
>
> Beneath all fancied hopes and fears
>   Ay me, the sorrow deepens down,
>   Whose muffled motions blindly drown
> The bases of my life in tears.

'The sorrow' of XLIX is not the Muse-like 'Sorrow' of XLVIII. This rejection of all fancies, whether of hope or fear, is followed by the near despair of L. The beginning of the desire for reunion with Hallam sounds more like an end than a beginning; at one time he thought of ending the sequence with LVII.[9] 'Be near me when my light is low, / When the blood creeps, and the nerves prick / And tingle; and the heart is sick, / And all the wheels of Being slow': it is the reality of a mortal sickness.

In three closely related sections, LIV, LV and LVI, it is not a matter of personal despair, but of urgent questioning about life, 'the living whole'. Tennyson felt that there was 'a deeper tone about' LVI, and there is a feeling that the sequence is moving towards questions to which some kind of answer must be given.[10] What there is of faith, and the desire for faith, is weak beside the fear that the indifference of Nature may mean the indifference of God, and the nothingness of man. The trust struggled for in LIV – 'That not a worm is cloven in vain; / That not a moth with vain desire / Is shrivelled in a fruitless fire, / Or but subserves another's gain', where the repeated negatives dull what they support – turns to the negation of 'Behold, we know not anything'; to the faltering commonplace of 'I can but trust that good shall fall / At last – far off – at last, to all, / And every winter change to spring'; and finally to the rejection of even this:

> So runs my dream: but what am I?
> An infant crying in the night:
> An infant crying for the light:
> And with no language but a cry.

The structure of these three sections, which present one of the most vital questions of the age, is that of a precarious balance achieved in the first two, which is destroyed by the third. The movement is first from the qualified 'Oh yet we trust' of the opening of LIV, to the insignificance in the last stanza of the inarticulate being that dreams this good; then from the opening lines of LV – 'The wish, that of the living whole / No life may fail beyond the grave, / Derives it not from what we have / The likest God within the soul?' – and the immediate qualification of this by the vision of God and Nature at strife, to LV's final statement of trust:

> I stretch lame hands of faith, and grope,
>   And gather dust and chaff, and call
>   To what I feel is Lord of all,
> And faintly trust the larger hope.

'Faintly trust' is somewhere between 'faint trust' and the strength of a trust achieved against great odds. LVI (one of the sections added after the trial edition) destroys the balance, with the flat denial by Nature of something accepted without question in the argument of LV.

> 'So careful of the type?' but no.
>   From scarpèd cliff and quarried stone
>   She cries, 'A thousand types are gone:
> I care for nothing, all shall go.

> 'Thou makest thine appeal to me:
>   I bring to life, I bring to death:
>   The spirit does but mean the breath:
> I know no more.'

This, and the ringing despairing stanzas that follow, with their declaration of all that man has achieved, present the tormented debate between nineteenth-century man and nature, between 'science' and the divine in man, 'the likest God within the soul'. The verse is magnificent, with the continuing purpose of those declamatory active verbs – 'Who rolled . . . Who built . . . Who trusted . . . Who loved, who suffered . . . Who battled' – passing at a blow to the double passive of 'be blown . . . or sealed', and the whole locked within the scarpèd cliff and iron hills. The questioning of LVI is something of a climax; the answer is only the bitter 'Behind the veil, behind the veil'. Speculation about the terms of this (which veil, and so forth) is hardly relevant. The meaning is in the repetition: this life at least offers neither answer nor redress.

Having put the question about man's splendid purposes and battling will, *In Memoriam* seems to change course. What follows has a good deal to do with day-to-day living on this side of the veil, and it is the simple ability to contain grief that begins to make itself felt. Tennyson observed of LIX ('O

Sorrow, wilt thou live with me'), a slight and charming poem of accommodation and even of hope, that 'a time has now elapsed and he treats sorrow in a more familiar and less dreading way'.[11] And the mild continuity of àrgument in some of the sections which follow is consistent with this feeling of adaptation and acceptance. So, in a different way, is the technical and emotional assurance of LXIV ('Dost thou look back on what hath been'), where the question of the single twenty-eight-line period moves quietly to the poignant, but bearable, 'Does my old friend remember me?' The structure records the progress of the lost boyhood friend, from village boy to world-renowned statesman, and seems to express acceptance, however comfortless, of the great difference between them. (The poem is rather like a counterpart of Gray's *Elegy*, and the substitution of 'vocal springs' for the MS first reading of 'native springs' is suggestive. 'The limit' (MS first reading 'limits') 'of his narrow fate' is also faintly suggestive in its context of 'the limits of their little reign' in Gray's *Ode on a Distant Prospect of Eton College*.)[12] There are various other signs of the ability to live with grief: the half-mocking self-quotation of LXV; the moving image of the blind man's accommodation to his lot in LXVI; the quiet insistence in the first and last stanzas of LXVII on what is known – in effect, that Hallam is dead, and that he, Tennyson, is alive, however mystic the glory of the moonlight on the lettered tablet, however the night begins and ends with thoughts of Hallam. It is in keeping with the apparent absence now of any effort of will that the mental action becomes that of dreams. Earlier, sleep brought no relief, and the angry will cried out against his surrender. What he yields to now will help to remake him. The effect of this is evident in the rather Blake-like dream poem LXIX (perhaps the least slow-moving of all the sections), where the mysterious angel of the night brings some comfort, and seems to promise more.[13] LXX is a dream poem of a different sort. It demonstrates (perhaps a little too demonstratively) the failure of the conscious will, and the re-creating power of sleep, with its final image of a dream of waking after nightmare, and the reassurance of a loved face whose features at first he could not imagine. The reassurance hardly matches the force of the nightmare into which he is drawn as he lies between waking and sleep, in which images of the living mass of industrial man, and the hell-like modern city where individuality is lost, pass into regressive images of prehistoric bulks and lengths of alien life.

> Cloud-towers by ghostly masons wrought,
> A gulf that ever shuts and gapes,
> A hand that points, and pallèd shapes
> In shadowy thoroughfares of thought;
>
> And crowds that stream from yawning doors,
> And shoals of puckered faces drive;
> Dark bulks that tumble half alive,
> And lazy lengths on boundless shores.

LXXI, which ends this sequence of dream poems, brings together the 'night-long Present of the Past' now forged (in both senses) by sleep, and the distance of 'The days that grow to something strange', and ends with the almost unrelated imagery, as of something out of time, of 'The cataract flashing from the bridge, / The breaker breaking on the beach'.

Perhaps, and surprising though it may seem, the uncharacteristically violent LXXII ('Risest thou thus, dim dawn, again') shows, almost as clearly as any of the dream sections, a deeper control than that of will. The anniversary of Hallam's death is celebrated by a kind of commination service; the day which 'howlest, issuing out of night' is a hellish birth. 'Day, when my crowned estate begun / To pine in that reverse of doom, / Which sickened every living bloom, / And blurred the spendour of the sun': the audacity of the outburst is remarkable. The day's only business is to die, and the section ends on a cursing dismissal:

> Climb thy thick noon, disastrous day;
> Touch thy dull goal of joyless gray,
> And hide thy shame beneath the ground.

What is of interest is that the turbulence which matches the fortuitous storm is more rhetorical than mental. The violence, coming where it does, is like a last effect of the violence of extreme grief.

If these sections show some readiness to find content on this side of the veil, much of what follows suggests a movement towards a closer involvement in the passion and the mystery of life. In LXXIX ('More than my brothers are to me') Tennyson admits a duty to the living by addressing his brother Charles, and tactfully and deftly removing the issue of his greater love for Hallam from the idea of greater love to that of greater need. This section is something of an occasional poem, but LXXXV (*pace* Bradley, p. 25) is not, and the long answer to the questions of Edmund Lushington states Tennyson's concern with the living as well as the dead. The questions are crucial: in effect, he is asked whether he is spiritually crippled, or is able to love and act. The formality of its recapitulation – Hallam's Lycidas-like reception by the 'great Intelligences fair' – removes the experience by placing it in a classic elegiac mode, and the movement of those exclamations of 33–6 from 'O friendship, equal-poised control' to 'O solemn ghost, O crownèd soul!' has the effect of a renewed farewell. What follows is revealing.

> Yet none could better know than I,
> How much of act at human hands
> The sense of human will demands
> By which we dare to live or die.

The twenty-fourth stanza – 'So hold I commerce with the dead; / Or so methinks the dead would say; / Or so shall grief with symbols play / And pining life be fancy-fed' – will return to the sense of fancied consolation, less bitter here than it would have been earlier. But with that strong insistence on human act and human will – the actuality of 'human hands' – it seems that he is ready to respond to the challenge, and take hold.

The prolongation through eighty lines of the argument for life with the living reflects something of the difficulties of such a transition. But in the three sections which follow, Tennyson achieves an intensity, and a variety, which present him at his most assured. LXXXVI ('Sweet after showers, ambrosial air') is one of his most brilliant single-period performances; its position also shows something of the skill with which he arranged the sequence. The ambrosial air sweeps from west to east, and in passing breathes new life into him, moving on towards the 'orient star'. So far from circumscribing everything by his sorrow, he plays a passive role. It is not quite the response it seems to be to the 'expectant nature' of LXXXIII ('Dip down upon the northern shore, / O sweet new-year delaying long'): it is very much a performance, and the studied richness at first seems too ornate to be honest. This begs more than one question, but 'Doubt and Death, / Ill brethren' at first seem ill indeed, until we realise what their function is: to 'let the fancy fly // From belt to belt of crimson seas'. For perhaps the first time, a fancy is to be accepted. The lyric is, in fact, predictive and auspicious, rather than an indication of anything that has been achieved, and the slight over-ripeness is particularly apt. LXXXVII, a very different poem, works in its own way towards delight in life. This is not Arcady and Argive heights, but the place itself – Cambridge – and Tennyson delighting to recall Hallam as he was. The present is like a dream, the past is very near. The conjunctions of the opening stanzas create a dream-like continuity, moving quietly to the mystery of time past and relived, so simply conveyed by that 'and felt / The same, but not the same' (like the 'every thing seems double' and 'mine own, and not mine own' of *A Midsummer Night's Dream*), and giving something of the elusiveness of an experience that he wants to hold entire, but cannot. But in the closing stanzas, where Hallam for the first time appears as he was – the master-bowman among his peers – the conjunctions quicken their pace to carry us up to a conclusion which unites the acclamation of that youthful band, and the conviction of the older man looking back on what might have been.

> Who, but hung to hear
> The rapt oration flowing free
>
> From point to point, with power and grace
> And music in the bounds of law,
> To those conclusions when we saw
> The God within him light his face,

> And seem to lift the form, and glow
> In azure orbits heavenly-wise;
> And over those ethereal eyes
> The bar of Michael Angelo.

(The widening, and touch of awe at the close, are aided by the hint of something unrelated from the absence of a verb after the last conjunction, where he seems to turn from the strong play of conjunction and verb throughout; it is an effect that Tennyson is master of.) In this context of pulses that begin to beat again, LXXXVIII is something of a climax.

> Wild bird, whose warble, liquid sweet,
> Rings Eden through the budded quicks,
> O tell me where the senses mix,
> O tell me where the passions meet,
>
> Whence radiate: fierce extremes employ
> Thy spirits in the darkening leaf,
> And in the midmost heart of grief
> Thy passion clasps a secret joy:
>
> And I – my harp would prelude woe –
> I cannot all command the strings;
> The glory of the sum of things
> Will flash along the chords and go.

This superb lyric, which at one stage he seems to have thought of omitting, is the real response to the questionings of LXXXV.[14] The appeal to the wild and darkling nightingale, the very voice of life, is for knowledge of himself. The answer comes with the almost dismissive 'And I', and the unwilled participation in the great fullness of life.

With this comes a renewed desire for contact with Hallam's spirit, 'Spirit to Spirit, Ghost to Ghost'. At the same time, the living presence of Hallam at Somersby, recollected in the idyllic LXXXIX, is very much in his mind. Hallam is closer now than he has ever been. Not that he says much that is brilliant; this is not the master-bowman of the Cambridge Apostles, and he is all the nearer for it. The contact is achieved, so far as it can be achieved, in XCV. But it is easy to be misled by what happens in XCV. The calm of the opening stanzas, and the excitement of the senses in the almost unnaturally intense observation of the breasts and eyes of the moths, is like a preparation. The movement of the long closing period, with the breeze that is 'sucked from out the distant gloom' to rock the elms and swing the rose and fling the lilies to and fro, is that of a sense of life which has been quickened by the intervening trance. But the nature of the contact during the trance should not be misunderstood. Tennyson is left alone on the lawn at Somersby rectory at the end of a day like one of those whose memory he lingers over in LXXXIX. A hunger for what has been seizes him, he reads Hallam's letters, and 'word by word, and line by line, / The dead man touched me from the past'. But it is not the mystical 'descend, and touch, and enter' desired in XCIII. The line 'The noble letters of the dead' means precisely what it says, and after so much of eddying fancy it strikes home: the man was noble, and is dead. 'And strangely on the silence broke / The silent-speaking words, and strange / Was love's dumb cry defying change / To test his worth; and strangely spoke // The faith, the vigour . . .': the insistence on the strangeness is similarly factual, and so with 'The dead man touched me from the past', where the touching is kept firmly in the context of the fact of death.

> So word by word, and line by line,
>   The dead man touched me from the past,
>   And all at once it seemed at last
> The living soul was flashed on mine,
>
> And mine in this was wound, and whirled
>   About empyreal heights of thought,
>   And came on that which is, and caught
> The deep pulsations of the world,
>
> Aeonian music measuring out
>   The steps of Time – the shocks of Chance –
> The blows of Death.
>
> (XCV. 33–43)

This is the central moment of the experience, marked by the chiastic structure of 36 and 37, which spans two stanzas. (The original reading of 'His living soul' for 'The living soul' and 'his' for 'this' seems preferable.) But even this is kept in control by 'it seemed at last', which confirms that hunger like this must in the end find something to feed on. Whatever the preparation for mystical communion, the contact in XCV is created by a yearning which works on the absence of Hallam from the place itself, and his equivocal presence in the letters. In the end, the experience of XCV is almost as much that of a heightened participation in the mystery of life around him, the sense of which has been growing for some time. (There is a similar effect in CXXII, which may refer to the experience of XCV, but where the cry 'enter in at breast and brow' brings a quickening of the blood, by which 'every thought breaks out a rose'. The delighted apprehension of the last two stanzas, the quickening of life – 'And all the breeze of Fancy blows, / And every dew-drop paints a bow, / The wizard lightnings deeply glow, / And every thought breaks out a rose' – seems to come with the mere thought of commingling.) What the nature of this contact confirms is that this is as far as he can go in this region, that direct communion with the dead is no longer to be thought of, and that strength from Hallam must be sought by other means.

One unmistakable turning point, in this sequence in which human will, and the separation from and return to human kind, play so great a part, is CVII, in which Tennyson seems to identify himself with the will to live of the human race. And perhaps it is the abandonment of the hope of a spirit-to-spirit meeting that is working in the vaguely allegorical (and unequal) CIII, with its strange meeting and setting sail with a giant Hallam, which takes place in the world of dreams, and leaves his waking 'after-morn content'. The fact that the dream occurs the night before he left Somersby has its own significance. The idea of the human root in place has become stronger. Now a disengagement from grief as from place, and a feeling for the continuity of human experience, begins to make itself felt. It finds one kind of expression in the exquisite CI ('Unwatched, the garden bough shall sway'), which has been strangely misread by one recent critic, and another in the rejection in CV of ancient forms and dying use before the promise of the rebirth of the human race, the coming of 'the closing cycle rich in good'. The faith in this, and his part in the collective faith of the Christian world, rings out (literally enough) in the clanging imperatives of CVI, where the Christmas festival is triumphantly taken out of an outworn domestic context and carried into that of the great closing cycle: 'Ring in the Christ that is to be'. After this formal statement of his faith, a major theme until the end of the sequence will be 'that great race, which is to be', which was sung in CIII, and of which Hallam was a type or forerunner. But this faith in higher will, human or divine, can be of little value without the simple will to live, the acceptance of the fact that life, as everyone says, must continue. Somewhere between the desperate appeal to the dead, and the idea of Hallam as what he will call in CXXX a diffusive power, there must be a moment when the living are living, and the dead, though gratefully remembered, are dead. Tennyson gives us such a moment, in CVII.

> It is the day when he was born,
>   A bitter day that early sank
>   Behind a purple-frosty bank
> Of vapour, leaving night forlorn.
>
> The time admits not flowers or leaves
>   To deck the banquet. Fiercely flies
>   The blast of North and East, and ice
> Makes daggers at the sharpened eaves,
>
> And bristles all the brakes and thorns
>   To yon hard crescent, as she hangs
>   Above the wood which grides and clangs
> Its leafless ribs and iron horns
>
> Together, in the drifts that pass
>   To darken on the rolling brine
>   That breaks the coast. But fetch the wine,
> Arrange the board and brim the glass;

> Bring in great logs, and let them lie,
> To make a solid core of heat;
> Be cheerful-minded, talk and treat
> Of all things even as he were by;
>
> We keep the day. With festal cheer,
> With books and music, surely we
> Will drink to him, whate'er he be,
> And sing the songs he loved to hear.

It is a new anniversary, that of Hallam's birth. The will is that of a family group strengthening itself against the besieging cold. The curtly dismissive 'The time admits not' sets the tone of acceptance, even defiance. The widening outward movement from the ice daggers at the eaves and the iron woods, to the cold seas that break the coast, explores the fear of frozen nature, but there is no shrinking. Against this are the confident imperatives urging us to board and hearth (the 'solid core of heat'), and culminating in the stubborn 'We keep the day'. After so much of reaching and speculating, 'whate'er he be' and 'even as he were by' indicate a common purpose of acceptance. The roots of this firm poetry of statement are in the human will not only to endure, but to reshape: the will which for Tennyson was 'the higher and enduring part of man'. Once again he draws on Horace. The difference between the Horatian of IX and XVII, and the Horatian of this section, is that between a charming away of agony by an appeal to a reassuring cosmos, and an acceptance of time and human seasons.[15]

However diffuse the general movement of *In Memoriam* is, it is obvious that CVII, with CVIII ('I will not shut me from my kind'), marks some sort of end to destructive sorrow, and unrealistic hopes. The rejection in CVIII is categorical: 'What find I in the highest place, / But mine own phantom chanting hymns? / And on the depths of death there swims / The reflex of a human face.' Much of what follows is almost valedictory in tone. The assurance of CXX is that of irony ('I trust I have not wasted breath: / I think we are not wholly brain, / Magnetic mockeries . . .'), which turns in the last stanza to contempt.

> Let him, the wiser man who springs
> Hereafter, up from childhood shape
> His action like the greater ape,
> But I was *born* to other things.

Tennyson pointed out that his irony was directed against mere materialism, not evolution, but his reference to this 'wiser man' sounds strangely against the references to the crowning race.[16] He did not italicise 'born' until 1872, and did so presumably to confirm both the contemptuous dismissal of materialism, and the insistence on that greater will expressed by human birth. In thinking now of Hallam as he was, and would have been, he sometimes speaks in unconvincing superlatives and orotundities. 'Heart-affluence in discursive talk / From household fountains never dry; / The critic clearness of an eye, / That saw through all the Muses' walk': the floridity of this wrecks the amplitude intended. In CXII, after the high glazing of the first stanza's confusing periphrasis, the sudden 'For what wert thou?' compels attention. But what follows is a fair example of what can go wrong in *In Memoriam*.

> Large elements in order brought,
> And tracts of calm from tempest made,
> And world-wide fluctuation swayed
> In vassal tides that followed thought.

It is a translation of Hallam in terms of creation, but it is choked by words. But uninspired and uninspiring though they are, the sections which pay tribute to the Hallam who fascinated his contemporaries imply, if only by example, that man may make himself; the wordy vision which ends CXII seems to escape from its immediate reference, and to suggest infinite possibilities. Man who may make himself is the hero of CXVIII. In LVI the strife of God and nature left man a monster, a dream, a discord. CXVIII is both celebration and exhortation, and has an air of delighting in its power, as in that of man. 'Contemplate all this work of Time, / The giant labouring in his youth; / Nor dream of human love and truth, / As dying Nature's earth and lime': there is optimism in *In Memoriam* long before the closing stages, but assurance like that of 'the giant labouring in his youth' is something new in the sequence. The section begins and ends with imperatives, none of which is more confident than the opening 'Contemplate', and it is dominated by the image of labouring and working, which culminates in the purpose of shape and use. Tennyson brings theories of evolution to the service of the idea of man as the herald of a higher race: 'They say, / The solid earth whereon we tread // In tracts of fluent heat began, / And grew to seeming-random forms, / The seeming prey of cyclic storms, / Till at the last arose the man . . .' 'They say' suggests that although this evidence is important, he hardly needs it, and the scientific reference is secondary to a much older concept: that of the created world as man ('this work of Time, / The giant labouring in his youth'), and man as the world, man who can, if he will, 'type this work of time // Within himself, from more to more'. Admirable though the concept is, however, there is a hint of large utterance here and there, and the sixth stanza seems forced. Life 'is not as idle ore, // But iron dug from central gloom, / And heated hot with burning fears, / And dipt in baths of hissing tears, / And battered with the shocks of doom // To shape and use . . .': there is a compelling force of purpose in the infinitives, and the figure brings that century of iron-masters and industrialists before us, but its extension, and the picturesque equivalences, show uncertainty.

The complex of certainty and uncertainty in CXXIV, on the other hand, reads no lesson to us. After the opening lines ('That which we dare invoke to bless; / Our dearest faith; our ghastliest doubt; / He, They, One, All; within, without; / The Power in darkness whom we guess'), it is the past tense which predominates. It is not argument, but conclusion, with the weight of *In Memoriam*'s experience behind it. The movement is typically cyclic, from darkness and that which may hardly be named, to darkness again in the last stanza, and the naming in terms appropriate to human understanding.

> And what I am beheld again
>   What is, and no man understands;
>   And out of darkness came the hands
> That reach through nature, moulding men.

CXXIV is the declaration of a man who has survived the worst effects of doubt, and has preserved his faith. CXXVII, on the other hand, is a vision of social and telluric upheaval, of the great Aeon sinking in blood, and of a human race largely ignorant of that assurance that all is well within which the vision is framed. If Tennyson's idea of progress towards the great race of the future means anything at all, these colossal upheavals of CXXVII are inevitable. But in spite of the consummate skill of the verse, and the double authority of the Book of Revelation on the one hand, and contemporary scientific thinking on the other, one is left with the impression of a *tour de force*, and with it of the difficulty he finds in relating his own recovery to his faith in the future: a difficulty not resolved until the Epilogue, and even then at some cost.

In CXXIX and CXXX, at once valediction and rejoicing, we have the mystery of Hallam as he now is, and Tennyson, as one feels he must, meets this directly, without benefit of analogy.

> Dear friend, far off, my lost desire,
>   So far, so near in woe and weal;
>   O loved the most, when most I feel
> There is a lower and a higher;
>
> Known and unknown; human, divine;
>   Sweet human hand and lips and eye;
>   Dear heavenly friend that canst not die,
> Mine, mine, for ever, ever, mine;
>
> Strange friend, past, present, and to be;
>   Loved deeplier, darklier understood . . .

The complex of paradoxes reaches a climax with the modulation of the last cry of passion in the sequence into the simplest of all paradoxes, 'strange friend', which embodies the distance and nearness, the loss and possession. The final paradox, in CXXX, is that of a Hallam mixed with God and nature, yet possessed by his living friend. Earlier embodiments, like those of XLVII, or Hallam's whisper in LXXXV, rejected there as fancy, have been outgrown.

What art thou then? I cannot guess;
   But though I seem in star and flower
   To feel thee some diffusive power,
I do not therefore love thee less:

My love involves the love before;
   My love is vaster passion now;
   Though mixed with God and Nature thou,
I seem to love thee more and more.

Far off thou art, but ever nigh;
   I have thee still, and I rejoice;
   I prosper, circled with thy voice;
I shall not lose thee though I die.

What those complementary 'seems' mean is that the account given is a true one, and that at this supreme moment the self is not deceived. With CXXXI ('O living will that shalt endure') he passes beyond paradox to prayer and affirmation, to the recognition of that participation by human will in divine will towards which the sequence has been slowly working. The living will invoked rises in the spiritual rock of Christ, the divine made human; the faith is created by 'self-control', that resolutely willed direction of the self to which so much of *In Memoriam* testifies.

The Epilogue, as most readers since Bradley (and Genung) have agreed to call it, stands both outside and inside *In Memoriam*, exemplifying, by the marriage which is described, the will of humanity not only to survive, but to grow until the coming of the crowning race. Hallam has gone beyond bounds, and now 'A soul shall draw from out the vast / And strike his being into bounds'. The participation in the marriage is the elegist's formal indication of his return to the race. But the Epilogue does present problems. The stanzas describing the marriage day are those of an epithalamium, but an epithalamium in which Tennyson seems to want to avoid either the actual or the transcendental, so much is turned to favour and prettiness. (And also to bad verse, like 'O happy hour, behold the bride / With him to whom her hand I gave', where the second line moves like a wooden leg.) John Dixon

Hunt, speaking of how Tennyson tries 'consistently to render highly individual experience in terms of a more public typology', suggests that the marriage 'is offered in very general terms, in almost the clichés of such events . . . because it was needed as a *type* that recurs in life and art'.[17] This is persuasive, but one suspects that the fact that the marriage will be seen as a type of greater growth leaves Tennyson free to indulge the sentimentality often found in his domestic idylls. With the thought of the absent Hallam, the 'stiller guest', the mood begins to change. Then with his own withdrawal from the festivities the verse itself changes dramatically.

> . . . And last the dance; – till I retire:
> Dumb is that tower which spake so loud,
> And high in heaven the streaming cloud,
> And on the downs a rising fire . . .

The transformation of the jangling village spire is so sudden that for a moment we are left behind. The inversion, and the vatic note of speaking tower and cloud and fire, marks the moment at which Tennyson turns from the description of the marriage day, to that of which the day is type, as the long period which ends the sequence begins to move to its climax. The division between the event and its meaning is so explicit that we are almost ready to believe that he weakened one to strengthen the other by contrast. As so often in *In Memoriam*, the cost is forgotten, as we are carried in a single sweep of forty-four lines from the event of the marriage, through the conception of the child which links us with the crowning race, to God as represented by 'one far-off divine event, / To which the whole creation moves'. It is a movement in which the last word on Hallam is necessarily subordinated to the idea of the coming race,

> Whereof the man, that with me trod
> This planet, was a noble type
> Appearing ere the times were ripe,
> That friend of mine who lives in God . . .

After so much of the Christ-like Hallam, and Hallam as a

diffusive power, and at the heart of the looking to the future, the first two lines of the penultimate stanza, marked by the calm turn of that 'Whereof', come with the simple authority of what has been known.

Tennyson's last word is not here, but in the Prologue of 1849. This is not so much of a paradox as some readers have believed; Lermontov, introducing *A Hero of Our Time*, remarks that in every book the preface is the first and also the last thing, serving either to explain the purpose of the work, or to justify it and answer criticism. That grave forward-moving beat, so often felt in the verse in spite of its circlings, is stronger in the Prologue than anywhere else: 'Strong Son of God, immortal Love'. But despite the beat, the Prologue does not look forward to *In Memoriam*, except to ask forgiveness for it. There is inevitably so much of 'I' in the poem; the Prologue rings with 'Thou', which is all that can be known. Tennyson considers his elegies in the Prologue, insofar as he considers them at all, from a position where all human effort seems feeble. In dismissing them as 'wild and wandering cries, / Confusions of a wasted youth', he is distinguishing between the source of spiritual life, and the little that men achieve.

Stylistically *In Memoriam* is often faulty. There is a tendency to hide behind large utterance: we learn to suspect words like 'large' or 'ample' or 'ripe'. 'A lord of large experience, train / To riper growth the mind and will' (XLII); 'the soul exults, / And self-infolds the large results / Of force that would have forged a name' (LXXIII); 'Till slowly worn her earthly robe, / Her lavish mission richly wrought, / Leaving great legacies of thought' (LXXXIV): it is not really unjust to bring these together, since they present something which occurs often enough to be obtrusive. The strain of Augustan diction often reflects an attempt at control, or a fear of isolation, and is sometimes the effect of a timorous apprehension of the phenomenal world. But there are times when it fails badly.

> And all the train of bounteous hours
> Conduct by paths of growing powers,
> To reverence and the silver hair.

It is not difficult to point to weaknesses, and most critics at some stage feel obliged to do so. One finds so much to admire, but missing the ground-swell of the greatest poetry turns on the faults of the sequence. Much of its eddying movement is that of speculation, of a looking for ways and means, often frustrated, but gradually working towards a reality within which he can live. But some of it is decorative rather than effectively speculative. Decoration spoils several sections in rather a revealing way, in that each of them might be better without its last stanza. The ending of LXXVI ('Take wings of fancy, and ascend') is adventitious, a wordy and diluting insistence. With the fourth stanza of XX ('The lesser griefs that may be said') he has said all that he has to say: the contrast between lesser griefs that may be voiced, and greater griefs that may not, and the effective conclusion of this with the image of the silent children by the hearth, suffers from the commonplace of what follows. And in LI ('Do we indeed desire the dead'), the four lines that hammer out the conviction answering the questioning of the first eight –

> I wrong the grave with fears untrue:
> Shall love be blamed for want of faith?
> There must be wisdom with great Death:
> The dead shall look me through and through

– are similarly weakened by the conclusion:

> Be near us when we climb or fall:
> Ye watch, like God, the rolling hours
> With larger other eyes than ours,
> To make allowance for us all.

Perhaps it is not so much that the last stanza is adventitious – it responds to the heart-sick 'Be near me' of L – as that its manner is that of rolling commonplace.[18]

Nor is there much more than decoration or incidental illustration in most of the domestic idylls in the sequence. Arguments that there is a sustained development in the domestic analogy, or that its recurrence helps to express the voice of the race which Tennyson claimed for his elegies, lack

conviction, since these passages mostly lack the only author-
ity worth considering, that of language. The triviality he is
capable of when he uses such analogy is evident in VI. 'And,
even when she turned, the curse / Had fallen, and her future
Lord / Was drowned in passing through the ford, / Or killed
in falling from his horse': instead of giving a fatal certainty,
the repetitive rhythms and syntax turn the event to mere
alternatives, and bathos. What happens in XL, as in XX,
suggests that there is something in the domestic idyll as
analogue which weakens his grasp. The ending is impressive:
'But thou and I have shaken hands, / Till growing winters lay
me low.' But the image of the dead as a bride owing other
duties than to her parents is given in the language of cliché:
'When crowned with blessing she doth rise / To take her latest
leave of home, / And hopes and light regrets that come / Make
April of her tender eyes.' And when, after the reference to
Hallam's fruitfulness in other realms, we have the heavy
difference, that unlike the daughter who will visit her parents
and show her child, Hallam may not return – introduced as it
is by the ponderous 'Ay me, the difference I discern!' – we
feel Tennyson is cheating himself, and us.

In Memoriam is an unequal performance, and any ex-
amination which does not take this into account is an ex-
amination of an abstraction from it. Nevertheless it is Tenny-
son's most considerable achievement. Perhaps too much has
been made of his remark to Knowles twenty years after its
publication, that it was too hopeful, 'more than I am
myself'.[19] Like Dickens, he became more despondent with
age, and 'too hopeful' may simply be the voice of an older
man with less to hope for. But the poetry of absence and
despair in the sequence on the whole carries more weight, and
we often feel that the poems which speak for life do so by a
kind of reflux or reaction. It has been argued that late addi-
tions after the trial edition, such as VII and LVI, reflect his
uncertainty.[20] And perhaps our feeling that VII and LVI were
not intended to counter baseless optimism, but to give direc-
tion, only means that it would be difficult for us to imagine *In
Memoriam* without them. But CXXI ('Sad Hesper o'er the
buried sun'), a notable late addition, makes these arguments
seem rather empty. This very beautiful poem is one of his last

words in the sequence on the cyclic, and the seasonal. 'Sad Hesper' and 'bright Phosphor' become 'Sweet Hesper-Phosphor, double name / For what is one', reassuring us of a singleness which was always there. As so often towards the end, distance and nearness come together, not only in the planet on the one hand, and the lives of men on the other, but within either. The planet watches and listens, hears and sees; the human closing door of the second stanza echoes strangely, and the team in stanza 4 becomes something other than the horses that draw the wain, by the abstracting and dissociating 'the moving of the team'. The watching and listening Hesper is ready to die in a dying world, whose features are forgotten in the haunting 'And life is darkened in the brain'. Phosphor's hearing and seeing is that of a more passive role in an awakening world: 'By thee the world's great work is heard / Beginning, and the wakeful bird; / Behind thee comes the greater light.' The greater light is from Genesis, the first and last in the last stanza is the Alpha and Omega of Revelation: the singleness in Hesper-Phosphor is complete.

But in spite of 'fresher for the night' and what follows it, and although 'brain' in the eighth line subdues 'darkened' to a suspension which distinguishes it from an image like Hopkins's 'each day dies with sleep,' it is likely that 'life is darkened in the brain' remains in our minds longer than anything else in the section. Denis Donoghue, speaking of Eliot's *Four Quartets*, Stevens's *Notes Toward a Supreme Fiction*, and Pound's *Cantos*, remarked that a long poem is necessarily a dogmatic poem, going on to say that the first embarrassment in these three poems is that they are dogmatic in an undogmatic age, and to speak of our feeling in the twentieth century, 'that long dogmatic poems must be particularly wary'.[21] *In Memoriam* is dogmatic in some senses, in others not; how far it could be described as wary is open to question, but there are varying and conflicting currents in it, and, as many readers have recognised, currents moving in different ways at different depths. The severe concentration on form is often like someone under great strain doing his best to control himself by moving as carefully as possible. In our less than dogmatic age a good deal of attention has been paid to effects of despair and disintegration which are sometimes apparent when the sense of conscious control which is one of the poem's most striking features seems to be strongest, or least ambiguous. Some of this critical attention, it should be said, has paid rather heavy dues to syntax, a word which has come to contain a curious principle of absolution.[22] *In Memoriam* is all the more an act of will, since the absence is stronger than the presence. Under that shock which 'stunned me from my power to think / And all my knowledge of myself', the self is threatened. Identity will not be restored until it is felt to be part of a greater will; and at the moment when the poem turns finally from the dead to the living, there is a revulsion not only against vacant yearning, but against the idea of self which has possessed him.

> What find I in the highest place,
>   But mine own phantom chanting hymns?
>   And on the depths of death there swims
> The reflex of a human face.

Patricia Ball has pointed to the differences between *In Memoriam* and that other long egotistical Romantic poem *The Prelude*, which was published in the same year. Tennyson 'faces the most un-Wordsworthian fear that the lone self, so exposed, is without meaningful identity in the universe. Only at the end of the poem . . . has he reached assurance that [the isolated creature] possesses within itself the vital powers of consolidation, the creative mastery of its own condition. Tennyson travels painfully to end at the point where Wordsworth began . . .' She shows how section XLV illustrates 'the changed temper of the egotistical idea . . . apparent in the poet's choice of the word "isolation" to convey the growing conviction of individual being'.[23] There could hardly be a greater difference than that between this defining by isolation, and the passage in Book II of *The Prelude* where (unlike Tennyson's baby who comes to separate mind by isolation) the soul of the Babe who sleeps on his mother's breast 'claims manifest kindred with an earthly soul'. 'No outcast he, bewildered and depressed: / Along his infant veins are interfused / The gravitation and the filial bond / Of Nature that connects him with the world. / Emphatically such a Being lives, / An inmate of this *active* universe . . .' Besides this, the identity guaranteed in *In Memoriam* seems cold, and fearful. The self and the world are recovered. But against that 'interfused' of Wordsworth, the idea of Hallam as a diffusive power is like an unconscious desire for escape.

CHAPTER VI

Maud

In Memoriam attempts a direction of self. *Maud*, which appeared five years later, is an expression of selfhood. Where *In Memoriam* contains an active principle, the dramatised hysteria of *Maud* expresses passivity, as does its continuing wry shrug of 'as I think' . . . 'as I guess' . . . 'as I divine'. *Locksley Hall*, written some seventeen years before, is also a rendering of lost love in a blighting age, and there is the same effect of passivity in its hysteria. But whether as monodrama or dramatic monologue, *Locksley Hall* is finally unsatisfactory, in spite of some brilliant passages. It begins and ends with posturing: 'Comrades, leave me here a little, while as yet 'tis early morn: / Leave me here, and when you want me, sound upon the bugle-horn' . . . 'Let it fall on Locksley Hall, with rain or hail, or fire or snow; / For the mighty wind arises, roaring seaward, and I go.' Its eloquence is spun from a dismal lingering: 'Knowledge comes, but wisdom lingers, and I linger on the shore, / And the individual withers, and the world is more and more.' *Maud* speaks of the withering of the individual in 'the days of advance'. But its posturing and self-pity are grounded in neurosis, or worse, and the dramatic method, as Tennyson explained it, is that 'different phases of passion in one person take the place of different characters'.[1] *Locksley Hall*, on the other hand, is a single speech by an irresolute egotist, and in spite of their dramatic swoops and recoils the long drifting and hammering couplets tend to dissipate themselves. Sometimes there is a neurotic intensity in the posturing.

And an eye shall vex thee, looking ancient kindness on thy
pain.
Turn thee, turn thee on thy pillow: get thee to thy rest again.

Nay, but Nature brings thee solace; for a tender voice will
cry.
'Tis a purer life than thine; a lip to drain thy trouble dry.

Baby lips will laugh me down: my latest rival brings thee rest.
Baby fingers, waxen touches, press me from the mother's
breast.

O, the child too clothes the father with a dearness not his due.
Half is thine and half is his: it will be worthy of the two.

O, I see thee old and formal, fitted to thy petty part,
With a little hoard of maxims preaching down a daughter's
heart.

'They were dangerous guides the feelings – she herself was
not exempt –
Truly, she herself had suffered' – Perish in thy self-contempt!

That is, Amy reaping what she has sown turns to Amy's
comfort in her child; which turns to jealousy of the baby as
the narrator's latest rival; which becomes in the same couplet
jealousy of a domestic reconciliation through the child, and
contempt for rival, lost mistress, and child alike; which dips
into the future to see Amy as hypocritical tyrant, and her
daughter as victim. The effect of a suspicion that feeds on
itself is most artfully conveyed by the rapid transitions. The
narrator presents himself as a man scarred by his earliest
experiences of life, yet full of generous impulse, triumphing
in thoughts of man's future, 'nourishing a youth sublime /
With the fairy-tales of science, and the long result of Time',
until this latest rejection.[2] Recollections of his youth are
dramatically interrupted by the tale of his love affair, and he
returns to them after some ninety lines of self-pity and

invective. He seems to hold the 'Mother-Age' before him as his natural state, and in one sense it is, since it means youthful dreaming: one tends to forget how large is the claim of 'I dipt into the future, far as human eye could see'. And the return to himself which he wills is in effect a cry for a retreat into those dreams of man's future ('Men, my brothers, men the workers') by which he glorifies himself: 'Hide me from my deep emotion, O thou wondrous Mother-Age!' His final appeal is ecstatic.

Mother-Age (for mine I knew not) help me as when life
                                 begun:
Rift the hills, and roll the waters, flash the lightnings, weigh
                                the Sun.

O, I see the crescent promise of my spirit hath not set.
Ancient founts of inspiration well through all my fancy yet.

Howsoever these things be, a long farewell to Locksley
                                  Hall! . . .

The rhetoric of this image of primary upheaval is such that the couplet which follows looks for one moment like self-mockery, and in the next like bathos. The actor's gesture of 'Howsoever these things be' is a tight-lipped direction of attention to thoughts that lie too deep for further eloquence, before he takes his leave with a last arm-tossing gesture:

Let it fall on Locksley Hall, with rain or hail, or fire or snow;
For the mighty wind arises, roaring seaward, and I go.

Impressive though much of it is, with that long trochaic line that so often holds us for a moment irresolute before confirming its intent, *Locksley Hall* is something of a dissipation.

   Maud's 'phases of passion', on the other hand, are solidly grounded, and through them it sets out a coherent action. Some readers have thought it incoherent, or have found in it no sense of movement, or have believed that the drama is subordinated to the lyrics, and that meaning lies in the development of some of the symbols rather than in the action that is indicated. On a deeper level than that of the lily and the rose, this last may be true. The fear of sexual love in *Maud* is apparent both in the jealous hatred of men – most obviously of the 'oiled and curled Assyrian bull', Maud's brother – and the elevation of women, notably Maud herself, by some peculiar mystic grace child only of her mother, who was 'a thing complete'. And the part played by the red-ribbed hollow, as Jonathan Wordsworth has argued, could mean a different action from that which the obsessed narrator sets out.[3] As for the lily and the rose, on the level at which we may be reasonably sure that Tennyson knew what he was doing, it is obvious that these recurrent symbols are an important part of this substitute for dramatic action. But it is one thing to say that image and symbol in *Maud* contribute to the dramatic meaning, and another to say that at this level the implied event means less than the symbol. E.D.H. Johnson observes that 'Symbols, and notably that of the rose, carry the burden of Tennyson's meaning to a far greater extent than does the actual course of the narrative, either explicit or implied.'[4] This seems to be an overstatement, which does less than justice to Tennyson's use of other methods. The flower symbols, incidentally, in particular the rose, are twice undercut by another symbol, which differs from lily and rose in that its role is that of something external which the narrator's imagination tries to make its own. I. xiv ('Maud has a garden of roses / And lilies fair on a lawn') opens with a glowing and tender vision of Maud's garden, passes to thoughts of how little separates them, then moves through the inevitable doubts to a strange foreboding of death. It is when he hears in the silence the rivulet, and the sea towards which it falls, that he thinks of death. He cannot understand why, and calls himself a fool. But the secluded garden in which Maud moves like a beneficent spirit, guarded by the heraldic stone lion ramping over her gate and clasped by a passion-flower, is virtually his creation, and it is this that the rivulet, as cold as that other rivulet at Somersby, must disturb. The contrast is even sharper in I. xxi ('Rivulet crossing my ground'). A rose is caught above 'a tinkling fall' of this stream that runs down from the hall, and with tender fancy he reads into it a message of love from Maud, whom he will meet that night. But it is

again the unsuspected meaning of the rivulet rather than that
of the rose which is important, since, however apostrophised
and brought into his passionate world ('forgetful of Maud
and me' is like a playful rallying of the messenger who has
done his job and wants to get away), it is merely following its
own path to the sea, part of the external world which no
pathetic fallacy will help him to come to terms with.

Nor is there much profit in thinking of *Maud*, or the only
parts of it that supposedly matter, as 'lyrics'. It is not simply
that the style varies so much, ranging from lyrical verse to
verse which Tennyson said should be read as if it were prose.[5]
The purpose is consistently dramatic, and the lyricism of a
supreme moment of emotion can pass into something less
lyrical, and more attuned to the whole event, so easily that we
hardly notice it. The eighteenth section of I ('I have led her
home, my love, my only friend') is a case in point. It has
sometimes been praised in part for the wrong reasons, for it is
a great love poem only for the first three stanzas. The five
stanzas that follow, moving though they are, are generally
inferior, and with them the section is subordinated to the
needs of the monodrama. This is not to say that Tennyson
conscientiously wrote fifty or sixty lines of inferior poetry;
he thought well of the last stanza's '*I* have climbed nearer out
of lonely Hell.'[6] It is likely that he did not want to maintain
the intensity of the first three stanzas, which, according to the
same source, he said 'might not be divided'.

Except for the inadequate third part, and perhaps one
section in Part I, his control over his drama is sure. The more
dramatic verse is sometimes misunderstood.

> Strange, that I felt so gay,
> Strange, that *I* tried today
> To beguile her melancholy;
> The Sultan, as we name him, –
> She did not wish to blame him –
> But he vext her and perplext her
> With his worldly talk and folly:
> Was it gentle to reprove her
> For stealing out of view
> From a little lazy lover

Who but claims her as his due?
Or for chilling his caresses
By the coldness of her manners,
Nay, the plainness of her dresses?
Now I know her but in two,
Nor can pronounce upon it
If one should ask me whether
The habit, hat, and feather,
Or the frock and gipsy bonnet
Be the neater and completer;
For nothing can be sweeter
Than maiden Maud in either.

My experience of reading that first stanza of I. xx with university students has been that they usually seize first on the badness of the verse, and when something of its dramatic purpose has been suggested, invoke the wrongs of women, and fall triumphantly on the masculine condescension as Tennyson's own. (Paull Baum, incidentally, believed that the little lazy lover is the speaker.)[7] So far from being sentimentalising bad verse, it is an ironic presentation of the hero's unbalanced joy as reflected by Maud, a girl of sixteen who seems wiser than her twenty-five-year-old lover. The context is that of the return in I. xix from the deep content of I. xviii to the world of society and its claims, and to that rancour between the two families which, in a line like 'The household Fury sprinkled with blood', suggests a curse out of ancient tragedy. It seems Maud's brother, who has spurned the fathers' bond and the mother's dying wish, now holds their happiness in his hands. The hero's response to this in I. xix is a struggling movement of the mind between extremes: the fierceness of 'Mine, mine – our fathers have sworn', the talk of plots against him, and the generosity which finally meets Maud's womanly desire for reconciliation, and by which he settles for the debt not only to Maud, but to what is hers – her brother. But the 'fantastically merry' of I. xix is ominous, and Maud's melancholy is a response to this, as well as to the pressures exerted by her brother and the moneyed and titled wooer he approves. Her melancholy is misunderstood: the condescension in that stanza, the soft rhythm of its commonplaces, the complacency of the feminine rhyming, speak of a new and dangerous confidence. The brother will be gently mocked; the padded booby of the cockney castle easily endured; the animal imagery of the second stanza will end with nothing more dangerous than the titmouse. Understanding the twin functions of the ball – the securing of the country, and the ensuring by marriage market of the *genus* Tory – the hero can look down from a height on this gathering of the men of many acres, to which he has not been invited. It is Maud who is apprehensive, seeing farther than he does, and (with good reason) fearing something more dangerous than worldly talk and folly.

Whatever else may be said of it, dramatic verse of this sort is hardly incoherent. The dance movement of I. xxii, on the other hand, is the lyrical climax of the first part, which has moved from despair to this sensuous ecstasy among the flowers of Maud's garden. The completeness of this feverish delight, so soon to be shattered, is brilliantly embodied in these eleven stanzas. This section imposes its form on us as perhaps no other section of *Maud* does. Basically it is that of a series of six- and sometimes eight-lined stanzas, with a close *a b* rhyme scheme in each, and lines of either three or four stresses. The rapid three-beat line dominates the beginning and end of the poem, in the first three and last two stanzas, but there is an even balance of four- and three-beat lines from the fourth to the ninth stanza. Some form of lyrical extension or repetition, a rapturous lingering over the occasion, occurs at the end of most of the stanzas: 'To faint in the light of the sun she loves, / To faint in his light, and to die'; 'Now half to the setting moon are gone, / And half to the rising day; / Low on the sand and loud on the stone / The last wheel echoes away.' The exceptions are stanza 7, itself an amplification of the closing lines of 6, and stanza 9, which ends with the imperatives and strong enjambment of 'Shine out, little head, sunning over with curls, / To the flowers, and be their sun.' Such patterns might be of no particular interest if it were not for what Tennyson does in the last stanza. The anapaestic rhythm of the lines has been crossed throughout by a falling movement within the stanzas, which seem to run or dance from the opening line until stayed by the repetition which concludes them. In the last stanza, the movement is reversed.

> She is coming, my own, my sweet;
>   Were it ever so airy a tread,
> My heart would hear her and beat,
>   Were it earth in an earthy bed . . .

The opening line repeats the central statement of the preceding stanza, creating a pause or moment of *recueillement* before the action of the conclusion, which begins with 'Were it ever so airy a tread'. That is, there is a rise at the end of the poem, which, together with the growing intensity of these repetitions, reverses a dominant feature of its form, matching the challenge to mortality with which I ends:

> My dust would hear her and beat,
>   Had I lain for a century dead;
> Would start and tremble under her feet,
>   And blossom in purple and red.

The dramatic force of I. xxii is in the ominously single delight, before the catastrophe of the duel with Maud's brother. It is a joy from which every other consideration is shut out, and the form is a masterly expression of its intensity, and its bounds. The power of I. xviii, on the other hand, is that of a present spaciousness reaching back to Eden, to the sheltering cedar's 'great / Forefathers of the thornless garden', and which, so far from urging claims on the future, is already part of what is to come.

I

I have led her home, my love, my only friend.
There is none like her, none.
And never yet so warmly ran my blood
And sweetly, on and on
Calming itself to the long-wished-for end,
Full to the banks, close on the promised good.

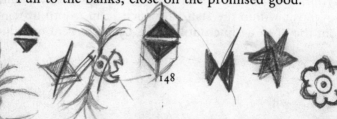

II

None like her, none.
Just now the dry-tongued laurels' pattering talk
Seemed her light foot along the garden walk,
And shook my heart to think she comes once more;
But even then I heard her close the door,
The gates of Heaven are closed, and she is gone.

III

There is none like her, none.
Nor will be when our summers have deceased.
O, art thou sighing for Lebanon
In the long breeze that streams to thy delicious East,
Sighing for Lebanon,
Dark cedar, though thy limbs have here increased,
Upon a pastoral slope as fair,
And looking to the South, and fed
With honeyed rain and delicate air,
And haunted by the starry head
Of her whose gentle will has changed my fate,
And made my life a perfumed altar-flame;
And over whom thy darkness must have spread
With such delight as theirs of old, thy great
Forefathers of the thornless garden, there
Shadowing the snow-limbed Eve from whom she came.

The movement and structure have the formality of an ode,
notably in the long period of the third stanza, where cedar
and woman are returned to the passion and the delight of that
first garden. Lebanon and the cedar are from the Psalms, and a
phrase like 'thy limbs have here increased' also draws on
Scripture. But with the repeated 'There is none like her, none'
it is the Hebraic tone of the verse itself that dominates. The
plainness of the opening lines is striking: nothing seems
needed after the first statements but the fact of the figure
('Full to the banks, close on the promised good'), and the
measure. Varied at first by the recurring 'none like her, none'
and 'sighing for Lebanon', the unaccustomed grave iambics

Maud

take over, and carry the period to its close. The deep content
has momentarily liberated the hero from himself; what fol-
lows is more personal. Some of the phrasing sounds as if
Tennyson had in mind Spenser's great marriage ode. The
dreamful wastes of the last stanza, and the prayer for the
sleeping girl ('May nothing there her maiden grace affright')
have something of Spenser's 'Let no deluding dream, nor
dreadful sights / Made sudden sad affrights.' This provenance
is probably the reason for language like 'dreamful wastes
where footless fancies dwell', which has not pleased every-
one. 'And you faint stars that crown a happy day / Go in and
out as if at merry play' is a rejection of the modern sad
astrology of distant fires. But the brooding over what is
rejected – 'Innumerable, pitiless, passionless eyes, / Cold
fires, yet with power to burn and brand / His nothingness
into man' – tells where part of the truth still lies, accepted in
the 'space and hollow sky' of which he has found the counter-
charm. The defiance of 'But now shine on, and what care I'
and '[I] do accept my madness' is in accord with the reaching
out at the end for the assurance of an older harmony no longer
possible to man: the concomitance of human and planetary
pulses, in the appeal of 'Beat, happy stars, timing with things
below, / Beat with my heart more blest than heart can tell.'
But the one assurance he has sought is found. 'I have led her
home, my love, my only friend' is a formal recognition of
this, and of the possession to come which, with 'home',
presents itself almost as fact. (The opening line is that of a
marriage song, but it is to her own home, the Hall, that this
bride is returned.) 'My only friend' is the greatest as it is the
simplest of reassurances. But the 'undercurrent woe' that
gathers at the end – and closes the poem with an echo of the
figure with which it began – can be answered only by the most
general of prayers: 'let all be well, be well'.

In this drama of different phases of passion, the Bedlam
scene of II. v is the obvious counter to I. xviii. Tennyson said
that he wrote it in twenty minutes, but we do not need this to
realise how close he was to the experience.[8] Broken by the
death of Maud, the hero believes himself thrust down into an
earth that swarms with the chattering dead, and pleads for
deeper burial. His mind leaps and darts – ('Who told *him* we

150

were there?' ... 'But what will the old man say?') – trans-
forming and re-creating events with its own strange logic, as
in the nightmare of Maud's garden, where the brother appears
as keeper, and completes his action by linking dead man and
spectral bride. In the long opening period with its rumbling
wheels and beating hooves and feet, the hooves beat not
merely into his brain but into his scalp: perhaps no other
word could give us that sense of aching bone and fevered skin.

> But up and down and to and fro,
> Ever about me the dead men go;
> And then to hear a dead man chatter
> Is enough to drive one mad.

The poem is alive with hatred of babble and blabbing:
ironically enough, since it seems that he himself is chattering
like the rest, the one silent thing being the phantom of Maud,
'from another stiller world of the dead, / Stiller, not fairer
than mine'. Throughout he has appealed for kindness, the
human creature crying out for its kind even as it turned from
it. But this phantom is neither beautiful nor kind, and the last
office of kindness must be to bury him a little deeper, so that
he may escape those voices of the dead.

> See, there is one of us sobbing,
> No limit to his distress;
> And another, a lord of all things, praying
> To his own great self, as I guess;
> And another, a statesman there, betraying
> His party-secret, fool, to the press;
> And yonder a vile physician, blabbing
> The case of his patient – all for what?
> To tickle the maggot born in an empty head,
> And wheedle a world that loves him not,
> For it is but a world of the dead.

Tennyson said that the last two lines were 'a glance at the
whole world', but the stanza itself is like a rendering through
madness of such a vision as Vaughan's in *The World*, which
has its doting lover, darksome statesman, miser,, and

epicure.[9] The world of the madhouse cell is the world as the hero knew it before; the diseased certainty of the earlier sections has now become crazed and visionary. And now again he harps bitterly on the public good, as a thing disregarded in this hell or out of it. Dead, he grumbles because he has not been properly buried.

> Wretchedest age, since Time began,
> They cannot even bury a man . . .

The rapid verse runs easily from a testy grumbling ('here beneath it is all as bad') and the dismissal of those responsible as a lazy careless lot, to the final indictment of this society.

> A touch of their office might have sufficed,
> But the churchmen fain would kill their church,
> As the churches have killed their Christ.

The churchmen stand for the open neglect of 'the public good': the phrase itself occurs in the context of the enigmatic prophecy which 'given of old / And then not understood, / Has come to pass as foretold'. (A little later a familiar maggot, that of the triumph of the cheating yardwand over the older England, reappears in the British rat of the Hanover ship.) When he summons himself to judgment, it is to distinguish between the public merit of striking down the public foe, and the crime of private vengeance. Of 'I swear to you, lawful and lawless war / Are scarcely even akin' Tennyson observed 'he feels that he is getting a little too sensible in this remark'.[10] The sense, such as it is, is overtaken by a renewed and whimpering plea for deeper burial, for the real burial over which he had postured at the beginning ('I will bury myself in myself, and the Devil may pipe to his own'):

> I will cry to the steps above my head
> And somebody, surely, some kind heart will come
> To bury me, bury me
> Deeper, ever so little deeper.

These three sections, all with an air of being complete in

themselves, of representing separate scenes, are climaxes to movements within the drama, and so correspond to different phases of passion. The third section of Part I, on the other hand ('Cold and clear-cut face, why come you so cruelly meek?'), though formally entire, is transitional. The stylistic development from the first to the third sections of I is a fair illustration of Tennyson's technique, in the sense in which R.P. Blackmur has described it as lacking in Hardy's poetry: 'the craft of his profession – technique in the wide sense; that craft, which, as a constant, reliable possession, would have taught him the radical necessity as it furnished the means, of endowing every crucial statement with the virtual force of representation'.[11] For a moment, in the opening lines of I. ii, we are still within the movement of the bitterly sermonising quatrains of I. i: 'Long have I sighed for a calm: God grant I may find it at last! / It will never be broken by Maud, she has neither savour nor salt.' Then the pace begins to slow, with the closer observation of the supposed dead perfection of Maud, and with it changes perceptibly that neurotic defining of self with which he came before us in I. i. The attempt at dispassionate observation compromises itself phrase by phrase, and the sonnet of I. iii represents a reflux, in which the extended and intricate rhyming begun in I. ii comes into its own. It is a sonnet, of a single period, because it is no longer, as in the first section, a matter of an obsession repeated through stanza after stanza, but that of a new complexity which he must struggle to apprehend, and hold entire.

Cold and clear-cut face, why come you so cruelly meek,
Breaking a slumber in which all spleenful folly was drowned,
Pale with the golden beam of an eyelash dead on the cheek,
Passionless, pale, cold face, star-sweet on a gloom profound;
Womanlike, taking revenge too deep for a transient wrong
Done but in thought to your beauty, and ever as pale as before
Growing and fading and growing upon me without a sound,
Luminous, gemlike, ghostlike, deathlike, half the night long
Growing and fading and growing, till I could bear it no more,
But arose, and all by myself in my own dark garden ground,
Listening now to the tide in its broad-flung shipwrecking
      roar,

Now to the scream of a maddened beach dragged down by
the wave,
Walked in a wintry wind by a ghastly glimmer, and found
The shining daffodil dead, and Orion low in his grave.

The recurring *b* rhyme of 'drowned', 'profound', 'sound',
'ground', 'found' is like a ground bass, which fades on a
desultory preterite. On the one hand, there is the action of the
dominant participles of the octave, by which the thought of
the woman grows and imposes itself on him; on the other, the
preterites of the sestet ('arose' . . . 'walked' . . . 'found') by
which he can only gesture at action. If the tides and stars of I.
iii are a wider world than the place and the pit and the fear of
the first section, what is most evident by the end of it is the
raw cold of the world in which he finds himself, with its dead
spring flowers and dying stars.

I. iii is probably the finest of Tennyson's sonnets, a form not
generally congenial to him, although he experimented fairly
widely with it. The variety of form in *Maud* is extraordinary.
He described the poem as 'a monotone with plenty of change
and no weariness', which suggests a rapidity of change that in
one way relieves, and in another confirms, the monotone.[12]
Yet its success is not that of virtuoso work, nor should 'phases
of passion' be taken to mean a handful of scenes linked by
operative *recitativo*. In a way, the risks taken command
respect. After many readings, that opening section with its
uncompromising vulgarity still comes as something of a
shock. Its theme is 'the place and the pit and the fear'. 'Were it
not wise if I fled': after the burden of the sixteen stanzas that
precede it, the self-questioning is a statement of impotence,
since these things are within the hero, and he feeds on them.

I hate the dreadful hollow behind the little wood,
Its lips in the field above are dabbled with blood-red heath,
The red-ribbed ledges drip with a silent horror of blood,
And Echo there, whatever is asked her, answers 'Death.'

The compulsive repetitions of the opening stanza are accom-
panied by a suggestion in the end-stopped lines of reflection,

or deliberation; the mood of brooding revulsion is tinged with something like wonder at this state. Elsewhere the agony finds release in a kind of passionate sermonising.

Why do they prate of the blessings of Peace? we have made
                                them a curse,
Pickpockets, each hand lusting for all that is not its own;
And lust of gain, in the spirit of Cain, is it better or worse
Than the heart of the citizen hissing in war on his own
                                hearthstone?

The linguistic vagueness of 'hissing in war' suggests popular rhetoric, with the assonance and heavy alliteration half concealing the grotesque image, and in the third line an internal rhyme to drive home the authority of Scripture. The agony is inescapable: the heath bleeds, the bankrupt woods shed their gold, the wind wails like a broken worldling. The morbid vision seems partly induced, like a dozing nightmare half relished by the sufferer. The grinding of the house-breakers' centre-bits in the silent city is like the gnawing of worms in a doomed fabric; the eye ranges from the blood-red of the heath to the pallor of the chalk and alum and plaster reflected in the faces of the poor, and back to the crimson lights of the murderous apothecary. The effect is of something generalised, yet intense, for which the relentless hammering of the language seems the only vehicle. And then the introspective vision which began with and returns to the place and the pit and the fear is disturbed by a human movement outside itself: 'Workmen up at the Hall'. It is the simplest of observations, but it is an indication of the dramatic art which will persuade us.

Following the acknowledgment of his fascination with Maud, and the belief that she has slighted him, the verse of the fourth section, with the measured sweep of the six-lined *a b c a b c* stanzas, reflects an attempt at control, at something of a larger view. Men are a little breed, and the self-burial of the first section is now to be translated into the calm of philosophic detachment, the 'temperate brain' of *nil admirari*: 'if a man could learn it', he says, with something of a melancholy swagger at the likelihood that a man cannot. The philosophy of withdrawal from the world of an inscrutable Creator rings out in one declamatory stanza after another, and rings false: the truth is in the fear of the new madness, of love. The philosophising is underpinned by a provincial Byronism: 'I keep but a man and a maid, ever ready to slander and steal; / I know it, and smile a hard-set smile, like a stoic, or like / A wiser epicurean, and let the world have its way.' It is the sort of hard-set smile which is practised before a mirror.

A million emeralds break from the ruby-budded lime
In the little grove where I sit – ah, wherefore cannot I be
Like things of the season gay, like the bountiful season
                                                            bland . . .

With the neurotic intensification of sense in the jewel imagery comes the common romantic view, of man as the single flaw in nature: 'to me alone there came a thought of grief'. Twenty lines later, however, the grove is neither gay nor bland. 'For nature is one with rapine, a harm no preacher can heal; / The Mayfly is torn by the swallow, the sparrow speared by the shrike, / And the whole little wood where I sit is a world of plunder and prey.' Maud's supposed slighting of the hero perhaps has confirmed that the strong despise those on whom they prey. The idea of nature as one with rapine invades his refuge, and before the vision of a nature red in tooth, beak, and claw, the peace of the grove vanishes as if it had never been. Until, that is, it reappears as a support for the *nil admirari* formula: 'Be mine a philosopher's life in the quiet woodland ways, / Where if I cannot be gay let a passionless peace be my lot . . .' As so often the formula is the expression of a deep fear: 'And most of all would I flee from the cruel madness of love, / The honey of poison-flowers and all the measureless ill.'

With the sixth section, and the thought of the touch of Maud's hand (that 'treasured splendour') in the village street, the nightmarish visions and large mouthings ('Our planet is one, the suns are many, the world is wide') give way to a sense of what is actually around him. Which does not save him from being acutely affected by the weather, like most depressives.

Morning arises stormy and pale,
No sun, but a wannish glare
In fold upon fold of hueless cloud,
And the budded peaks of the wood are bowed
Caught and cuffed by the gale:
I had fancied it would be fair.

There is a conversational ease in the verse, with the rendering
in commonplace of the wistful sense of why this day of all
days should have been fair; a quickness of response in place of
the unfaltering delivery of the first and fourth sections. It is
perception, however twisted, not self-justification. Now ful-
ly conscious of the other, he begins to be properly conscious
of himself, and to take stock. Wryly enough, in 'Ah, what
shall I be at fifty / Should Nature keep me alive, / If I find the
world so bitter, / When I am but twenty-five?' But there is a
responsibility to self in these lines, which sound oddly like a
Shropshire lad come of age, or the figure of doomed youth
brought up short by the recognition that life does not end at
twenty-five, or thirty, or forty.[13] The raven croaking of 'Keep
watch and ward, keep watch and ward' is unexpectedly
countered. 'Yea, too, myself from myself I guard, / For often
a man's own angry pride / Is cap and bells for a fool.' He has
come some way from burial in self, and this 'a man's' is free
from swagger. Suspicion, generalised in fears that Maud may
be a coquette, has sought reason in her brother's campaigning
for place and party, and how another vote may be gained.
His morbid fears – 'What if . . . What if . . . ?' – fight to the
last, and only yield to the hesitant affirmation of 'perhaps'
when something of what made him is declared.

Perhaps the smile and tender tone
Came out of her pitying womanhood,
For am I not, am I not, here alone
So many a summer since she died,
My mother, who was so gentle and good?
Living alone in an empty house,
Here half-hid in the gleaming wood,
Where I hear the dead at mid-day moan,
And the shrieking rush of the wainscot mouse,

And my own sad name in corners cried,
When the shiver of dancing leaves is thrown
About its echoing chambers wide,
Till a morbid-hate and horror have grown
Of a world in which I have hardly mixt,
And a morbid eaten lichen fixt
On a heart half-turned to stone.

O heart of stone, are you flesh . . .?

The turning point here is the recognition of kindness in Maud's 'womanhood', so different from the 'womanlike' of the third section, and which, manlike, is supported now by the thought of 'My mother, who was so gentle and good'. The outpouring is a naming of himself, and the voice drops after it to the tone of a gentler self-colloquy, a weighing of possibilities – 'Ah well, well, well, I *may* be beguiled' – in which the quick rancorous 'what if?' turns to an 'if' that could be accepted: 'if she were not a cheat, / If Maud were all that she seemed . . .'

With the appearance of her officially sanctioned wooer, and the fear that she is after all part of the world of Mammon, like her brother, the floodgates are opened, and in I. x what looks like the truth is told. The 'morbid-hate and horror . . . of a world in which I have hardly mixt' expressed self-censure as well as self-pity. Now, from the contemptuous roughness of what made the 'new-made lord' – 'left his coal all turned into gold' makes him sound like a Dummling or other hero of folktale who has come into his kingdom – he passes to self-disgust and self-justification in the same breath.[14]

. . . a lord, a captain, a padded shape,
A bought commission, a waxen face,
A rabbit mouth that is ever agape –
Bought? what is it he cannot buy?
And therefore splenetic, personal, base,
A wounded thing with a rancorous cry,
At war with myself and a wretched race,
Sick, sick to the heart of life, am I.

England is 'a blatant land'; this bought commission is its
defence. 'Therefore' has something of the rhetorical force of
an older usage. The bitterness of recognition turns back to the
'Sick, am I sick of a jealous dread?' of the opening line of the
section in such a way that the answer comes like a violent
release. Bitter accusation of England is accompanied by
self-accusation: he is right and wrong, right to be the thing
that he is. And of course we do not quite believe the eloquent
'therefore'; it is the neurosis of the opening section again,
with the professed observer now directly involved, and pro-
portionately more bitter, calling for a hero who might yet
regenerate this England where nobody is well, and yearning
for his own regeneration:

> And ah for a man to arise in me,
> That the man I am may cease to be!

That the risks Tennyson takes command respect is prob-
ably as true of this section as of the first. There are others
where it seems that he could easily slip into bathos.

> So dark a mind within me dwells,
>   And I make myself such evil cheer,
> That if *I* be dear to some one else,
>   Then some one else may have much to fear;
> But if *I* be dear to some one else,
>   Then I should be to myself more dear.
> Shall I not take care of all that I think,
> Yea even of wretched meat and drink,
> If I be dear,
> If I be dear to some one else.

I. xv is self-scrutiny, after the ominous premonition of death
in I. xiv. The fourth line, with the repetition of 'some one
else', sounds momentarily like a false note. Unguarded by
wry humour, it seems to all but to ask for sardonic assent. But
the undertone in which he communes with himself somehow
precludes, or offers no opportunity for, such comment. The
repetitions and close rhyming attest the understanding hardly
achieved, of the need for responsibility in everything, and the

need to accommodate the 'I' to the other, before the voice fades on the unquiet 'if I be dear'. 'Before I am quite quite sure' in I. xi also dares a good deal in recapitulating the simplicity of the prayer for love ('Before my life has found / What some have found so sweet') against the fears of failing ground, and of a sky which may darken before its time. One section where Tennyson almost certainly fails is I. xvii: 'Go not, happy day.' T.S. Eliot thought it one of the most beautiful lyrics in *Maud*; many have thought otherwise. J.H. Buckley considered it one of the 'great arias of the monodrama', and observed that in it 'the image of the rose is repeated like a full note in music and the sound conquers all sense.[15] Perhaps a sense of the dominance of the image has overridden other considerations. For the first twenty lines the song maintains itself with some success, partly because of the expectations it arouses. The drugged trancelike quality of the trochaics – all but one of its twenty-eight lines are of five syllables – and the repetition of word and rhyme, give something of the voice of a man who cannot quite believe his good fortune. (In 'Over glowing ships; / Over blowing seas' Tennyson originally had 'blowing' for both ships and seas, but being denied 'blowing ships' by a reviewer retained as much of the original sound as he could with 'glowing,' so admitting to these sunset-touches a further effect of fancy to be contained by the gentle rise and fall of the verse.)

> . . . Till the red man dance
> By his red cedar-tree,
> And the red man's babe
> Leap, beyond the sea.

The babe may have been inspired by Wordsworth's *Intimations Ode* ('And the Babe leaps up on his Mother's arm'), where 'land and sea / Give themselves up to jollity'. Although often singled out for mockery, the hyperbole is not offensive. But in the four lines that follow, the poem loses its footing.

> Blush from West to East,
> Blush from East to West,
> Till the West is East,
> Blush it through the West . . .

It is a little difficult not to think of Enobarbus's drinking song
('Cup us till the world go round'); the repetitions which end
Tennyson's song die as they are uttered.

Slight though these sections are, the appeal in the eleventh,
and the searching of the fifteenth, turning on the repeated 'if'
as the self comes near to recovering its object, help to ensure
the dramatic effect, within the poem's phases, of the depth of
assurance and foreboding in I. xviii, and the intensity of I.
xxii. Part II returns us at a blow to the red-ribbed hollow
where *Maud* began. The action that torments him, the killing
of Maud's brother, is narrated in lines that crack like a whip
('And he struck me, madman, over the face, / Struck me
before the languid fool, / Who was gaping and grinning by: /
Struck for himself an evil stroke; / Wrought for his house an
irredeemable woe; / For front to front in an hour we
stood . . .'), until the old horror of the place possesses him,
with its million bellowing echoes of the shots, and his mind's
echo of Maud's cry. With the second stanza of II. i we may
again feel that Tennyson is daring a good deal.

> The feeble vassals of wine and anger and lust,
> The little hearts that know not how to forgive:
> Arise, my God, and strike, for we hold Thee just,
> Strike dead the whole weak race of venomous worms,
> That sting each other here in the dust;
> We are not worthy to live.

There is something in this of the moralising commonplace,
the heartfelt pulpit language turned to when our own words
fail; either that, or spongy sermonising by Tennyson. Yet the
large condemnation after what has been done is in character,
and the first reading seems the fairer. In II. ii ('See what a
lovely shell') the voice drops, and the sight sharpens strange-
ly, the tiny object momentarily arresting the circlings of the
diseased mind, its artifice rendered in the extended intricacy
of the *a b c d a b c d* rhyming of the opening stanza.[16]
Tennyson remarked that 'the shell undestroyed amid the
storm perhaps symbolises to him his own first and higher
nature preserved amid the storms of passion', but this sounds
like a later and tentative rationalisation.[17] The shell is design

in the midst of chaos. Though empty, it is eloquent of life, and of survival by a perfection of organic form. Then with the sudden blink of 'Breton, not Briton', vision changes to the haunting by the 'hard mechanic ghost' that 'moves with the moving eye, / Flying along the land and the main'. Sight and brain are diseased. And with that the poem enters its closing movement, which culminates first in the madhouse burial, then in the departure for the Crimea. 'She is but dead, and the time is at hand / When thou shalt more than die.' That is, madness; the 'comfort her though I die' which ended the preceding section offered the final atonement before its time.

What follows in II. ix reaches the depth of guilt and loss, as I. xviii came as near the felicity of possession as the event allowed. In place of the great traditional forms that echo within that section, there is the ballad-like poignancy of

> O that 'twere possible
> After long grief and pain
> To find the arms of my true love
> Round me once again!

The section derives from the lyric 'Oh! that 'twere possible,' written twenty years earlier, which Tennyson took as the nucleus of *Maud*. Unpublished since its separate appearance in 1837, the poem inspired by Hallam's death now found its place. As with the seventh section of *In Memoriam*, the effect is that of a starkness of loss against and aggravated by the swarming mass of men. London is chaos and the death of the individual: 'the shouts, the leagues of lights, / And the roaring of the wheels'. Wordsworth's type or image of the city in the seventh book of *The Prelude* is the spectacle of Bartholomew Fair; a dream, a hell for eye and ear, a parliament of monsters. For Tennyson's guilt-ridden hero it is a place of rejection, a raw reality in which he is haunted by a phantom, 'without knowledge, without pity'.

> But the broad light glares and beats,
> And the shadow flits and fleets
> And will not let me be;

> And I loathe the squares and streets,
> And the faces that one meets,
> Hearts with no love for me.

The apparent last of his existence above ground is the tormenting shadow, 'the faces that one meets', and the intolerable light. As so often in drama, whether of one voice or many voices, the truth in commonplace renews itself: 'and will not let me be'.

In 1859, four years after its publication, Tennyson divided *Maud* into two parts. The further division of II in 1865 confirmed, if anything, the single section of III as an epilogue, in which the hero's lost rose returns as a blossom of war, and the language returns to the style of the beginning.

> My life has crept so long on a broken wing
> Through cells of madness, haunts of horror and fear,
> That I come to be grateful at last for a little thing.

The little thing is the dream of Maud as one of the blest, who urges him to the coming wars. Love and service have been transferred, and Maud of the starry head is associated with the blood-red Mars. The promise to live a life of truest breath becomes what seems to be a promise of sacrifice in the Crimean War has been presented in the monodrama as a consequence of evil rather than a cause, and as preferable to the civil war of commerce and exploitation. Britain is to recover her soul in a war against Russian tyranny, and the hero will be made whole by his part in it.

> And I stood on a giant deck and mixed my breath
> With a loyal people shouting a battle cry . . .

That is, his solitary breath is now mixed with that of a people righteously in arms.

There has been some preparation for this, on one level, but Tennyson's readers have remained unconvinced. The ringing conviction after the whimpering in Bedlam will always sound false. Some justification can be found in the psychology of the hero, for whom England's peace has been a sickness (the 1855 reading of 'the long, long canker of peace' in line 50 is like the 'longae pacis malae' of Juvenal's Sixth Satire), and whose cry of relief is like a cry for vengeance on the past. Perhaps the hectic oratory is that of the hero's obsession, and the hammering simplicity of his reduction of things to 'the good' and 'the ill' is a matter of violence done on himself. Perhaps, after all, we are not to think of the bitterness of comments like Victor Hugo's *Au dessert* from *Les Années Funestes* (1852–70), which presents a post-war exchange of courtesies between the Czar and the French Emperor: 'Causerie entre czars et rois, propos de table / Qui font rire les morts d'un rire épouvantable'. (Tennyson's comment, that his hero was 'sane, but shattered', and was giving himself up to work for the good of mankind, offers no consolation whatever.)[18] The most convincing statement of this interpretation is that of Roy Basler, who suggests that the hero is not completely cured, and that an obsession with self-sacrifice takes the place of an obsession with self-destruction.[19] (Basler also argues that the recapitulative epilogue of III is a major structural defect: 'although Tennyson saw clearly the necessary resolvement, perhaps he could not trace the steps leading away from dementia with an imagination equal to that which sustained his portrayal of the steps leading to it'. It is unlikely, however, that Tennyson could not have shown some kind of convincing recovery.) The argument about a transferred obsession is attractive, if only because the closing lines, in spite of their clanging repetition of identity and decision, represent an escape. In 'I embrace the purpose of God, and the doom assigned', 'embrace', apparently so strong in its intent, is another burial of self, in the submission to divine direction (notably absent throughout) which sanctifies this devotion to a cause. And if anything is clear about *Maud*, it is that it is not a way or progress of the soul. Whatever phases the hero has passed through, and in spite of his firmness about Maud's appearance being only a dream, and his rejection of 'that old hysterical mock-disease', perhaps we are to understand that he is at the end substantially what he was at the beginning, except that his death will now have a purpose; that he has not changed, presumably because few of us do change; that the victory is credible enough, whether it has to do with suppression or sublimation.

But though psychologically credible, this is not very much more than a critical solution of the wrong problem. What is wrong with III is that Tennyson is either asking too much of us, or too little, and the second seems more likely. The conclusion is a makeshift, and though we cannot say that the effective end of *Maud* is in Bedlam, madness is a better end to these mental processes than patriotism as the last refuge of a neurotic. Our age is of course preoccupied with alienation, and *Maud* is very much of our age, from the flux and shiftings of reality in a single mind, to the greed and social injustice of industrialism. The phenomenon of a raw sensibility afflicted by externals which it can neither control nor accept, and which become surfaces on which the mind can obtain no hold, is something which in fact we accept a little too readily, and to the exclusion of much else in our time. It may be yet another argument for a critical solution, that the solution Tennyson's hero proposes for himself is peculiarly modern: that is, the attempt to associate oneself with a collective or national movement. The assuaging of individual guilt and fears by joining in collective action (mixing one's breath with that of others) is something which this century is well able to understand. But there is hardly any doubt that the monodrama pays a heavy price for Tennyson's escape from it. It should not prevent us from recognising its quality. R.J. Mann, in a defence of *Maud* which Tennyson approved, said that 'in its general form of severe dramatic uni-personality, the poem . . . is absolutely unique'.[20] Not that there has ever been general agreement about this, and there has recently been some disagreement about the sources of its themes and form. It has been suggested that it is not an expression or rejection of Tennyson's early life, since there is no evidence that he was still preoccupied by his early difficulties; that what mattered was 'the purely literary question of how to express the passionate morbidity which he felt infected the land', and that the solution was found in the monodrama as invented by Rousseau.[21] It is not enough to reply that the evidence for Tennyson's continuing preoccupation with his early difficulties on some level is in *Maud* itself, but that his real feelings about Rosa Baring (with whom he fell in love, and who rejected him for a wealthy suitor) may not have been very strong, does not mean that we should not see the morbidity as his own as well as England's. His own insistence on the originality of *Maud* need not in this context be an argument of weight on one side, any more, perhaps, than is a reference of his practice to established monodramatic form on the other. The form of *Maud* suggests rather that the mode is being re-formed or renewed by the particular nature of the material; given the nature of the material, and Tennyson's continuing morbidity (and perhaps also the difficulty of distinguishing among morbidities), it seems a little odd not to associate it also with the personal difficulties which he had known. 'No other poem (a monotone with plenty of change and no weariness) has been made into a drama where successive phases of passion in one person take the place of successive persons.' Some of Tennyson's comments on *Maud* are unhelpful, but here as elsewhere he seems to have recognised his achievement. Of the strong personal reasons for his fascination with the poem, for the continual readings of it which he gave to (and sometimes inflicted on) friends and strangers, there would seem to be as little question.

CHAPTER VII

Idylls of the King

In 1887, speaking of modern acts of heroism performed in spite of the decline of 'the old reverence and chivalrous feeling' in the present age ('this . . . awful moment of transition'), Tennyson said 'the truth is that the wave advances and recedes', and added 'I tried in my "Idylls" to teach men these things, and the need of the Ideal'.[1] If nothing else, this confirms that his purpose in *Idylls of the King* was public. At the same time the death of Hallam, the other Arthur, is part of their inception, in the *Morte d'Arthur* of 1833. The great gift and loss are acted out again, but the large cycles give little consolation. Fairly obviously, he wanted to use idyll to give the effect of narrative on a large scale, while keeping the allusiveness of idyll. The narrative is about the decline of man's kingdom, and the stasis we sometimes associate with idyll is that of inertia: Merlin sunk in melancholy before the resolute Vivien; Lancelot leaning 'in half disdain / At love, life, all things, on the window ledge' while the dead Elaine passes on the river; Tristram lying in the beechen lodge, and thinking idly of a past as dishonourable as the present; Geraint drowsing while Enid weaves the grass 'into many a listless annulet, / Now over, now beneath her marriage ring'. The long afternoon in which the dishonour of the Order accomplishes itself is the longest of Tennyson's many afternoons. This alone would make us suspicious of allegorical interpretation, which is generally rejected, though at one time he was interested in Arthurian allegory. Something of it remained; Arthur as the soul can sometimes embarrass the finer processes of what he called the 'parabolic drift', and 'the thought within the image'.[2] He returns to allegory in two late idylls, but on his own terms: mockingly in *Gareth and Lynette* (' "Ugh!" cried the Sun'), where the fools' allegory of time is part of the burlesque of romance, and with a grim intensity in *Balin and Balan*, where, however, it is only one of the levels on which the idyll can be read.

Tennyson's achievement in the *Idylls* remains something of a smouldering issue. Some readers think they are the greatest English poem of the age. Others point to radical weaknesses of style, and to the forty years of straggling composition. F.E.L. Priestley has played a major part in reassessing the *Idylls*, and the comparison between his early analysis, and what he said more than twenty years later, is of some interest. In 1949 he remarked that 'however unified the total structure has been made thematically, the treatment remains heterogeneous', and, speaking of their quality as that of 'dramatic allegory', said, rather cautiously, 'the total dramatic effect seems to me to have considerable power'. In 1973 he described their structure as 'highly complex and very experimental', and called them 'a dramatic parable of enormous variety, richness, and complexity', which yet '[retains] the strong and relatively simple shape of tragedy'.[3] It is a fair example of how the *Idylls* have taken hold of the imagination. Some of the hoarier objections can be set aside, like the forty-year period, and Tennyson's complaints about the difficulties inherent in a fragmentary mode of treatment; if we knew more about what other writers thought of work in progress, there might be some strange revaluations. (His remark, after finishing *The Holy Grail*, that he would write 'three or four more of the "Idylls"', and link them together as well as I may', could be a harder nut for defenders to crack.[4] But *The Holy Grail* is something of a key idyll in the scheme; Tennyson had hesitated for years over writing it, and afterwards probably felt he had turned a corner.) It is pointless to argue that the *Idylls* fail because they set out decline; Arthur is deceived in Guinevere nearly from the beginning, but this has everything to do with the concept of Arthur as the soul, and of his task in the world as an impossibility. It is also a

waste of time trying to confound Tennyson by holding him
sternly to Arthur as Soul and Guinevere as Sense, since it is
not allegory, and even if it were, allegory often allows a good
deal of latitude. And lastly, given his interest in idyll, it is
probably better not to think of these idylls as watered epic, in
spite of his early plans for Arthurian epic. More arguments in
favour could be put forward, but it is almost certainly true to
say that the large claims which have been made for the *Idylls*
are exaggerated. (Some of them have been so skilfully prom-
oted as to suggest a minor critical industry: 'Excalibur Enter-
prises'.) The decline of Arthur's kingdom seems an ideal
subject for Tennyson's intense backward looking and for-
ward boding. But the style is often uncertain or dull, and
although the scheme is coherent, the effect is sometimes that
of arrangement rather than shaping.

Since Tennyson admitted he found it difficult to put the *Idylls*
together, because of the fragmentary mode, it may be worth
considering first how he faced some of the difficulties over the
beginning and end. The conclusion was already there, either
in *Guinevere*, last of the four 1859 idylls, or in *Morte
d'Arthur*. He chose to end with the *Morte* as *The Passing of
Arthur*, and to begin the cycle by matching it with the advent
and recognition of the spirit, in *The Coming of Arthur*. The
Morte, whose heroic style had been accommodated to the age
by *The Epic*, was now isolated as legend, and the new frame
turns inward. The King's passing is presented as 'That story
which the bold Sir Bedivere, / First made and latest left of all
the knights, / Told, when the man was no more than a voice /
In the white winter of his age, to those / With whom he dwelt,
new faces, other minds.' So prefaced, the last event in the
cycle has receded, and become a tale. (Tale, not monologue,
despite a fairly prevalent opinion; there is every reason for the
absence of immediacy, and 'story' is unequivocal.) In the 169
lines of the opening that brought the 1833 poem into place,
Tennyson rises to the occasion. Some of it has a dreamlike
quality, appropriate to this legend to be: with 'I hear the steps
of Modred in the west', or 'this blind haze, which . . . / Hath
folded in the passes of the world', we are out of ordinary time

and place. It also has the concentration of recapitulation, of truths finally apparent.

> There came on Arthur sleeping, Gawain killed
> In Lancelot's war, the ghost of Gawain blown
> Along a wandering wind, and past his ear
> Went shrilling, 'Hollow, hollow all delight!'

The dying resonances are Tennyson's, but so is the almost lapidary conjunction of the three names and what they represent: Arthur apart in his own world; Gawain, like Wordsworth's 'simple pleasure foraging for death'; Lancelot, whose betrayal meant war. With the dying King stands Bedivere, who will live on in a world ignorant of what has been. *The Passing of Arthur* ends with the line (and period) 'And the new sun rose bringing the new year.' So much has been destroyed that it would be difficult to find in this anything but the bleakness of what the new light reveals. Perhaps the 'new' of 'new faces, other minds', and of the 'new men, strange faces, other minds' of Bedivere's last words to Arthur, affects its meaning, but there seems to be little strength in the line. The central caesura makes it drag, and for once in the cycle truth seems to be divorced from season. (It is arguable that the dragging movement is that of a weary gathering of strength, which carries its own conviction, but there is often room for argument for and against in the *Idylls*.)

Tennyson had a harder task with the idyll which begins the cycle, and would have had a harder task even if the *Morte d'Arthur* had not been written. The cold void of the last idyll is matched in *The Coming of Arthur* by a birth in men's minds, the genesis of a myth, and the human needs and desires that help to create it. (He gives us only one passing, but more than one coming: when Arthur, riding to battle, feels 'Travail, and throes and agonies of the life, / Desiring to be joined with Guinevere', the context is that of a second birth, in which 'the life' names Arthur as the instrument of a purpose.) The body of the idyll gives us the processes by which King Leodogran, father of Guinevere – very much the average man, with his pithy apothegms, and thinking mainly of his daughter's welfare and his own dignity – passes from doubt to the illumination of a dream. The ten Round Table idylls are contained in the coming and passing of the spirit, and *The Coming of Arthur* is made to look foward to this construction. It begins and ends with an evocation of historical time, of which Tennyson's age was strongly conscious. His nineteenth-century parable has what C.S. Lewis, distinguishing between Spenser and Ariosto, called Ariosto's when and where, but the way it is presented reflects the fact that the past has swallowed up his hero, leaving little more than a name.[5] He assumes the voice of an old chronicler, to tell us of the ruin of the land among the petty warring kings, the swarming heathen, and the savage beasts, 'till Arthur came'. The expectation in the repeated 'ere Arthur came . . . till Arthur came' is suddenly neutralised by the factual 'for a space'.

And after these King Arthur for a space,
And through the puissance of his Table Round,
Drew all their petty princedoms under him,
Their king and head, and made a realm, and reigned.

The greatness of the Order which challenged time lies hidden in the dry naming of historical time. Then out of the renewed and gabbling account of waste lands and swarming heathen hordes and beast-like men, there rises, as a human cry sometimes rises sharply from the dullest of chronicles, Leodogran's 'Arise, and help us thou! / For here between the man and beast we die.' With this the action of the *Idylls* begins, an action which will complete its heroic early stage in this idyll, with the marriage of Arthur and Guinevere, and the defeat of the Saxon hordes. The accents of the chronicler are heard again at the end of the idyll, in a passage which closely parallels the first, so that the present in which the spirit weds the flesh, and the knights sing before their lord, is contained in the flatness of historical time: 'for a space' . . . 'for a space'. But the rejoicing in what is almost defeats the chronicler's time of the last paragraph, where the power of the victorious single will seems to open into a future of infinite possibility.[6]

And Arthur and his knighthood for a space
Were all one will, and through that strength the King
Drew in the petty princedoms under him,
Fought, and in twelve great battles overcame
The heathen hordes, and made a realm and reigned.

The living myth, the cycle which has begun, is held within chronicle, and freed from it to take its course with us.

The Coming of Arthur contains impressive passages, and is skilfully constructed.[7] Whether its total effect is anything more than that of a skilful response to the *Morte d'Arthur*, and a methodical preparation for the Round Table idylls, is another matter. Problems like this hardly arise with the later *Gareth and Lynette*, which was published three years later in 1872, and took its place as the second idyll. This youthful dream of action is a genial parody of romance, which fails with Camelot, where it cannot afford to fail. *Balin and Balan*, completed in 1874, is a dark internalised conflict. The comedy of *Gareth and Lynette* is an externalisation appropriate to the still golden time of Camelot as seen by joyous youth. Gareth is a type of integrity, whose impetuous strength must be given to a higher purpose. When he sleeps, 'all his life / Past into sleep'; when he takes the horn of Death, he sends through it 'all his heart and breath'; facing the figure of death made terrible by bones and fleshless laughter, he dismisses these as 'imageries / Of that which Life hath done with'. At first he has to contend only with the rough seneschal Sir Kay, whom he twice defeats, first by cheerful service in the kitchen, then by overthrowing him. Although Lynette, whom he accompanies on his quest, has missed the only way, the country through which they ride is not so dangerous as the waste lands where Geraint will adventure Enid and himself. There is, of course, the hollow with the round mere, where Gareth saves the stalwart Baron. But the worst of the mere is the sound it makes when the murderous stone is tumbled in. 'Oilily bubbled up the mere': the onomatopoeia is like a child's delight in imagined danger. The three brothers who guard Castle Perilous typify the temptations of the three ages of life.[8] But Lynette calls them fools who have sucked their allegory from a rock-carving of the war of time against the soul of man. To

Morning Star, glorying in himself and the blue arms given him by his 'daughters of the Dawn', Gareth opposes his own morning of youth, and overthrows his opponent after a brief if savage combat, in which his maiden shield is cloven, presumably so that he can take the other's shield, to which he has a better title. The Noonday Sun, with his red face gleaming out of blinding mail, is a different matter. Probably he represents the strong complacency of middle age, apparently secure within its limitations. As such he gives few but mighty blows, until his horse slips in the stream, and 'the Sun was washed away'. (Like ' "Ugh!" cried the Sun', the phrase tells us most of what we need to know about this easy allegorising.) The deadliest combat is with Evening Star, who springs up as often as he is struck down, seeming to grow young as Gareth grows old with weariness. Tennyson glossed his hardened close-fitting animal skins as 'allegory of habit'.[9] What he represents is plain enough, and if it had not been, there is an uneasily explicit simile to help us: Gareth, half despairing, 'seemed as one / That all in later, sadder age begins / To war against ill uses of a life, / But these from all his life arise, and cry, / "Thou hast made us lords, and canst not put us down!" ' It ends in a deadly wrestle (each combat is closer than the one before) and the hurling of Evening Star over the bridge. Unlike the other two, he is not sent to Arthur's court: whether he sinks or swims, this animal-like figure of age who has wrestled 'all unknightlike' is beyond redemption. In the last encounter, Death is revealed as 'a blooming boy' lost in his night-black armour, whose plea is the boy's excuse, 'my three brethren bad me do it'. The action is that of charade, and Tennyson's contemporaries must have responded to it as charade: a common New Year's show was a child as the New Year breaking out of the frail husk of the old year. It is not by accident that the word 'unhappiness' (taken from Malory, and glossed by Tennyson as 'mischance') occurs so frequently, for in no idyll is there less 'unhappiness'.

There is considerable charm in all this, with some subtlety in the equivocal defeat of time by youth, and what seems to be a lurking suggestion of time's revenges. Gareth's strength is put forth against a masquerade. (Earlier there was a disquieting image of age in his father, Lot, 'a yet-warm corpse, and yet

unburiable'.) Time's only defeat is by young love, as in that
heightening of the present when Lynette bends over the
sleeping Gareth, delighting in him, and in the world. It is
unexpectedly moving, this sense of permanence which these
two have found in their youth, guided to their refuge as they
have been by the rock which still presents 'in slowly waning
hues . . . / The war of Time against the soul of man': a silent
comment both on the fools who took only the form, and
those who overcame. Not that Lynette's last battle has been
fought, and reckonings up of her new-found ability to dis-
tinguish between appearance and reality are not very impor-
tant. At first she was all compact of youthful and shrewish
pride, telling Arthur that he sits there to do nothing, and
when brought to the point, announcing her nobility to the
King, who had not asked about it. Later she threatens to
return to court and shame him. Denied Lancelot for her
champion, she hates Gareth all the more because, though
knave, he combats like a knight. After the defeat of Evening
Star, she recognises his worth, and asks pardon. But his
overthrow and naming by Lancelot reduces her again to
petulance, and to a most shrewish rejection of Gareth under
all of his titles, including a fourth which Lynette tends to
confer very freely: 'knight, knave, prince, and fool'. She is
still smouldering when Lancelot tells her Gareth's story: 'Ay
well – ay well – for worse than being fooled / Of others, is to
fool one's self.' Of course, she has not had the easiest of times,
first with Arthur's offer of a kitchen-slave instead of Lance-
lot, and now with Lancelot and the kitchen-slave turned
prince exchanging compliments over her head. It is all very
human, and Tennyson takes a hand in it when at the end he
adapts his narrative formula of 'he who tells the tale' to say
that he prefers his own version to Malory's: Gareth will
marry Lynette, not her besieged sister Lyonors, and perhaps
there is a hint that some of their quarrels are still before them.

The charm of this tale perhaps leads one too far. The
play-acting of earnest youth, and the darkness of time behind
it, are one thing; Arthur's court is (unhappily) another.
Merlin's double vision of reality is a check to play-acting, and
in his description of Camelot as a city 'built / To music,
therefore never built at all, / And therefore built for ever', the

riddling that works through 'built' uses one of the oldest of myths to present a simple truth, that the city's strength is in the continuity of what inspired it. But the working of Camelot, though strained through boyish eyes, does not convince. 'And evermore a knight would ride away' has the dullness of the expected, but 'the listening eyes / Of those tall knights, that ranged about the throne' is facile artifice. In other respects it is fairly clear that in following out his burlesque of romance, Tennyson risks a good deal. There is more bad verse in *Gareth and Lynette* than in any of the idylls, except *Lancelot and Elaine*. 'But he spake no word; / Which set the horror higher: a maiden swooned . . .' Perhaps the bad verse is part of the parody, like the weaker passages in Eliot's *Four Quartets*, of which it has been said 'it is thus that the incompetence turns out to be dazzling virtuosity'.[10] At one stage Tennyson thought that with *Gareth and Lynette* he had finished with the *Idylls*, and it would have been natural for him to turn to parody. But there is no way by which an unconvincing Camelot could help the *Idylls*. His comment that the idyll was written 'to describe a pattern youth for [my] boys' may mean very little. It cost him much time and labour; he found it 'more difficult to deal with than anything excepting perhaps *Aylmer's Field*', and perhaps this fiction of joyous youth was hammered out in rather a joyless way.[11]

Some years ago F.E.L. Priestley suggested that critical misunderstanding of the *Idylls* had arisen largely from the reading of detached idylls.[12] Since then, so much has been written about their cyclic structure and complex reference of image and event, that it may be of use to examine several of them without such wider reference, to see how they stand up. The transformation of the *Morte d'Arthur* was entirely successful. But of the two late idylls discussed, *Gareth and Lynette* has serious weaknesses, and although its concentric structure is impressive, something is lacking in *The Coming of Arthur*. Perhaps we are so much aware of Tennyson's needs – a birth to match the passing – that it is difficult to have an honest opinion about the poem in which he met them. But perhaps, after all, not much more can be learned from how he met the difficulties of beginning and ending the cycle, than that a comparison of the first and last poems suggests a methodical and wistful response to early poetry which deals with the one part of the story which profoundly moved him. I propose to examine five more poems, in the hope of reaching some balanced estimate of Tennyson's failure in the *Idylls: Guinevere*, which he thought highly of, and wanted at one stage to use as a conclusion; *Lancelot and Elaine*, which in spite of its faults has greater integrity than some of the later and superficially more sophisticated idylls; *Merlin and Vivien*, one of the best of the idylls, and central to the scheme; *The Holy Grail*, and *The Last Tournament*, which though skilful are unconvincing.

The usual criticism of *Guinevere* is that the King, or soul, is now an outraged husband. The real difficulty with it is that, though sumptuous in language and often moving, it is clogged by overt device, like the novice. Her continual harping on the evil wrought by Guinevere reaches its climax on her prattling distinction between the noble lady before her and the Queen, and the narrative comment – 'So she, like many another babbler, hurt / Whom she would soothe, and harmed where she would heal' – does little to help. Some exception has been taken to the loathing of Arthur's flesh for Guinevere, but it is not this which is wrong, or the passionate reasoning of his rejection. *Guinevere* is one idyll in which the cycle suffers from serial composition; it was originally the last of the four 1859 idylls dealing with the true and the false: Enid, Vivien, Elaine, and Guinevere as true wife, harlot, true maid, and false wife. That Tennyson did not know what his purpose was, or was content with approximation, is clear from his use of the *Guinevere* of 1859 as the second last of the *Idylls*. The method was appropriate to the earlier idylls, but in the larger scheme parabolic or allegorising soul and sense have survived at this level only by being kept apart, and the powerful eloquence seems even more oppressive than in a context merely of true and false.

> 'Yet must I leave thee, woman, to thy shame.
> I hold that man the worst of public foes
> Who either for his own or children's sake,
> To save his blood from scandal, lets the wife
> Whom he knows false, abide and rule the house:

For being through his cowardice allowed
Her station, taken everywhere for pure,
She like a new disease, unknown to men,
Creeps, no precaution used, among the crowd,
Makes wicked lightnings of her eyes, and saps
The fealty of our friends, and stirs the pulse
With devil's leaps, and poisons half the young.
Worst of the worst were that man he that reigns!

That there is no mean between a lapsed wife and a whore may simply reflect the understanding of what Guinevere's example has been, but 'makes wicked lightnings of her eyes' is hysteria. The indictment, of course, is plain ('The children born of thee are sword and fire, / Red ruin, and the breaking up of laws'), and in spite of Vivien there is not much point in condemning Arthur's imputation of all blame to Guinevere, since it was her example which weakened the vows for many of his Order, and helped Modred, who took advantage of Arthur's wars against Lancelot to revolt. But whatever the indictment, the style is unconvincing: the Miltonising of 'She like a new disease, unknown to men, / Creeps, no precaution used, among the crowd' is at odds with the plain strength of Arthur's opening words, and the authority of much of this speech. Obviously Tennyson is using more of Milton than his language. *Guinevere* in its stiff way presents a fallen world; Modred, like Satan, climbs the garden wall, though what he sees is hardly Eden. Nevertheless something is being hammered home by the style, and it is a reflection of this that the three speeches of Arthur and Guinevere degenerate progressively. They were at the centre of the Order, distantly conceivable as soul and sense. Now at the breaking up of the Order each is made to explain the other, and the effect is to weaken meaning. One has only to compare Guinevere's soliloquy of repentance with Lancelot's musing at the end of *Lancelot and Elaine* to recognise its stiffness. Tennyson, after a simile that flashes out like the mountain stream he speaks of, draws attention to her speech as 'passionate utterance'. But 'It was my duty to have loved the highest: / It surely was my profit had I known: / It would have been my pleasure had I seen' is theatrical. Like nearly all the idylls, *Guinevere* is unequal, and the quiet nobility of her reply to the novice's questions about the manners of Lancelot and the King has something to tell us about patience, and repentance.

> Then the pale Queen looked up and answered her,
> 'Sir Lancelot, as became a noble knight,
> Was gracious to all ladies, and the same
> In open battle or the tilting-field
> Forbore his own advantage, and the King
> In open battle or the tilting-field
> Forbore his own advantage, and these two
> Were the most nobly-mannered men of all;
> For manners are not idle, but the fruit
> Of loyal nature, and of noble mind.'

Perhaps what is most moving about this in its context is what it does not say. And the novice's recounting of the wonders in the land at the founding of the Order (the spiritual so aptly degraded now to signs and wonders) is almost enough to make one forget the weaknesses. But the limits of the idyll, stylistically and in its contribution to the cycle, are clearly defined.

The faults of *Guinevere* are important, because in the end they are those of its conception. There is no such formula for failure in *Lancelot and Elaine*, which is of the same period. Yet none of the *Idylls*, except perhaps *The Holy Grail*, shows so clearly Tennyson's weaknesses as well as his strengths. It begins and ends brilliantly, with the symbolism of Elaine in her high tower, poring on Lancelot's shield, and the bitterness of Lancelot's soliloquy. Much of it is on a lower level. The slow pace of the narrative is an afternoon effect; even so, it tends to sprawl. But unequal though it is, the idyll is an impressive tale not only of youth destroyed by attachment to doubting middle age, but of ageing itself, of suspicion and *ennui*. Lancelot, great and greatly flawed, is at the heart of this tale of a Camelot in which courtesy is passing into courtliness, and where the womanising Gawain now comes to the fore. Except for the imprisoning of Merlin, there is no great event in any of the ten Round Table idylls, which present a progressive decline. But here the absence of great event is palpable. There is only Lancelot speaking speciously to Guinevere of how his 'loyal worship is allowed / Of all men', puzzled about how he may decently appear at the tournament, then riding angrily off to lose his way, and losing it, to find Elaine. His account of the wars against the heathen is a glowing chronicle of what is past, a story told after dinner. The present is full of doubt, of malice which sharpens scrutiny, and self-defence. This is the Order of Guinevere's 'There gleamed a vague suspicion in his eyes: / Some meddling rogue has tampered with him.' (The idyll is full of the act of scanning and reading faces, and of faces masking feeling from curious eyes.) The final judgment is that of Lancelot on himself. There is also Guinevere's coarse criticism of Arthur; Gawain's mockery of Lancelot; the courtiers' greedy scanning of the faces of Arthur and Guinevere, and the sidelong eye that glimpses the shadow of the quivering lace belying Guinevere's calm; above all, the embittered mutual appraisal of Guinevere and Lancelot. Arthur's sharp rebuke to Gawain is later followed by the gentlest of rebukes to Lancelot, who has failed himself, and Elaine: his 'Free love will not be bound', though easily justifiable, sounds like prevarication, and Arthur's 'Free love, so bound, were freëst' is unanswerable. One may wonder, of course, what else Lancelot could have done: 'to be loved makes not to love again'. Yet he seems less than intelligent when, knowing that she loves him, he presses Elaine to tell him her one desire. The end of it is his admission of a sterile love, and a bitter self-appraisal in terms we have heard before from Merlin: use, and name, and fame. As for the unschooled lily maid herself, it is too easy to restrict her role to fantasy, and no doubt a good deal could be made of the naked shield read behind barred doors. But it is passionate love, not fantasy, which creates response: not the sobriety of Jane Eyre, but not mere egotism. There is youthful self-dramatisation in her preparations for her one appearance before the court which she still thinks 'gentle', but her death is the effect of despair. Her offer of her love has the directness first of innocence, with the suggestion that Lancelot wear her favour, and at last of desolation, with her appeal (like and unlike Juliet's promise) 'to serve you, and to follow you through the world'. She has, after all, saved Lancelot's life, and whatever her dreams and fantasies she represents a principle of life, and finally of life denied.

The purposes of *Lancelot and Elaine* are very clear, and Elaine and Lancelot themselves are memorable. But it tends, like many of the others, to hold up its effects before us: 'Then rose the dumb old servitor, and the dead, / Oared by the dumb, went upward with the flood.' Later the 'tongueless man', whose twisted rock-like face is turned from the babbling courtiers, turns when the King appears 'From the half-face to the full eye', which seems for a moment to draw together all the eyes and faces in the idyll. The dialogue is often impressive, the narrative less so: the stubborn clear voice of innocence in Elaine's 'Of all this will I nothing' is real, the insistence on Elaine as 'a little helpless innocent bird' is merely sentimental. The most famous lines in the idyll start up and strike an attitude before us.

> And peradventure had he seen her first
> She might have made this and that other world
> Another world for the sick man; but now
> The shackles of an old love straitened him,
> His honour rooted in dishonour stood,
> And faith unfaithful kept him falsely true.

One purpose of the idyll is to show what should have been, and the clanging oxymorons describe the imprisoned self, incapable of action. But they ring out too readily, like rhetoric directed at an audience confirmed in admiration. It is arguable that the language is suitable to an idyll which deals in courtliness as distinct from courtesy, but this may be no more than the kind of critical solution we have heard before in connection with the third part of *Maud*. There are many lapses of style: here, as with the Latinate sounds in Guinevere's lips 'severely placid' before the watchful court, Tennyson is straining after effect.

These three idylls – *Gareth and Lynette*, *Guinevere*, *Lancelot and Elaine* – obviously contribute to the design. But in spite of this, and all the arguments about uses of romance modes, parody, and so forth, they have serious faults; the gesture of act in poetry sometimes becomes gesticulation.

Apart from anything else, *Guinevere* of course is unfit for the final scheme. But we can think of it as an ending, less because of the ghost-like passing of the King, which Tennyson liked, than because the Queen achieves self-knowledge, or rather because soul and sense come to know each other. The objections to this have already been stated, but some form of it was inevitable at that late stage. The most powerful word on self-knowledge is in fact the last written of the *Idylls*: Balin and Balan, who make up one self, know each other only at the point of death, and this allegorising is very different from the stiff extremes of *Guinevere*. This is the crisis of individuality, of the self which is not to be known, which *The 'How' and the 'Why'* had expressed at its own level of perplexity: 'How you are you? Why I am I?' As in section XLV of *In Memoriam* ('The baby new to the earth and sky'), the self is known by a defining isolation from others, and from things, and the question of how to live is overtaken by the question, who am I who live? Coleridge could speak of the dread watch-tower of man's absolute self almost as Wordsworth's refuge and place of strength. There is no such refuge for Tennyson, haunted as he is by doubt about what the self might be, and how it might be known, a doubt reflected by his passionate desire to believe in personal immortality. *In Memoriam* explores the workings of a self, and its possible relationship with the world and the cosmos, whose solitude has been redefined by what has been lost. *Maud* presents an obsession with self, briefly relieved by love, and at the end a sinking of the self in race and nation and cause, together with what looks like a final solution in the prospect of death. In the *Idylls* knowledge of self works within the framework of the degrees of self-reverence, self-knowledge, self-control of a community entered by the spirit, and coming to reject it. Looking on the dead after the last battle, Arthur cries 'I know not what I am, / Nor whence I am.' It is one of Tennyson's deepest chords, although here it may have something to do with uncertainty about his purpose. From the beginning, in the *Morte d'Arthur* (where Bedivere is 'clouded with his own conceit' and even the King's mind is 'clouded with a doubt') and the 1859 *Idylls*, the issues of the true and the false naturally tend to be expressed in terms of degrees of self-knowledge, and (it must be said) with varying degrees of conviction: Geraint, unlike the 'simple noble nature' of Enid, coming to some kind of self-knowledge only after many trials; Elaine, whose single purpose contrasts with self-tormenting and self-deceit; Guinevere, and of course the unavailing first and last of knowledge in Merlin, struggling with Vivien as with himself.

Merlin and Vivien was the second of the idylls to be written, after the *Morte d'Arthur*, and probably the first to be written with the knowledge that this was not going to be epic. It is the sixth of the twelve poems, and is in other respects central to them. Its qualities are of some interest in any consideration of why the *Idylls* are an unequal performance. *Lancelot and Elaine*, though powerful in symbol, rambles, and tends to present dissolution by diffuseness. The substance of *Merlin and Vivien* is a hesitation before a catastrophe, but its symbolism is supported by its form, which is that of a debate, recognisably within the self, and exteriorised by the figure of Vivien. Vivien is conceived as one of the principal destroyers of the *Idylls*, a creature of the elements, invoking fire and water, and pagan in the language of her claim that her truth is 'as clean as blood of babes, as white as milk'. Merlin's fall represents the defeat of the mind that informs the kingdom, and readers are sometimes puzzled by the fact that there is no effective reason why he yields to Vivien, since from the beginning he knows what she is. But this is the failure of human wisdom simply because it is human, subject to time and bound to the flesh. Earlier Merlin's age meant wisdom; now no sooner is he presented than he decays. In *The Coming of Arthur* his 'vast wit / And hundred winters [were] but as the hands / Of loyal vassals toiling for their liege'. In *Gareth and Lynette* he is the old Seer who expounds Camelot to Gareth, and mocks him in riddling speech. In *Merlin and Vivien* he is presented as 'the most famous man of all those times, / Merlin, who knew the range of all their arts, / Had built the King his havens, ships, and halls, / Was also Bard, and knew the starry heavens . . .', and within a dozen lines he has crumbled to a figure of doubting and flattered age.

The beginning is in age's knowledge of the 'world-war of dying flesh against the life', and (an interesting touch) the ominous enthusiasm for purity among the younger knights. Merlin is shown as having no illusions about the Table Round. Although he defends those Vivien defames, except Lancelot and the Queen, he describes his friends as 'All brave, and many generous, and some chaste': this is spoken without rancour, and to himself, and it tells us what we need to know about the Order whose founding was once sung of by the oak where they sit. 'Use and name and fame' recurs like a refrain, a brooding over a self already surrendered in thought. 'Right well know I that Fame is half-disfame, / Yet needs must work my work . . . I rather dread the loss of use than fame': his accents are as tired as those which expressed his purpose a few lines earlier: 'I fain had given [men] greater wits.' The words admit failure, and 'needs must work my work' is less rigour than dull acceptance. This is the conscious will, so strong in Tennyson; earlier, in the fine simile of 228–31 ('So dark a forethought'), there was the forethought that left Merlin mute before Vivien, a simile which indicates the sources of so much of his strength, and weakness. In the late poem *Merlin and the Gleam* he speaks as Merlin; here his wizard, while not a projection, is almost certainly, and for various reasons, far more of a reflection than Prospero was. But this is failure, not a laying down of power. Much of what Merlin says once Vivien has talked him into some kind of security seems to come very easily from Tennyson, like the description of the 'little glassy-headed hairless man, / Who lived alone in a great wild on grass', to whom 'the wall / That sunders ghosts and shadow-casting men / Became a crystal, and he saw them through it, / And heard their voices talk behind the wall', and the wizard's book of which he is the last interpreter, with its 'text no larger than the limbs of fleas'. The subtleness of this is that there is a growing disparity between what is said and what is happening, and that the disguise on both sides deceives neither. But its charm is also that of the Tennyson who doubted his powers, and sometimes wrote too easily, now issuing in this idyll which expresses so much else of him. If so, the enemy was hardly Vivien. But he turns it to account: the consciousness of what is coming is like a shadow behind the tales with which Merlin counters her seduction, and which are a reliving of surrendered strength, and a dispersal of will against her purpose. Vivien kisses Merlin's feet, but he

> was mute:
> So dark a forethought rolled about his brain,
> As on a dull day in an Ocean cave
> The blind wave feeling round his long sea-hall
> In silence.

'Feeling', linked to 'forethought' by more than alliteration, and working at the heart of the figure by the verbal action continuing from 'rolled', then suspended, comprehends and brings together the blind wave, and forethought that is as much feeling as thought. We are made aware at the beginning of the debate of the issue of this melancholy: that is, the impossibility of real articulation, or action. The nearest Merlin comes to either is in the apologetic 'You seemed that wave about to break upon me' (of the wave, or doom, that was poised to fall), and the (significantly enough) commonplace of his summing-up before the end: the peasant wisdom of 'nine tithes of times / Face-flatterer and backbiter are the same', and the cumbrous analysis of the rancorous harlot mind to which he will yield. The gap between this, and his thinking and feeling in the simile about the wave, reveals as much of the nature of Tennyson's success and failure as perhaps anything he wrote.

Merlin and Vivien and *The Passing of Arthur* seem to me to be, with perhaps *Balin and Balan*, Tennyson's greatest successes in the *Idylls*. The last is a late dream or image of their action, and by this achieves a notable concentration. *The Passing of Arthur* is of course the *Morte d'Arthur* of 1833–34; *Merlin and Vivien* presents him twenty-three years or so after that promise. Both express Tennyson as the other idylls, generally speaking, do not. (If Tennyson were Dante, the argument would not mean very much; as things are, and though it may not be the crux of the matter, it is probably near enough to the crux.) The coherence of later idylls like *The Holy Grail* and *The Last Tournament* is of a lower order, which may be one effect of the pressure on him in the late 1860s and early 1870s to complete the cycle. (There was no such pressure on him when he wrote *Merlin and Vivien*, any more than when he wrote the *Morte d'Arthur*.) It is not that either of them sprawls, or confuses. On one level at least, *The Holy Grail* is a little too coherent. In spite of the fine visionary passages, and a conclusion which comprehends all the conflicting forces, and leaves that comprehension in a kind of vacancy, we are too often conscious of being advised, or instructed. The inequalities make it a key idyll in more senses than one.

Tennyson sets out the destructive Grail quest as a reversal of the process begun by the advent of the spirit in *The Coming of Arthur*. Galahad's authority is made to challenge that of the King; as for the others, Arthur's words are harsh enough: 'one hath seen, and all the blind will see'. In place of the chorus of *The Coming of Arthur*, there is a clamour of individual voices, and the desolate visionary landscapes of obsession. To Arthur's vision of a world regenerated by the active spirit is opposed a spirituality of frustration, and rejection. The beginning of it is with the nun whose thwarted human passion 'glanced and shot / Only to holy things', and who after her vision of the Grail passes her obsession to her brother Percivale, and to Galahad. Others are instructed, who 'fasted and prayed even to the uttermost, / Expectant of the wonder that would be', and the year of miracle duly follows. We are presented with a clear chain of cause and effect, by which desire born of frustration has its way with a community which is now willing to deceive itself. Tennyson said he had expressed in *The Holy Grail* 'my strong feeling as to the Reality of the Unseen'. But speaking of the symbolic meaning of Camelot, he said that there was 'no single fact or incident in the *Idylls*, however seemingly mystical, which cannot be explained as without any mystery or allegory whatever'. Some of the meaning of this idyll depends on our rejection of one kind of mystery, and to prevent misunderstanding he added a number of glosses. Of the storm that breaks round Galahad and Percivale before Galahad passes to Sarras, the spiritual city, he said 'It was a time of storm when men could imagine miracles, and so storm is emphasised'; on Bors's vision of the Grail there is the laconic comment, 'it might have been a meteor'.[13] The glosses insist on what the text makes sufficiently clear. Bors, square-set and honest, is made to represent normality, and in fact is like a gloss which has crept into a text. Loving and grieving for his kinsman Lancelot, he would have been happy to leave the vision to him. Although he thinks he saw the Grail, his quest does not denote any internal confusion; he falls among pagans, and bears witness to his faith. His love and humility are in sharp contrast with Percivale's wavering between despair and pride, and with the madness of Lancelot, who, devoured by guilt, tries to lose himself in the great sea. As for Percivale, the former member of the Order who tells the tale, we are not left in any doubt about his obsession, since Arthur rejects him as firmly as he has rejected the Order. The answer he gets to his announcement of his 'fresh but fixt resolve / To pass away into the quiet life' is first silence, and later Arthur's description of him as one who 'leaving human wrongs to right themselves, / Cares but to pass into the silent life'.

The climax of these visions is that of Lancelot, presented as a man burned and blinded by what he saw and did not see. Then the libertine Gawain, bound and swearing by his senses, and so the apostle of the rational, breaks the silence that follows, and, addressing Percivale, returns us to the origins of the quest.

> 'The holy nun and thou have driven men mad,
> Yea, made our mightiest madder than our least.
> But by mine eyes and by mine ears I swear,
> I will be deafer than the blue-eyed cat,
> And thrice as blind as any noonday owl,
> To holy virgins in their ecstasies,
> Henceforward.'

By a single deft movement, the reductive interpretation of the glosses is stated and (Gawain being what he is) discredited, so that the King, having rebuked Gawain as one 'being too blind to have desire to see', may reasonably, if distantly, relate Bors, Lancelot, and Percivale to the prophets and bards of old, in that they have seen according to their sight. Obviously some such balance had to be found before what Tennyson said he intended as 'the summing up of all in the highest note by the highest of men', which is a concept of vision sanctioned by duty, of the King as the hind who must not leave his work for visions.[14] This is greater than anything told by those who have followed wandering fires: 'this earth he walks on seems not earth, / This light that strikes his eyeball is not light, / This air that smites his forehead is not air / But vision'. (The physical reality of earth, light, and air is part of the play on vision and no vision; one kind of seeing has been emphasised, and an influence that passes from eye to eye, and perhaps it is no accident that Arthur should say, not 'eye', but 'eyeball'.) The King's faith triumphs in this speech, but it seems to be virtually his faith alone, to which he witnesses before 'a barren board, / And a lean Order'. It is not Percivale's, whose 'So spake the King: I knew not all he meant' ends the idyll.

It is likely that one of the strongest impressions left on us by the idyll is that of admiration for its form, as well as for its visionary poetry. The form is partly monologue, partly reported narrative, with an interlocutor, and many reported voices. It accommodates expertly a wide range of individual experiences, some directly opposing each other, others merely divergent, and one, the King's, inclusive and apart. (Although there is little point in rejecting Tennyson's various kinds of seeing as such, perhaps Galahad is not quite accommodated, in all the range of the true and the false.) But in spite of the authority with which Tennyson adapted the legend of the Grail quest for this stage of his cycle, the form sometimes betrays itself as device, which tells us where to stand if we want to see things to advantage. For most readers who are not committed to the opinion that *Idylls of the King* is the greatest poem of its age, there is probably some stage in *The Holy Grail* at which we begin, rather suddenly, to lose confidence. As, for example, when Percivale tells Arthur what has happened, on the King's return to Camelot after the appearance of the Grail and the swearing of the oaths, and Arthur's face 'Darkened, as I have seen it more than once, / When some brave deed seemed to be done in vain, / Darken'. The King will not be too dark a prophet, for brave deeds will be done in vain, but this reading of Arthur's foreknowledge through a Percivale already devoted to the quest – and told by a Percivale who believes he saw the Grail – rings false. Once one has lost confidence, all sorts of doubts begin. Bors's sight

of the Grail (that might have been a meteor) 'by miracle –
what else?' is the voice of faith, contemptuous of anything
less, but it also comes out of the monologue and pushes at us.
Even the stratagem of making Gawain's words recall the
origins of the collective madness loses something by the
careful preparation for it.

> 'So speaking, and here ceasing, Lancelot left
> The hall long silent, till Sir Gawain – nay,
> Brother, I need not tell thee foolish words, –
> A reckless and irreverent knight was he,
> Now boldened by the silence of his King, –
> Well, I will tell thee . . . '

This too is in character, but it seems less Percivale's hesitation
than a tactical hesitation by Tennyson to show what follows
to advantage. Percivale can tell Ambrosius 'what said each,
and what the King', because 'the living words / Of so great
men as Lancelot and our King / Pass not from door to door
and out again, / But sit within the house'. These lines reach
back with assurance to a past when great men spoke, and were
remembered; they are not 'epic' circumstance. But by the
time we come to them we are almost ready to take them for an
overt support (or excuse) for the form of the poem. Almost
ready, it is true, but we do find ourselves justifying, and also
rejecting argument, and shrewd device. Ambrosius questions
shrewdly enough, with his 'Came ye on none but phantoms
in your quest?' But the rambling insistence on (or the insis-
tent rambling about) the warmth of common life which leads
up to the question, with the relentless beating of the adjectives
– 'little thorpe', 'old walls', 'honest face', 'homely secret' –
reaches out of the text like a finger-post. Again it is in
character: Tennyson used to call attention to these 'babbling
homely utterances'.[15] But the idea is so driven home as to
make us suspect either that Tennyson does not trust us, or
does not trust himself: perhaps there is no real distinction.

The Holy Grail is probably the most striking single inst-
ance of Tennyson's characteristic success and failure in the
Idylls. *The Last Tournament*, published first in 1871, and its
near contemporary, is in many ways comparable: a skilfully

handled narrative whose action brings before us much that is
at the heart of the *Idylls*, but in which there is a good deal of
expert contrivance. The idyll presents the decadence of the
Order; it echoes with the language of frustration and con-
tempt. The most marked of its oppositions is that of the
self-knowledge of Dagonet, the King's dwarfish fool, and the
emptiness of the splendid Tristram. Tristram is not a Pelleas,
swinging from one extreme to the other, but the kind of
natural man to be met with any day, claiming equality with
Lancelot with his 'Great brother, thou nor I have made the
world; / Be happy in thy fair Queen as I in mine.' That is, if
this is the world, then live in it: the doctrine is common
enough, and Tristram, like Gawain, is the apostle of things as
they are. His first love song means take what you can while
you can, and the 'Ay, ay, O ay' of his second song, like the 'O
aye' of his earlier 'The vows! / O ay – the wholesome madness
of an hour', is a half-cynical, half-rueful recognition and
rejection. This light of common day is that of a new genera-
tion: a hard-headed view not unsympathetic to what it re-
gards as a necessary illusion which has had its day. His dream
of the two Isolts means nothing to him, and he wakes
untroubled and ready for action. His justification of the
marriage with Isolt of Brittany is the rough gesture of 'the
night was dark': however qualified by 'the true star set', it is a
show of virile pragmatism. But thinking of Queen Isolt's
love or hate, he confesses 'I know not what I would': this
latter hero is ignorant of motive and of self, trusting only in an
idea of 'full man'. It is skilfully handled, as is the opposition
with Dagonet. The music to which the Order moved is now
in the mind of a skipping fool, and renowned though Tris-
tram is as harper, Dagonet refuses to dance to his music. (But
it is here, perhaps, that we have to make a distinction. The
most revealing thing about the long dialogue between
Dagonet and Tristram is the level on which it succeeds: the
contrivance, not to say the pastiche, is expert.) As for Arthur,
his heroic enterprise with the souls of men is nearly over. He
fears that his realm will 'Reel back into the beast, and be no
more', but in a sense the fall has already taken place. His
courtesy to the mutilated churl, and his orders to the vulgar
Kay to tend him like a king's heir, ring strangely now.

Lancelot seems divided from him, and is haunted by his boding words. The formal utterance of their last encounter – ' "Is it well? . . . "It is well . . . it is well" ' – which turns to Arthur's 'Is it then so well?' directs us quietly to all that has been lost.

Elsewhere the direction is less quiet. The entrusting of the mutilated churl to Sir Kay rings strangely; it also rings hollow. We know how Kay will treat 'my churl, for whom Christ died', and are scrupulously left to know. 'The sudden trumpet sounded as in a dream / To ears but half-awaked, then one low roll / Of Autumn thunder, and the jousts began': even without the gloss 'The autumn of the Round Table', the syntax suggests instruction.[16] There is a great deal of over-insistence, and it cannot all be met by the large assumption that idyll works like that, or does not work like that.

> 'For feel this arm of mine – the tide within
> Red with free chase and heather scented air,
> Pulsing full man . . . '

The vulgarity of that second line is surprising. It may seem wrong-headed to point to the weaknesses of *Lancelot and Elaine*, and then to censure Tennyson for demonstrating in *The Last Tournament* the structural skill which the earlier idyll lacks. But *Lancelot and Elaine*, for all its wanderings, is nearer the heart of things than the over-wrought and officious *The Last Tournament*. Though the turning back of the narrative, and the interweaving of the various plots, give an effect of firm control, we often feel the direction more than we want to: as with the interlocking of the narratives of Tristram and Arthur, Tristram dreaming of the two Isolts and the ruby necklace, Arthur riding to the burning of the Red Knight's hold. 'Then, out of Tristram waking, the red dream / Fled with a shout': we do not need to be alert to every possible weakness to feel that we are being manoeuvred into the right position. Or even to suspect that the reduction of spiritual strength to the figures of Fool and King is the skilful application of a formula, part of a virtuoso performance.

'It makes a silent music up in heaven,
And I, and Arthur and the angels hear,
And then we skip.'

This has its charm, but the fluency, and the archaising, have
produced something as rootless as the gesticulatory 'Behind
him rose a shadow and a shriek' of Tristram's death.

The expert contrivance in some of the later idylls defines
itself more clearly if we compare them, not only with *Merlin
and Vivien* or *The Passing of Arthur*, but with the last idyll
Tennyson wrote. *Balin and Balan* was finished by 1874, but
not published until 1885. It is not without faults, but is
probably the most complete statement within the *Idylls* of his
deepening pessimism, and one of his last words on self-
reverence, self-knowledge, self-control. The rational and
governing power of Balan, and the dark fierce energy of
Balin, are an image first of the unified, then of the disrupted
self, which ends in a mutual fratricide representing self-
destruction. The idyll returns to the old mode of the quest.
Any quest is in some sense internal; this one represents a
masterly direction of the mode by what for a later age, as in
Browning's *Childe Roland*, was its major principle. With this
it also returns, though on its own terms, to the earlier mode of
allegorising, a strain of which persists throughout the *Idylls*.
In *Balin and Balan* the shadow or reality of objective truth,
the reality or shadow of the projections of the mind, are so
near akin that each supports the other, and parable for once
approaches allegory without losing anything of its supple-
ness. Here, if anywhere, Tennyson trusts his readers; it is a
pity that they have not always responded. His greatest effects
are often achieved in dreams, and *Balin and Balan* often holds
us in the strange certainties of nightmare.

. . . leaves
Laid their green faces flat against the panes,
Sprays grated, and the cankered boughs without
Whined in the wood . . .

. . . At length, and dim through leaves
Blinkt the white morn, sprays grated, and old boughs
Whined in the wood.

The artistry is of a sort which should not be mistaken for dexterity, whether in the dreamlike compulsion in the curtness of 'He rose, descended, met / The scorner in the castle court', or the supple forward movement of Vivien on her way to Camelot, the advancing evil agency sure of its triumph:

> But now the wholesome music of the wood
> Was dumbed by one from out the hall of Mark,
> A damsel-errant, warbling, as she rode
> The woodland alleys, Vivien, with her Squire.

As most readers have recognised, movement is what is lacking, or only intermittently present in most of the *Idylls*. Their movement within stasis has had its defenders: complex references, idyllic convex mirrors, and so forth. *Balin and Balan* is a kind of stasis of frustration, but there is a deeper movement and urgency in it than in most of the others. It is not clear why Tennyson waited eleven years or so before publishing it. Sir Charles Tennyson suggested that he did not want to disturb the sale of the 1872 volume, which brought together the *Idylls* in nearly their final form, and thought it unfair to purchasers to issue a new edition so soon. J.M. Gray, in a brilliant paper, points to a shift in emphasis, in this *Doppelgänger* idyll, from the epistemological separation of appearance and reality in the *Idylls* generally, and suggests the consequent difficulty of interpretation as the main reason for the delay. If it were not for the fact that Tennyson thought *Guinevere*, with *Maud*, the finest thing he had written, one might wonder whether he hesitated over his last idyll because its dreamlike, even valedictory concentration made some of the virtuoso work of the other idylls suffer by comparison.[17]

The language of the *Idylls* is notoriously debatable ground. For some readers, the weaknesses prejudice any serious purpose; for others, no problem exists. What could be Tennyson's opinion is given in the sixth stanza of *Merlin and the Gleam*, that enigmatic poem of 1889 written, according to Hallam Tennyson, 'for those who cared to know about his literary history'.[18]

Then, with a melody
Stronger and statelier,
Led me at length
To the city and palace
Of Arthur the king . . .

The riddling of the poem makes it difficult to know whether
Tennyson is referring primarily to the *Morte d'Arthur*, but
perhaps the riddling also makes nonsense of such identifica-
tions and distinctions. A major problem in the melody of the
Idylls is the extensive use of archaism. Their archaising
language is among the most sustained of Tennyson's many
indirections, but its quality varies greatly, from the evocation
of a chronicler's language in *The Coming of Arthur*, to a
réchauffé of Malory like 'a marvellous great shriek and
ghastly groan'. The use of such a style in the first idyll, of
course, had a particular purpose. Generally speaking, the
need seems to have been for a language which would support
the parabolic drift by combining the remoteness of another
age with a certain intimacy. At its best, the archaising of the
Idylls does exactly that. But the continuing need for it
sometimes dulled Tennyson's responses.

O purblind race of miserable men,
How many among us at this very hour
Do forge a life-long trouble for ourselves,
By taking true for false, or false for true;
Here, through the feeble twilight of this world
Groping, how many, until we pass and reach
That other, where we see as we are seen!

This language is accepted by readers who are willing to
dismiss with ignominy large tracts of William Morris, or
(perhaps with an eye to its spelling) R.H. Barham's *As I Laye
A-Thynkynge*. (The odds against Barham's lyric are heavy,
but in its own rather peculiar way it succeeds.) It is not on the
level of Richard Watson Dixon's *Mano*: 'This Poem, in the
Italian's measure made, / Commended be, if it some deal
observe / The law which on his verse the master laid, / From
which the most do in our language swerve.'[19] But it is watery

and unmemorable, the more surprisingly since Tennyson is dealing – although discursively rather than by event or symbol – with an opposition central to the *Idylls*. It has the awkwardness and muffled effect of a bad translation from something we vaguely remember. The passage, or part of it – it is the opening lines of *Geraint and Enid* – has been described as an adaptation of the opening terzetto of Canto XI in the *Paradiso*.[20] This is hopeful rather than accurate, but it does read rather like an early attempt at translating Dante. Hallam Tennyson compared Lucretius, *De Rerum Natura* II. 14: 'O miseras hominum mentes, O pectora caeca' ('O pitiable minds of men, O blind intelligences').[21] The only thing confirmed by these comparisons is a sense of something borrowed, and debased; it is difficult to think that this is actually Tennyson. There is a considerable difference between this archaising and a line like 'And she by tact of love was well aware', from the passage in *Lancelot and Elaine* in which Elaine, rejected by Lancelot, looks down on him as he leaves, aware 'that Lancelot knew that she was looking at him'. This brings the event very near, while letting it keep the little distance that we love to cancel, in the familiar terminal effect of 'was well aware'. Sometimes the closeness is achieved by the sudden absence of archaic expression. In *Geraint and Enid*, Enid, weeping at the wayside by the wounded Geraint, is seen by the bandit Earl Doorm, who 'Bound on a foray, rolling eyes of prey, / Came riding with a hundred lances up; / But ere he came, like one that hails a ship, / Cried out with a big voice, "What, is he dead?"' The rolling movement of the antique language of action is impressive, but it is the contrast of 'What, is he dead?' which makes the effect. It resembles the high-born whore Ettarre's courteous greeting in *Pelleas and Ettarre* of Gawain, who enters on horseback ('as who should say him nay'), having supposedly slain Pelleas.

> 'Dead, is it so?' she asked. 'Ay, ay,' said he,
> 'And oft in dying cried upon your name.'
> 'Pity on him,' she answered, 'a good knight,
> But never let me bide one hour at peace.'
> 'Ay,' thought Gawain, 'and you be fair enow . . .'

The contrast is a little like a trick. But in the narrative of Lancelot's departure from Elaine, Tennyson used the archaic as only a poet alive to all the possibilities of his medium could have done. On the other hand, this from *The Marriage of Geraint* confesses itself nakedly: 'like a man abroad at morn / When first the liquid note beloved of men / Comes flying over many a windy wave / To Britain, and in April suddenly / Breaks from a coppice gemmed with green and red ...' 'Many a windy wave' is charming, but it is not much more than a deft bit of mediaevalising, as prettily glazed and patterned as Morris's drinking-pots in *A Dream of John Ball*. Not that this is Morris's mediaevalising at its best.

> And now, knights, all of you,
> I pray you, pray for Sir Hugh,
> A good knight and a true,
> And for Alice, his wife, pray too.

This, from the short poem *Shameful Death*, seems to reach us across the years. The ten-thousand-odd heroic lines of the *Idylls* give Tennyson no such advantage.

Admittedly critics of the language of the *Idylls* have sometimes overlooked Tennyson's purposes. It has been said that 'An armlet for the roundest arm on earth' falls like brawn; this is true, but it is also true that it is meant to fall like brawn, being part of an artificial speech which Lancelot is making to a suspicious Guinevere, who will presently throw the words back in his face.[22] Perhaps the burlesque of *Gareth and Lynette* has to be judged by different standards, though its unconvincing Camelot is another matter. But – since we have been looking at a passage from *Lancelot and Elaine* – it is difficult to accept a description of that idyll as a poem whose style as a whole is 'intentionally artificial', the effect being that 'in this world in which courtesy is a mere form and corruption the substance, the inflated style functions as a vehicle of moral judgment'.[23] The argument will go just so far. The descriptions of Guinevere as 'The flower of all the west and all the world' and of Lancelot as 'the darling of the court, / Loved of the loveliest' are not, in their context (248,

260–1), notably artificial, and none of the turns of speech
should blind the reader to Guinevere's directness, or Elaine's
simplicity. (It would take an unusually slow reader not to
understand 'Some meddling rogue has tampered with him',
or 'who loves me must have a touch of earth'.) There is a great
deal of confessed artifice – 'being lustily holpen by the rest',
'Diamond me no diamonds!', 'So fine a fear in our large
Lancelot / Must needs have moved my laughter'. There is
more of this than 'Ye will not lose your wits for dear Lavaine',
though admittedly this is like Gawain's 'Ay . . . and you be
fair enow'. But the style of *Lancelot and Elaine*, whether
judged separately or against other idylls, cannot merely be
called 'inflated', nor can the function described be attributed
to it other than occasionally, and in the most obvious sense.
Even the burlesque or parodic purposes of *Gareth and
Lynette* are not always helped by the language.

> 'She lives in Castle Perilous: a river
> Runs in three loops about her living-place . . .'

> 'The last a monster unsubduable
> Of any save of him I called . . . '

The effects of parody like this are dearly bought. But the
weaknesses elsewhere in the *Idylls* should make us cautious
about referring every piece of clumsiness to parody, or to
inflation or deflation reflecting various sorts of judgment.
With language like this, the suspicion of an uncertain or
divided purpose will always arise. Parody, self-parody,
irony, conscious artificiality, cogent uses for banalities and
gaucheries: it is still difficult to imagine the function of this,
again from *Lancelot and Elaine*:

> 'Lo!
> What is he? I do not mean the force alone –
> The grace and versatility of the man!'

'The flash and motion of the man' which scatters the follow-
ers of Limours in *Geraint and Enid* is the sullen rage of
Geraint in action, but these lines are almost unbelievably
wooden.

There is at least one unexpected stylistic failure among the extended similes.

> Thus, as a hearth lit in a mountain home,
> And glancing on the window, when the gloom
> Of twilight deepens round it, seems a flame
> That rages in the woodland far below,
> So when his moods were darkened, court and King
> And all the kindly warmth of Arthur's hall
> Shadowed an angry distance.

The verse is assured, but the simile seems both decorative and confused. The terms are in one sense too near (hearth, kindly warmth), and in another too distant; the reflected fire in the woodland is inadequate to express the courtesies of the Order as they seem to the violent Balin, haunted by the fear that he will only prove the worse for them. The weakness inherent in the conjunction of the two kinds of seeming is only partly disguised by 'rages' and by the expert phrasing of 'shadowed an angry distance', where we are left wondering how much work 'distance' has to do. Nor is it, perhaps, too severe to find decoration in a single word in *The Coming of Arthur's* 'And thus the land of Cameliard was waste, / Thick with wet woods.' The King will drive the heathen, slay the beast, and fell the forest to let in the sun; in *The Marriage of Geraint* a forester comes before Arthur 'wet from the woods'; at the end of *The Last Tournament* Arthur returns 'All in a death-dumb autumn-dripping gloom': so much could be said in its defence. And the wetness of England, reclaimed or unreclaimed, is one of its least endearing features. Yet there is little in 'wet woods' (as distinct from woodland swamps, or simply 'woods', the enemy of man the cultivator) that suggests much more than physical discomfort.

The stylistic successes need no advocacy, but the uncertainty of much of the language should not be ignored. Many critics have ignored it, influenced perhaps by the thematic coherence, or wanting to do justice to a work which they thought had been unfairly neglected. It is possible that some critics have been influenced by the fact that the material was originally that of epic. T.S. Eliot spoke in 1942 of the 'great British epic material' magnificently handled by Malory, and skilfully adapted by Tennyson to 'suitable reading for a girls' school'.[24] In a rather oblique way, Eliot's remark about what Tennyson did with great epic material is less interesting than the date. The critical reassessment of the *Idylls* which began about thirty-five years ago has had a good deal to do with the recognition that the decline of Tennyson's kingdom is an image of the decline of Western civilisation, which anticipates Spengler and Yeats. It may also have something to do with Britain's political decline after the Second World War, and a consequent growing interest (particularly in America) in a 'matter of Britain', of the sort which has interested writers from Kipling to David Jones.[25] I suggest this only as one reason why so many critics since the 1940s seem willing to overlook the weaknesses of the *Idylls*. As to the reasons for the weaknesses, obviously we have to look beyond the serial composition, and inconsistencies caused by changes of attitude. The adulterous triangle of Lancelot, Guinevere, and Arthur at such a height as the destiny of the kingdom probably troubles us less than we think it ought to trouble us. Nor do the *Idylls* suffer from the action (or inaction) of any of what have been described as the large ministering abstractions which recur in nineteenth-century thinking. For Tennyson, the spirit wars against savagery, whether of materialism or despotism, and against false or selfish spirituality. The idealism of the *Idylls* is a living thing, and Arthur's words at the end of *The Holy Grail* are not far from what he intended them to be: 'the summing up of all in the highest note by the highest of men'. Tennyson was capable of fine mythopoeia, in the *Idylls* as elsewhere. His narrative formula of 'he who tells the tale' is both a tactical retreat into the form of a fiction which must make its claim for the authority of fiction, and a claim from fiction to a body of racial knowledge and experience of which he is only the latest interpreter. And in spite of our reservations, there are things which return to question us when we are at our most censorious; not only the unmistakable successes, but lines like

lying bounden there
In darkness through innumerable hours
He heard the hollow-ringing heavens sweep
Over him . . .

– with the assurance that comprehends the early English of 'lying bounden', and the Virgilian of 'hollow-ringing heavens'. But the impression of an uncertain purpose remains: at almost any moment some blankness, or clumsiness, will make us realise what is lacking. His long-drawn-out creation of the *Idylls* reveals the dilemma of a nineteenth-century Romantic intent on what Wordsworth called 'some work of glory', deeply troubled, as Wordsworth describes himself at the beginning of *The Prelude*, by the inability to find the local habitation and the name, and desperately persisting in the hope that all will be well. The effect of translation one often catches (and not merely in lines like the beginning of *Geraint and Enid*) is not only a matter of language, unless everything is; it has to do with a direct translation from concept or invention, which is perhaps most of what we need to know about the general failure.

CHAPTER VIII

Later Poems

Five years after the Arthurian idylls of 1859, Tennyson published two long domestic idylls, *Enoch Arden* and *Aylmer's Field*. Mackail, discussing his use of Theocritean idyll, rightly criticised this large-scale application of enriched idyllic treatment: 'in these poems we cannot but feel that the balance between subject and treatment is on the point of being lost, and that the rule of the half being more than the whole is forgotten'.[1] Both deal in human contrivance for the future, and what comes of it, with the addition in *Aylmer's Field* of the dull hand of Mammon and pride of race. Wordsworth's 'The blind walk of mortal accident' might serve as epigraph for either, and in the light of this, and of such a predecessor as *Michael*, it is probably wiser to forget the constraints and purposes of idyll, and think of them as tales. 'Him running on thus hopefully she heard, / And almost hoped herself': this is the authentic voice of domestic epic, of those annals of the poor, at once heightened and subdued, passionate and prosaic, in which the age delighted, in Europe as in England. *Enoch Arden* offers the spectacle of poetry turning to the concerns of prose fiction, and justifying itself to huge numbers of readers. The second nutting passage, with the bending or breaking of the 'lithe reluctant boughs', suggests Wordsworth, and Tennyson often writes with Wordsworth's music in his head.

In him woke,
With his first babe's first cry, the noble wish
To save all earnings to the uttermost,
And give his child a better bringing-up
Than his had been, or hers; a wish renewed,
When two years after came a boy to be
The rosy idol of her solitudes,
While Enoch was abroad on wrathful seas,
Or often journeying landward; for in truth
Enoch's white horse, and Enoch's ocean-spoil
In ocean-smelling osier, and his face,
Rough-reddened with a thousand winter gales,
Not only to the market-cross were known,
But in the leafy lanes behind the down,
Far as the portal-warding lion-whelp,
And peacock-yewtree of the lonely Hall,
Whose Friday fare was Enoch's ministering.

'Ocean-spoil / In ocean-smelling osier' is a most Wordsworthian periphrasis. 'In truth' just before it does not mean very much; with 'The rosy idol of her solitudes' it suggests a memory of the 'It is in truth an utter solitude' in *Michael*, and of the roses carried in his cheeks by young Luke. It is more than Wordsworth's music, of course. Behind the challenging insistence on 'the noble wish / To save all earnings to the uttermost', which is at the other extreme from the grocer's saving and prayer of Yeats's *September 1913*, is the thrift and 'honourable gain' of *Michael*, a poem profoundly concerned with utmost effort, and utmost pain. Tennyson's line reminds us of the scriptural payment to the uttermost, but since the fatality of event has little to do with payment, unless for the sin of forethought, it is a little like a sounding-board. The fatality of some of the poem's repetitions – Annie first with Enoch, then with Philip 'Just where the prone edge of the wood began / To feather towards the hollow' – works continually against the planning and hoping of its actors. And where the prosaic style takes wings – momentarily, as in 'Philip glancing up / Beheld the dead flame of the fallen day / Pass from the Danish barrow overhead', or more formally in the magnificent island passage, or in the grey world of

Enoch's homecoming, where 'The dead weight of the dead leaf bore it down' – it is with the certainty of the indifference of time or nature to the human.

Against this stands Enoch's courage, and his submission to divine will, but not every reader has admired his refusal to declare himself to wife and children, however upheld by 'Prayer from a living source within the will'. According to the happy liberal conviction that every problem can be solved by discussion, Enoch should have declared himself, by this (as someone once said) making an entire family miserable instead of one man. (Judging by Annie's change of heart after she has borne a child to Philip, when 'that mysterious instinct wholly died', she is less haunted than the gossiping Miriam Lane believes.) Tennyson has been blamed for sponsoring neurotic behaviour in his hero, and although Enoch conceals his wife's bigamy he remains in the same town, however much he looks forward to his death.[2] Six years later Tennyson skilfully mingled devotion, neuroticism, and heroism in *The Holy Grail*; in *Enoch Arden* all that is clear is the insistence on heroism. The final heroic act is Enoch's refusal to see his children again, confirmed by the stern 'let me hold my purpose till I die', which resembles the 'my purpose holds / To sail . . . until I die' of *Ulysses*. The last line (' . . . the little port / Had seldom seen a costlier funeral') has had its defenders, including Tennyson: 'The costly funeral is all that poor Annie could do for him after he was gone.[3] Enoch, so often named in the tale with a continuing reverence for these plain actors, becomes 'the strong heroic soul', and the insistence makes us resist. We understand well enough that the money lavished on the dead Enoch would have preserved the family when he was alive; the difficulty is that there has been so much unechoing plainness in the nine-hundred-line domestic epic of suffering, self-inflicted suffering, and release, that whatever echoes there are in this plainness are hardly roused.

Aylmer's Field, which is nearly as long as *Enoch Arden*, expresses a theme present in some of the earlier English Idyls, notably *Audley Court* and *Walking to the Mail*: that of the downfall of the great house. The sin of pride of race and wealth, present in *Locksley Hall* and *Maud*, finds late expression in a strangely violent tale. The source, as with *Enoch Arden*, was Tennyson's friend, the sculptor Thomas Wool- ner; he may have taken the episode of Leolin's intuition of Edith's death from a similar episode in Charles Reade's *The Cloister and the Hearth*, which, enlarged from its first ver- sion, had been published in 1861. The 'grizzled cripple, whom I saw / Sunning himself in a waste field alone', and who tells the tale (having 'been himself a part of what he told'), is a Wordsworthian figure. This, on the other hand, despite the blank verse, reminds us of Crabbe.

'O brother, I am grieved to learn your grief –
Give me my fling, and let me say my say.'

At which, like one that sees his own excess,
And easily forgives it as his own,
He laughed; and then was mute; but presently
Wept like a storm . . .

. . . till at length the two,
Though Leolin flamed and fell again, agreed
That much allowance must be made for men.

The last two lines are like an adaptation of a Crabbe couplet: 'Agreed, though Leolin flamed and fell again, / That much allowance must be made for men.' Elsewhere the quality of the satiric observation is variable. The reference to the outraged Sir Aylmer and his lady as 'the Powers of the House / On either side the hearth' is alive with the indignation that prompts it, and the 'ordeal by kindness' to which Sir Alymer subjects his daughter Edith is a memorable stroke. But the 'black republic' of rooks on his elms is on the brink of lighter comedy. So with Sir Aylmer having the position explained to him, and 'slowly stiffening' as he spoke: we feel the phrase would have done well in *Edwin Morris*, but that here Tenny- son's eye is too closely on 'that almighty man, / The county God' as a rewarding object. He seems to have attempted to support the violence of the tale by setting it in 1793: 'Harder the times were, and the hands of power / Were bloodier, and the according hearts of men / Seemed harder too . . . ' The climax is the sermon directed at the guilty Aylmers after the death of Edith and her landless lover Leolin. The text chosen by Lady Aylmer to awaken pity becomes their condemnation: 'Behold, your house is left unto you desolate.' (Sir Aylmer has drawn aside the curtains of their seat, so that they may be seen by the congregation in their desolate state, thus ensuring that they are naked to all blame.) But much of the irony of retribution is lost in the melodrama of 'Darkly that day rose', of the dark church, the livid face above the pulpit, and the long denunciation. The earlier *longueurs* tend to be those of accurate but lavish instance, although the romanticising of the labourers' cottages ('each a nest in bloom' under the hand of Edith) would hardly have satisfied Crabbe's directions on the painting of cots. The occasional knottiness of the language, and its momentary obscurities, suggest the invitation and the constraint of another style. Words such as 'niggard', 'purelier', 'scarfskin' seem hardly to occur elsewhere in Tennyson. But though the fine conclusion owes something to Wordsworth, there is nothing in it of constraint.

> Then the great Hall was wholly broken down,
> And the broad woodland parcelled into farms;
> And where the two contrived their daughter's good,
> Lies the hawk's cast, the mole has made his run . . .

It is with something of the music of the conclusion of *Michael* – 'great changes have been wrought / In all the neighbourhood' – that Tennyson turns from the destruction wrought by human passions, to the wild creatures who seem as innocent as the 'gentle creature' whose death is on her parents' heads. In 'Lies the hawk's cast, the mole has made his run', the perfect tense of the second part answers the metrical inversion and slight lengthening of the first with unhurrying reassurance.

> . . . the thin weasel there
> Follows the mouse, and all is open field.

The earth abideth and the title in 'Aylmer's Field' is revealed for what it is.

One of the most interesting poems of the 1860s is unlike
Enoch Arden in nearly every respect, though its theatricality
resembles that of *Aylmer's Field*. *Lucretius*, Tennyson's only
Roman monologue, accomplishes the suggestion in 'Roman'
of eloquence, of austere restraint, and the passion behind it.
Baum has a valuable discussion of the poem, in which he calls
the introduction prosaic, the conclusion bathetic, and the
soliloquy a fine studio-piece rather than a masterpiece.[4]
However revelatory it is, it does not remain with us, as
Ulysses and *Tithonus* do; as with *The Holy Grail*, which
Tennyson wrote eight months or so after *Lucretius*, there is
something rootless about its brilliance. It is likely that Tenny-
son could not have shown sexuality formerly restrained, now
overmastering, other than at the distance both of frenzy and
of a bleak narrative setting. Perhaps decorum required that
the poet of the *De Rerum Natura* should remain at a distance,
the more so when maddening under the influence of a love
potion. Whatever the truth of this, *Lucretius* has something of
the nature of a spectacle, in which the lights and shadows
playing on the passages deriving from the *De Rerum Natura*
achieve a strange effect of recognition, and remoteness.

Tennyson may or may not have believed the doubtful but
persistent legend which he uses, of the suicide of Lucretius in
a fit of madness after drinking a love potion.[5] He seems to
have been drawn to the figure of Lucretius *furens* partly by
his interpretation of Democritean and Epicurean science, in
the light of nineteenth-century science, and partly by the idea
of the cracking of an iron control, and the coming to power of
the brute brain within the man's. His Lucretius is presented at
first as austere, and unimpassioned. Even before his frenzy,
however, he was a haunted man. The first of his dreams, a
nightmare of an eternity of destruction and creation, of
'frames of things' ruining and clashing together again, he
recognises as his own, unlike the new nightmares he goes on
to recall. But the 'twisted shapes of lust' he dreams of
represent the worst diseases of all those that man escapes by
suicide. He had thought he lived as virtuously, as 'securely' as
the Epicurean gods.

But now it seems some unseen monster lays
His vast and filthy hands upon my will,
Wrenching it backward into his . . .

For this fall from godlike calm there is only one remedy: let
Nature take 'Those blind beginnings that have made me man',
and do her will with them.

It may seem less strange that Tennyson's Lucretius should
suffer from nightmare visions of sexuality, than that he
should be haunted by the atomic Democritean and Epicurean
universe. In both cases the fear appears to be that of Tenny-
son, not Lucretius. The culminating passage of the fourth
book of the *De Rerum Natura*, sometimes thought to indi-
cate a lack of balance, is generally considered (and was
considered by Munro) as satire; Tennyson's response is
directed by his suspicion of 'double-natured love'. Epicurean
physics, on the other hand, though subservient to Epicurean
ethics, were meant to free man from fear of the gods and of
death. But for Tennyson, with his passionate belief in identity
and immortality, his rejection of the concept of a blind
governing will, and his conviction that knowledge of God
must come from within man, the Epicurean doctrine of the
material and mortal soul, and of creation by the fortuitous
concourse of atoms – whatever the insistence of Epicurus on
free will – meant only a soulless infinity of making and
unmaking. (The fact that his maddened Lucretius is an exem-
plary figure for the England of 1868, the England of commer-
cial materialism, and of Huxley's *Zoological Evidences for
Man's Place in Nature*, may make us a little uneasy with the
poem, as not merely spectacle, but directly edifying specta-
cle.) At the same time, there are some similarities between the
Roman and the English poet. The claim of Lucretius to have
plucked 'the mortal soul from out immortal hell', as Tenny-
son renders it, resembles that implicit in the close of *Demeter
and Persephone*, which looks forward to a race of kindlier
gods and godlike men. Lucretius believed that the miseries of
hell exist only in this life, and although Tennyson rejected
what he took to be Lucretius' atheism, he was far more
sympathetic to this doctrine, than to the atomistic doctrine
which resembled so much of what he rejected in contempor-

ary thinking. There is also some similarity of circumstance. Lucretius lived in the turbulent times of the first half of the first century BC, and may have been a member of the aristocratic *gens Lucretia*; Tennyson makes him say that he 'bears one name' with the Lucretia of heroic legend, whose suicide helped to bring about the commonwealth. Tennyson, an aristocrat by inclination and by genius, had little desire to see power pass from the aristocracy to the people, and saw the confirmation of his fears (expressed in the indignant, even bitter simile of lines 168–72) in the popular disturbances of 1866 and 1867.

The structure of *Lucretius* is that of a frenzied monologue within an austere and ironic narrative setting. His wife Lucilia, 'dreaming some rival' (her rival is the scrolls of Epicurus, whom her husband 'held divine'), gets an aphrodisiac potion from a witch.

> And this, at times, she mingled with his drink,
> And this destroyed him . . .

'And this . . . And this . . . ': the intent and the direction of a stupid mind are bleakly answered. There follows self-loathing, confusion, and loss of the power to shape, which we later learn was almost his only pleasure.[6] The narrative ending returns us to the irony of the beginning, with the contemptuous multiplication of the remorseful Lucilia's actions, which are predictable – 'ran in, / Beat breast, tore hair, cried out' . . . 'fell on him, / Clasped, kissed him, wailed . . . ' – and within this, the dry and heavily accented contractions of 'Beat breast, tore hair'. The frame does not mediate between ancient and modern. Its dryness insulates, and it presents the triumph of stupidity.

The monologue so framed, however much of the *De Rerum Natura* Tennyson put in it, is made of questioning and self-questioning, sardonic mockery and self-mockery, sharp interjections, and rambling defences, shot through with the longing for the divine calm of the new Epicurean gods, occasionally acquiescing in the features of the old. It is introduced by the recollection of three dreams, which are followed by a fourth, in which his terrors encroach on the day. The first dream, which he owns as his, 'Of and belonging to me', seems almost welcome in comparison with the second and third: the harlotry or hired animalisms born of Sulla's massacres, a monstrous parody of fertility and increase, and – a classic instance if destructive beauty – the fire that shoots from Helen's breasts. He asks Venus if he is punished because he refused to degrade her by sacrifice, and goes on to distinguish between her 'popular' name or names, and her reality as Nature. The description of the calm of the Epicurean gods is followed by a passage in which he is made to stumble over the paradox of the immortality of the Gods, and their atomic composition. Bitterly aware of his confusion, he turns back to the easy target of *religio* or superstition, in the figure of the mounting sun-god Hyperion, and with it to the ills of human life supposedly seen by the god, thence once again to the abominations that haunt him. He attempts to throw off the horror, but his mind returns to shapes of lust, if only to toy with them mockingly in the tale of Numa snaring Faunus and Picus. And with frightening speed his fears or desires return, with the vision of the Oread pursued by the satyr, seeming even to mean to 'fling herself, / Shameless upon me? Catch her, goat-foot: nay, / Hide, hide them, million-myrtled wilderness . . . ' On this, despairing of godlike calm on earth, he takes his Roman and aristocratic resolve, to find that calm the nearest way.

The impressive closing paragraph of the monologue, which gathers up much that has necessarily been disparate, and in which Lucretius formally utters his *beot* or heoric boast before what is to come, may help to appease some readers, but may confirm the poem for others as a set-piece, like *Tiresias*. As in *Maud*, which also deals in the borders of sanity, there is a certain bravura, perhaps inseparable from the subject. But the monologue is clearly more of a formulation than the monodrama. Like *Maud* again, there are extremes of style: on the one hand the hectic language of the nightmares; on the other, the gravity of instance as of doctrine in these lines, with their weight of monosyllables, where the rhythm varies with the deep delight in what is expounded and observed:

> . . . to shadow forth
> The all-generating powers and genial heat
> Of Nature, when she strikes through the thick blood
> Of cattle, and light is large, and lambs are glad
> Nosing the mother's udder, and the bird
> Makes his heart voice amid the blaze of flowers . . .

Just after this, there is a mannered emphasis which resembles Arnold: 'The Gods! and if I go *my* work is left / Unfinished – *if* I go.' (Lucretius has just referred to Empedocles, 'the great Sicilian', and there are affinities with *Empedocles on Etna*, which had been reprinted in 1867.) As with the apparent wandering of the monologue, so with what seem its compulsive linguistic repetitions. The second dream shows Lucretius 'girls, Hetairai, curious in their art, / Hired animalisms . . .': the fascination behind the disgust in 'curious in their art', encouraged perhaps by the lingering euphemism of 'Hetairai' or 'companions', is immediately disowned. 'Curious' is archaic, and Baum censures Tennyson for using such forms, as well as for being prosaic. 'Beardless apple-arbiter', of course, is sardonic as well as archaic, if rather heavily so. Since the language of the *De Rerum Natura* is often archaic, it is likely that in passages like the one about the dreaming dog, that 'With inward yelp and restless forefoot plies / His function of the woodland', Tennyson is following Lucretius. But 'Whose death-blow struck the dateless doom of kings' is attributable neither to this nor to extremes of style. The ranting in lines 233–42, before the last paragraph of the monologue, seems as unconvincing as the dull play on so much or so little in our little life a few lines earlier. It is perhaps the only passage in the poem where it is evident that composition is reducible to the skilful or unskilful handling of a subject. On the other hand, it is a little too easy to dismiss 'dire insanity' (1 line 163) as prosaic. The equivalence or near equivalence of 'animal heat and dire insanity' concludes a remarkable passage in which the disgust in 'harpies miring every dish' passes into the suspicion of what seems like a cosmic origin of this evil: 'The phantom husks of something foully done, / And fleeting through the boundless universe . . . ' Coming where it does, the phrase has something of the weight of its Latin origins behind it.

'A satyr, a satyr, see, / Follows; but him I proved impossible; / Twy-natured is no nature . . . ' The twy-natured satyr is a projection of his own state, but Lucretius is made to understand directly something of his plight. 'How should the mind, except it loved them, clasp / These idols to herself?' he cries. Although followed by an alternative explanation in terms of Epicurean physics – which passes into the simile of the crowds that push, 'their rags and they / The basest', into the council-hall – the question stands out because of the bitterness of recognition in it; it is the only time the word 'love' is used. The principal irony in the poem has to do with the nature whose workings he expounds. The *De Rerum Natura* opens with an invocation of Venus, whom Lucretius asks to be his partner in this undertaking, since 'you alone govern the nature of things, since without you nothing comes forth into the shining borders of light, nothing joyous or lovely is made'. Venus and Nature in the *De Rerum Natura* sometimes seem equivalent, and have been aptly described as the poetic and scientific formulation of the same idea.[7] Tennyson in turn makes Lucretius, 'poet-like', take the name of Venus 'to shadow forth / The all-generating powers and genial heat / Of Nature'. At the end of it, it is Nature, 'the womb and tomb of all', who will receive him. When he asked Venus if these torments were her vengeance on him, he seems, oddly enough, to have spoken more truth than he knew. By the terms of the legend as Tennyson interprets it, the Nature Lucretius expounds and the divinity he has invoked destroy him, despite the distinction he makes between the goddess of tradition who can be offended, and the Nature of all-generating powers, which supposedly cannot.

Tennyson continued to write up to within a few months of his death, in 1892. With some exceptions, his later poetry is markedly inferior to that of his youth and maturity, and the plays that he wrote between 1874 and 1882 – *Queen Mary*, *Harold*, *Becket*, *The Falcon*, *The Cup*, *The Foresters*, *The Promise of May* – must be regarded as self-tribute. The difference between *Ulysses*, written when he was twenty-four, and such a pedestrian exercise in monologue as *Col-*

umbus, written when he was seventy, is very great. What could be crudely called the exercise of technical skill on subjects for poetry is foreshadowed in the poetry of the 1860s, which shows signs of waning powers, in *Lucretius* and *The Holy Grail*, as in *Enoch Arden* and *Aylmer's Field*. He rises to the occasion in the opening of *The Passing of Arthur*, but it is a reworking of earlier poetry, a capitalising on earlier inspiration. There is undoubtedly a growing sense, as we follow him, of a lack of effective intellectual capital, as distinct from intellectual curiosity. Auden's remark, that Tennyson was the stupidest of English poets, has been the subject of angry rebuttals, but the briefest comparison with one of the greatest of his predecessors is illuminating.[8] We do not prefer Shelley to Tennyson because of his doctrine of necessity, or his concept of the expression of the changeless by the changing, or of men as portions of the one mind. But though Tennyson speaks in *In Memoriam* of 'the wheels of Being', we can hardly fail to understand the contrast, since Shelley's thinking about being and its reasons is a glowing core felt everywhere in his poetry. What is lacking in Tennyson is as evident if we think of his younger contemporary Baudelaire, with whom Auden compares him: of the range of experience in Baudelaire as well as its weight, of the complexities of his frustrations and releases, and the mind and the poetry which achieve a synthesis. Tennyson's poetry sometimes resembles a refuge from thinking, in the sense that it is an alternative to it, rather than an overplus from constant mental workings. The apparently wide range of his later poetry – the dialect poems, the epistolary poems, visionary poetry like *The Holy Grail* and *Balin and Balan*, new forms like *The Ancient Sage*, questioning and affirmation like *Vastness* or *Parnassus*, a comment on earlier preoccupations and earlier poetry like *Locksley Hall Sixty Years After* – is a little delusive. Nothing could seem more different from *Lucretius* than the dozen or so poems about common life, many of them in dialect, that he wrote between 1859 and 1890. But almost as we think of them as exemplifying a wide range, we have to retract, and recognise that many of them are brief raids, not necessarily on the inarticulate. The best of them are the earliest, the *Northern Farmer, Old Style* and *Northern Farmer, New Style* of the early and middle 1860s. (The exception, if we can accept its ending, is *Rizpah* (1880), with its grim yet human concentration on 'bone of my bone'.) Their immediate predecessor, *The Grandmother* of 1859, which like *Rizpah* is not in dialect, avoids losing itself in a morass of sentiment by the slightest of margins. The rambling monologue, seemingly held together by its rhymes, is full of death, yet somehow all these deaths make for a strong sense of life. The Northern Farmer poems never look like losing themselves. The dying man of the first recalls with satisfaction that he has 'stubbed Thurnaby waäste', even to the ghost in it.

Theer wur a boggle in it, I often 'eärd 'um mysen;
Moäst loike a butter-bump, fur I 'eärd 'um about an' about,
But I stubbed 'um oop wi' the lot, an' raäved an' rembled 'um
out.

That, and perhaps the voting 'wi' Squoire an' choorch an' staäte', is his comfort, against the fear that proper farming of Squire's land will end with him: 'Do godamoighty knaw what a's doing a-taäkin' o' meä?' The new style equivalent of land is 'proputty', and the slow querulous voice from the deathbed changes to the brisk accents of an independent man intent on extending it. 'Proputty' is also Mammon, and its crushing of love at this level of society is rendered with wonderful accuracy.

Thou'll not marry for munny – thou's sweet upo' parson's
lass –
Noä – thou'll marry for luvv – an' we boäth on us thinks tha
an ass.

And while the son gets a bit of ash from the hedge against the flies, the father's moralising takes its highest flight: 'Taäke my word for it, Sammy, the poor in a loomp is bad.' The attempt to repeat these earlier successes suggests the desire to open up a vein of alternative subjects. The observation remains accurate, as with the peasant impatience with trees in *The Village Wife, or, The Entail* (' "Drat the trees," says I, to be sewer I haätes 'em, my lass, / Fur we puts the muck o' the land an' they sucks the muck fro' the grass'), but they tend to read a little as if their subjects had sat for them. With some exceptions, like that of the Baptists leaving their sins in the pond to poison the cow in *The Church-Warden and the Curate*, we begin to feel the limitations of dialect-sardonic reflections on religion, marriage, and the lettered classes. The 'reäson why' of the new style farmer ('Could'n I luvv thy muther by cause o' 'er munny laäid by? / Naäy – fur I luvved 'er a vast sight moor fur it: reäson why') becomes the 'an' I'll tell tha why' of *The Northern Cobbler*, and the 'I ham wot I ham' of *The Church-Warden and the Curate*, written in 1879 and 1890: the true accents of the simple man are paraded before us, rather like boards at a protest march of simple men. By then, of course, Tennyson had had a lifetime of poetry, and was old and tired, and the habit of asking for and accepting ideas for poetry is evident in others besides the dialect poems.

More than once in his career Tennyson attempted to speak for the common man, as distinct from writing in dialect, or as official laureate. Some of the political poems of 1852, written when war threatened after Louis Napoleon's *coup d'état* of December 1851, are in the form of songs or ballads, like *The Penny-Wise*, and *For the Penny-Wise*, in the first of which 'ruin' and 'doing' stand stoutly forth to rhyme. On the whole, the warlike noises are less threatening than those of *Maud*; he was thinking of defence, not attack, and the references to the Caffre wars in the Cape Colony in *For the Penny-Wise* have something of the note of popular realism, of 'the kingdom's in trouble again': 'We meant to beat the Kaffirs, / We had the best intentions; / But the Kaffirs knocked us over, / With the last inventions.' Other poems represent more nearly the voice of what is described in *Suggested by Reading an Article in a Newspaper* as 'the thinking men of England'. Tennyson published this over the pen-name 'Taliessin', and as 'Taliessin' praised the poems he had published as 'Merlin' – *The Third of February, 1852*, and *Hands All Round! –* and called on himself to 'make opinion warlike'. In *Hands All Round!* (1852) there is some hasty accommodation of British royalty to American republican sentiment: 'You must not mix our Queen with those / That wish to keep their people fools.' *The Third of February, 1852*, on the other hand, written when the

House of Lords wanted to keep the press quiet about the state of the army, and the dishonesty of Louis Napoleon, is a grave rebuke, and a recalling of Britain to her duty: 'It was our ancient privilege, my Lords, / To fling whate'er we felt, not fearing, into words.' In one at least of the songs, the popular form released something in Tennyson; this is the unpublished *Rifle Clubs!!!* ('Peace is thirty-seven years old'). (Another and inferior poem of the same title, the original version of *Riflemen Form!* contains the remarkable description of the French as 'bearded monkeys of lust and blood'.) The title is a noisy shout, but the grim refrain beats out the reality behind the glib political formula of 'coup d'état'.

> 'Children and women – their wounds are red,
> And I wait for Louis', the ferryman said,
> 'To follow the dead, the dead, the dead,
>   Killed in the *Coup d'État*'.

Two years later the news from the Crimea inspired him to speak for his countrymen with compelling simplicity, in *The Charge of the Light Brigade*. Much of the authority of the poem is in the movement and sound of the charge, in the unhurrying pace of the repetitions which seem to dull individual feeling, after the bitter 'Some one had blundered', which needs no repetition.[9] With *The Revenge: A Ballad of the Fleet* of 1878, it is probably the best of Tennyson's poems of war and courage. Joanna Richardson speaks of the 'fine resounding jingoism' of *The Revenge*, which is a little misleading.[10] A defence against related charges might be the comparative in the 'swarthier alien crew' that manned the captured *Revenge*, which is less explicit than Evelyn Waugh's description in *The Ordeal of Gilbert Pinfold* of travellers in the Egyptian canal zone of the 1950s being passed from swarthy sullen English soldiers to swarthy sullen Egyptians. To read Tennyson's poem against Macaulay ('And tomorrow shall the fox, from her chambers in the rocks, / Lead forth her tawny cubs to howl above the prey') probably helps us to understand his achievement better. If individual feeling in *The Charge of the Light Brigade* is swallowed up in the collective action, and the national response to it, it is the range of feeling in *The Revenge*, and its varied rhythms, that most contribute to its success: not only the seamen at the end refusing to follow Grenville into death, but the sick men ashore brought on board 'Very carefully and slow, / Men of Bideford in Devon', though the danger pressed; fear overcome by resolution under Grenville's 'Let us bang those dogs of Seville, the children of the devil'; the tenderness of idiom as of feeling in 'Where they laid him by the mast, old Sir Richard caught at last'.

Of the laureate poems, the *Ode on the Death of the Duke of Wellington* stands alone. *A Welcome to Her Royal Highness Marie Alexandrovna, Duchess of Edinburgh* is fairly typical of the later laureate poetry. Tennyson had called her grandfather a liar in *Maud*, but now Tsar Nicholas I is merely 'him with whom we strove for power', and his son Alexander II the ruler 'Who made the serf a man, and burst his chain'. Two empires smile upon each other, and come together to the accompaniment of a roll-call of imperial regions: stirring Tartar tents, conscious Elburz and the Caucasus, Indian palms and 'loyal pines of Canada'. There is the hope that there will be 'truth and manful peace' between England and Russia, and there is also the quiet reminder that England is 'the stranger land, / Where men are bold and strongly say their say', and there is nothing very much more than the fluency and deftness with which it is all said. The *Ode Sung at the Opening of the International Exhibition* of 1862 has as little inherent interest as *Opening of the Indian and Colonial Exhibition by the Queen* of 1886, or *On the Jubilee of Queen Victoria* of 1887. The *Ode on the Death of the Duke of Wellington* of 1852, on the other hand, was written out of a deep anxiety, a fear for England's future, which was to find expression again in *Maud*. With Wellington's death, a long tradition of public service seemed weakened, and England, though 'a people yet' under her monarchy, was the poorer. In an impressive passage dropped after 1852, the emphasis is on decay and civil conflict.

Perchance our greatness will increase;
Perchance a darkening future yields
Some reverse from worse to worse,
The blood of men in quiet fields,
And sprinkled on the sheaves of peace.

A major theme of the *Ode* is England's manifest destiny; she is 'the eye, the soul / Of Europe', and her statesmen must save 'the one true seed of freedom sown / Betwixt a people and their ancient throne'. But although 'the mourning of a mighty nation' is given further voice at a moment when the race may soon be called upon to defend and justify her greatness, the occasion is also one for reassurance, and Tennyson's assurances are often stilted. When he speaks of Wellington's campaigns – appropriately, to Nelson, who died before Wellington was sent to the Peninsula – the invasion of France from Spain as 'England pouring on her foes' has the sound of a great event, a release of pent-up national force. But even in the context of loss the formal repetitions can ring hollow. 'His voice is silent in your council-hall / For ever; and whatever tempests lour / For ever silent; even if they broke / In thunder, silent.. . . ': there is not much more in this than solemn lingering. His method seems initially to have been to simplify, and to enlarge.

I

Bury the Great Duke
  With an empire's lamentation,
Let us bury the Great Duke
  To the noise of the mourning of a mighty nation,
Mourning when their leaders fall,
Warriors carry the warrior's pall,
And sorrow darkens hamlet and hall.

The simplicity of the first four lines is that of a compelling theme. That of what follows – where after the first edition, with its 'And warriors carry the warrior's pall', it is not quite clear if the 'when' of line 5 is to be carried foward to 6 – is achieved by the invocation of a heroic age, in 'hamlet and hall'

as in 'warriors'; the judicious omission of sorrow darkening
Seven Dials is quickly overtaken in II by the burial in
'streaming London's central roar'. The enlargement in IV is
proper to celebratory ode: Wellington as 'Whole in himself, a
common good', and 'In his simplicity sublime'.[11] But a point
is reached – perhaps after the memorable survey in strophe VI
of Wellington's deeds as 'leader in these glorious wars', but it
is implicit before then – when we feel that everything that
could be said has been said, and that the rest is hyperbole, like
the giant public statue of 'But while the races of mankind
endure, / Let his great example stand / Colossal, seen of every
land . . . ' To say this is probably to undervalue the eighth
strophe, where these lines occur, and in which the redirection
of Gray's sombre 'The paths of glory lead but to the grave', in
'Not once or twice in our rough island-story, / The path of
duty was the way to glory', achieves a memorable weight and
impetus. The choric repetitions frequently steady the irregu-
lar verse, and confirm it in its purpose. And such a mutation
as the ringing Hebraic opening of VI ('Who is he that cometh,
like an honoured guest, / With banner and with music, with
soldier and with priest?') is at once a striking shift of voice,
even of mode, from the choric ending of V ('O civic muse, to
such a name'), and a strengthening of its intent. But in the
Ode's slow periods we are too often conscious either of
strong recovery, or of a word or form which is being run
nearly to death: the continual insistence on one form or
another of eternity is weakening. Tennyson lengthened the
Ode by thirty lines after the first edition of 1852. Many of the
changes are improvements, with the exception of the lines
about the great example which were added to strophe VIII.
But we are left with a feeling that its music would have been
heard more clearly if it had been shortened.

A mode in which Tennyson excelled is the epistolary and
dedicatory poem of friendship and compliment, from *To E.L.,
on His Travels in Greece*, of 1853, to *To the Master of Balliol*
in 1892, the year of his death. The only early example which is
of value is *To J.S.* of 1832, an occasionally stiff poem of
moving consolation in bereavement. Tennyson once said that
he would as soon kill a pig as write a letter, and though he

attracted and fascinated many of his contemporaries, he seems to have been too egocentric to have any gift for friendship, and in fact was capable of neglecting old friends.[12] But the delicate and generous courtesy of the epistolary poems of his middle and late years has little to do with self, except as it may be honoured in honouring others. Nor is there anything comparable to Yeats's defining of the self through those he has known, as in *The Municipal Gallery Revisited*: 'Think where man's glory most begins and ends, / And say my glory was I had such friends.' (The nearest Tennyson approaches this is probably the elegiac *In the Garden at Swainston*, written after the death of Sir John Simeon: 'Three dead men have I loved and thou art last of the three.')

In the poem to Edward Lear, on the gift of Lear's *Journals of a Landscape Painter in Albania and Illyria* of 1851, Tennyson has a particular use for the *In Memoriam* stanza structure. At first he seems to be countering his friend's characteristic modesty, by giving the heights and lengths and depths of mountain landscape in his grandest manner.

> Illyrian woodlands, echoing falls
> Of water, sheets of summer glass,
> The long divine Peneïan pass,
> The vast Akrokeraunian walls . . .

In the slow beat of 'Akrokeraunian' – which is very different from the swing of Shelley's 'In the Acroceraunian mountains' in *Arethusa* – the wonder grows before 'classic ground' long known of, now revealed: 'I read and felt that I was there.' From the stately inversion of the first two stanzas, the mountains and passes 'shadowed forth' by Lear which Tennyson studies eagerly, the poem moves first to his delighted recognition of the golden age, then to an expansion of this in three more stanzas of description: 'For me the torrent ever poured / And glistened.' Its structure, in fact, follows the chiastic *a b b a* structure of the stanza. It is typical of Tennyson that the cycle does not end there.

> . . . From him that on the mountain lea
>   By dancing rivulets fed his flocks
>   To him who sat upon the rocks,
> And fluted to the morning sea.

With 'morning sea', after the nameless human figures that evoke something of the 'Who are these?' of the *Ode on a Grecian Urn*, the poem seems less to end, than to open out on a primordial freshness. *To Ulysses* of 1889, which uses the same stanza, turns an old man's willing ignorance of strange lands to memorable account, though in the description of himself as 'chaining fancy now at home / Among the quarried downs of Wight', there is perhaps the idea not only of restraint, but of failing powers. For much of its length the poem, written in return for W.G. Palgrave's gift of a volume of essays entitled *Ulysses*, maintains Tennyson's north against Palgrave's exotic south and east, more gently than Kingsley did in his *Ode to the North-East Wind* ('Tis the hard grey weather / Breeds hard English men'). Tennyson did not know Palgrave well, though he knew, and was sometimes irritated by, his brother F.T. Palgrave, and the poem has this much of self in it, that it is something of a laudation of his own endurance at seventy-nine, 'once half-crazed for larger light', now 'keeping leaf', like his giant ilex, in these harsher latitudes. When he turns at last to the 'rich gift' of the essays, it is to keep the wonders of south and east at an appropriate distance, in a litany of strange names ('Hong-Kong, Karnac, and all the rest') and a gracious compliment: 'your various book'.

It is a fair illustration of Tennyson's own variety, that the finest of the epistolary poems, *To E. Fitzgerald* (1885) and *To Mary Boyle* (1889), are markedly different in form. The 'birthday line / Of greeting' to Fitzgerald turned to mourning when Tennyson heard of his death; the greeting appeared as dedication to the early *Tiresias*, with a mourning epilogue to end it. Fitzgerald never concealed his preference for Tennyson's earlier work, and in the epilogue Tennyson sets his death against his own now useless fancy that he might disapprove of the 'opulent end' of *Tiresias*, and would 'defend his judgment well'. The contrast between death, and the preoccupations of the living, is not laboured; nothing is, for the art of this poem is to conceal its skill behind what looks like rambling. Delighting in its many 'ands' – of the twenty-one in its fifty-six lines, all but eight begin lines – the dedication moves gently from one memory of friendship to another: from Fitzgerald's doves to his vegetarianism, then to Tennyson's short-lived attempt at vegetarianism, and the extraordinary dream that marked his falling away; then by way of a plain distinction between Lenten fare and Lenten thought to the golden *Rubáiyát*, to old friends who praised it, and are now silent; to the living, on this birthday, and so to the early poem Fitzgerald will welcome for the 'gracious times' that are recalled. Before we know it, the musing accretion has become a current carrying us on to an end of whose plainness and fitness we have never been in doubt.

> When, in our younger London days,
> You found some merit in my rhymes,
> And I more pleasure in your praise.

'And I more pleasure': the last and strongest 'and' returns with quiet satisfaction on the others. The epilogue compares the dedication's 'rhymes, / That missed his living welcome' to unsuspecting guests who arrive too late, and 'find the gate / Is bolted, and the master gone'. Nothing in it is more moving, or more formally satisfying, than the slowing towards the end of the conjunctions that flowed so easily in the birthday greeting:

> Remembering all the golden hours
> Now silent, and so many dead,
> And him the last ...

To Mary Boyle of 1889 accompanied the gift of another early poem, the ode *The Progress of Spring*. The last stanza of the ode affirms man's hopes of eternal life ('hopes, which race the restless blood'), and the epistolary poem which introduces it is one of consolation in bereavement, and gentle exhortation. The first and third lines of the *a b a b* quatrains are five-foot, the second and fourth two-foot iambics, which tend to follow the long lines on a minor note, and are often composed of monosyllabic words. (In the fourth and fifth stanzas, which are central to the poem – the reminder of Mary's promise to visit him, and the insistence, in spite of grief – there are only two words which are not monosyllabic: 'memory', and 'Marian'.) The form of the birthday poem to Fitzgerald, with its four-foot iambics in undivided alternate rhyming quatrains, resembles an unbroken line of life. Here the alternating movements, and the sense of movement and delay, suits the lapidary, and the hortatory: 'Be needle to the magnet of your word . . . '; 'Is memory with your Marian gone to rest, / Dead with the dead?' The slow pace of the remembered, and the forgotten, is maintained with consummate skill through seventeen stanzas. The three stanzas or so spent on the memory of 'rick-fire days' in 1830, on how as an undergraduate he had helped by passing buckets, may sound like self-indulgence, but in fact are a story told of youth, of that other world of 'more than half a hundred years ago', to distract from present grief. We are conscious of how much time there has been in the lives of these two, who met so recently, when Tennyson's son Hallam and Mary Boyle's niece Audrey fell in love, and married. And something of the simplicity of age is perhaps an essential reason of the poem, in the ways it suggests by which life may be used, and death met: the use of 'change of place' in combating grief, the argument that golden youth may mourn, but age ('the silver year') may not, being itself close to death.

> And you, that now are lonely, and with Grief
> Sit face to face,
> Might find a flickering glimmer of relief
> In change of place.

('I thought of times when Pain might be thy guest, / Lord of thy house and hospitality; / And Grief, uneasy lover! never rest / But when she sate within the touch of thee . . . ': Wordsworth's fine lines in *To H.C. Six Years Old* may have influenced Tennyson here.) 'What use to brood?' he continues, and in the simple 'In change of place' (the phrase occurs in *In Memoriam* CV) there is perhaps the ghost of a judgment on one kind of human frailty, a hint of how little we need to keep us with the living.

The short dedicatory poems, *To Professor Jebb*, and *To the Master of Balliol*, are of the same period. Each presents to a classical scholar – Richard Jebb, and Benjamin Jowett – a poem on a classical theme: *Demeter and Persephone* of 1889, and *The Death of Oenone* of 1892. J.F.A. Pyre drew attention to their late mutation of the quatrain as a method of suggesting in English poetry the alien cadences of classical poetry.[13] The experiments began with *The Daisy* of 1855, whose metre Tennyson described as his invention, 'representing in some measure the grandest of metres, the Horatian Alcaic'.[14]

The first, second, and fourth lines of the iambic quatrain rhyme; the non-rhyming third line has a feminine ending, and the fourth line substitutes an anapaest for the third iamb. In the invitation poem *To the Rev. F.D. Maurice*, written a few months later, Tennyson carried his metrical experiment a stage farther, repeating the single rhyme, and the feminine ending of the unrhymed third line, but beginning the fourth line with two dactyls: 'Your presence will be sun in winter, / Making the little one leap for joy.' The poem to Jebb uses the same measure; *To the Master of Balliol* represents a farther stage.

> So may this legend for awhile,
> If greeted by your classic smile,
>   Though dead in its Trinacrian Enna,
> Blossom again on a colder isle.
>
>   (to Jebb, 9–12)

> And read a Grecian tale re-told,
> Which, cast in later Grecian mould,
>   Quintus Calaber
> Somewhat lazily handled of old.
>
>   (to Jowett, 5–8)

The third line becomes a trochee and a dactyl, the fourth a trochee, two dactyls, and a catalectic foot. Both poems are short enough for any lingering over syllables to have its full effect. Of the two, the poem to Jowett is the more Latinate, in part because of its more resolute syllabification in the third and fourth lines, where 'Bálliŏl', 'wárriŏr', and 'fúnĕrăl' are all trisyllabic. (The first short line, 'Thére ăt Bálliŏl', evokes Jowett's Oxford with something of a gentle playfulness.) But the real advance in the English accentual rendering of classical measure is that the trochees and dactyls of its third and fourth lines make up a unit which is less likely to suggest anapaests with anacrusis than the fourth line of the poems to Jebb and Maurice, where the iambic third line and its feminine ending seem to lead into the opening dactyls of the fourth line in such a way as to make room for the rise that lurks in English dactyls. The internal rhyme and consonance in the first part of the last line ('Stark and dark in his funeral fire') slows the line, and seems to seal as dactylic the rhythm which has closed each stanza.

Fine though it is, the poem to Jowett is not perfect; the monosyllabic fourteenth line ('To thoughts that lift the soul of men') is singularly dull. Nor, it has to be said, is what could have been the classic poem of address of this period, *To the Marquis of Dufferin and Ava*, whose alien cadences are not metrical – Tennyson uses the *In Memoriam* stanza – and which though private is also public. The occasion is the death of Lionel Tennyson, his second son; the poem introduces the 1889 volume, *Demeter and Other Poems*. Lord Dufferin, whom Tennyson had known for many years, had been Governor-General of Canada, and was Viceroy of India, where he had invited Lionel Tennyson, who had entered the India Office. Lionel had died on the way home of a fever contracted in India, and Dufferin had taken care of him at Government House during his last months there. The poem spans a great deal, without that vocabulary of 'large' or 'affluent' which Tennyson sometimes drops into when he is merely expansive: world empire in the east and west; power, and courtesy; service and truth; love and grief, and a near unquestioning acceptance of God's will. For eight of its thirteen stanzas it moves quietly forward, by way of Dufferin's service, the 'dear debt' 'from me and mine'; Lionel, his service, and his death. After the first two stanzas – the first adapted from the 1830s poem *Hail Briton!*, and now purged of its immediate warning, so that the second stanza may

answer it with the knowledge of what empire may achieve –
there is even some stiffness.

> Your rule has made the people love
> Their ruler. Your viceregal days
> Have added fulness to the phrase
> Of 'Gauntlet in the golden glove.'

Stanza III has something of the plainness of Ben Jonson,
but not his strength, and VII also falls away from the author-
ity of the beginning. ('Rule' and 'ruler' in III turn on 'love',
but remain flat. 'Viceregal days' and 'have added fulness' are a
little unconvincing, and fail to make us receive the aphorism
as Tennyson wants us to. Stanza VII, which is praise of
Lionel, is weak not because of its superlatives, which are
traditional, but because of the diffuseness of the language,
owing to the invariable position of the adjectives in the third
and fourth feet: 'earliest youth', 'brightening year', 'simple
truth'. A fair comparison with Jonson would be *The Under-
Wood* XXII, which uses this stanza.) Then with Lionel
Tennyson's last voyage it rises to a height which could not
easily have been predicted.

IX

> But ere he left your fatal shore,
> And lay on that funereal boat,
> Dying, 'Unspeakable' he wrote
> 'Their kindness', and he wrote no more;

X

> And sacred is the latest word;
> And now the Was, the Might-have-been,
> And those lone rites I have not seen,
> And one drear sound I have not heard,

XI

Are dreams that scarce will let me be,
    Not there to bid my boy farewell,
    When That within the coffin fell,
Fell – and flashed into the Red Sea,

XII

Beneath a hard Arabian moon
    And alien stars. To question, why
    The sons before the fathers die,
Not mine! and I may meet him soon . . .

'Your fatal shore' takes up the earlier 'your India was his Fate,
/ And drew him over sea to you' – which may have been
intended to lighten Dufferin's sense of guilt at having invited
Lionel to India – and the firm, even proud 'Not mine!',
however qualified by what follows it, both answers and
echoes the despair of 'Not there' six lines earlier. Inversion
plays an increasingly material part as the poem draws to its
close. In IV the suspension of meaning is Horatian: 'But since
your name will grow with Time, / Not all, as honouring your
fair fame / Of Statesman, have I made the name / A golden
portal to my rhyme.' But 'Unspeakable' in IX, preceded as it
is by 'Dying', and accentuated by the delayed 'wrote', follows
'fatal' and 'funereal' as if part of their context; there is a
moment when it might mean anything, and no sooner is the
movement complete than 'wrote no more' returns with final-
ity on word and action. The hesitation before 'Red Sea' crea-
ted by the metrical variations of XI. 4 is not the least moving
part of the poem. Though its end is silence, the affirmation in
XII rises above the speaking voice like a cry, and as with
Lionel Tennyson's words, inversion takes the place of verb;
this, though native as well as alien, is the true alien cadence of
the poem. The effect is of something hewn into shape, an
epigraphic force appropriate to death and loss, and to the
theme, or rather purpose, of service to the State, 'our Britain':
Dufferin's, Lionel's, that of Tennyson himself in writing and
making public the poem.

In the Garden at Swainston, a lament for lost friends written in 1870 on the death of Sir John Simeon, is in one sense more purely elegiac than *To the Marquis of Dufferin and Ava*. But though 'elegiac' may indicate a mode, it need not prescribe to the last syllable, and though the poem beats out the fact of death, its rhythm is not remorseless.

Nightingales warbled without,
  Within was weeping for thee:
Shadows of three dead men
  Walked in the walks with me,
  Shadows of three dead men and thou wast one of the three.

Arthur Hallam was another of the three dead men, the third being Henry Lushington. In *Break, break, break* the assurance was of loss, with not even a metaphor to explain or console, and the slow anapaests that rise from and question the opening words seeming to question pretensions to life and meaning. But in the later poem, with the second line's initial effect of inversion to guide us, the dactylic chant has a curious underlying effect, if not of lightness, of something other than grief. In section LXXXVIII of *In Memoriam*, the nightingale was the very voice of life; here

Nightingales warbled and sang
  Of a passion that lasts but a day;
  Still in the house in his coffin the Prince of courtesy lay.

Is it death which is contrasted with this brief passion, or is it the friendship of the dead 'Prince of courtesy'? The last stanza answers, with Tennyson's 'love that ever will be'. Much of the assurance in the poem is of what has been. When Tennyson sums up, although the end of it is plainly the end ('Three dead men have I loved and thou art last of the three'), there is a feeling of gratitude, of thanks returned for what has been known. He was sixty when he walked in the garden at Swainston, and perhaps sixty is not an age for a reversal of the Book of Common Prayer's 'In the midst of life we are in death.' But there is a deep and glowing pride in the men that he has loved, hardly, if at all, qualified by the haunting close:

'and thou art last of the three'. The command of rhythm is unsurpassed, even by Tennyson.

Several of the later elegies might have been written in support of the advice he gave Mary Boyle, that the silver year must cease to mourn. Nothing is avoided, but whether it is his own loss that he thinks of, or that of Catullus 'nineteen-hundred years ago', something of continuing life wells up in the poetry, some principle of sober yet tender acceptance seems to be at work in him. His gloom about England and about man's future deepened as he grew older, and his morbidity hardly seems to have lessened. Nevertheless we are often conscious, not necessarily of Tennyson in the role of calm seer or *vates*, though *The Ancient Sage* of 1885 is precisely that, but of a celebration of life before the fact of death. Whatever the sense of loss, something of this is present in the rhythms of *In the Garden at Swainston*, but (not surprisingly) there are other poems where it is more evident. Nine years earlier, in 1861, a visit to a valley in the Pyrenees which he had last seen in 1830 with Arthur Hallam had occasioned yet another word on his friend: *In the Valley of Cauteretz*. This poem began life as two quatrains, each of two couplets. In its final version it consists of five couplets, the third of which links the original quatrains, and presents the defeat of time. A glance at the two versions makes it clear that for Tennyson, as for other poets, refining is not rubbing and polishing, but a strengthening of meaning.

(i) Brook that runnest madly, brook that flashest white,
   Deepening thy voice with the deepening of the night,
   All along the valley, where thy mad waters go,
   I walked with Arthur Hallam two and thirty years ago.
   All along the valley thou ravest down thy bed,
   Thy living voice to me is as the voice of the dead,
   All along the valley, by rock and cave and tree,
   The voice of the dead is a living voice to me.[15]

(ii) All along the valley, stream that flashest white,
   Deepening thy voice with the deepening of the night,
   All along the valley, where thy waters flow,
   I walked with one I loved two and thirty years ago.

All along the valley, while I walked today,
The two and thirty years were a mist that rolls away;
For all along the valley, down thy rocky bed,
Thy living voice to me was as the voice of the dead,
‑And all along the valley, by rock and cave and tree,
The voice of the dead was a living voice to me.

The second version has less immediacy, and more power, than the first. 'Brook' in line 1 of the first draft becomes the more generalised and less domestic 'stream'; 'thy mad waters go' in line 3 similarly becomes 'thy waters flow', and the 'madly' and 'ravest' of lines 1 and 5 are excised; the ordering of the last two couplets, and their relationship with the rest of the poem, is made more clear by 'For' and 'And'; their present becomes past, as the experience defines itself. A. Dwight Culler's description of the metrical effects is accurate: 'the odd lines are of six feet, but with a caesura that occupies the time of a seventh, whereas in the even lines the caesura is filled up with sound, but the stressed syllables are alternately heavy and light so as to produce two rhythms, one superimposed upon another'.[16] To which may be added that unlike the repeated phrases of the fourth and fifth couplets, 'twŏ ănd thirtў yeărs ăgó' and 'thĕ twó ănd thirtў yeárs' vary metrically, alternating lighter and heavier stresses on 'two' and 'thirty'. The effect of the variations is to blur the denotated time, and the lightening of the stress on 'thirty' helps to make the years 'a mist that rolls away'. This poetry of statement is a long way from that of *Mariana*; apart from anything else, there are only three adjectives in the poem, one of them repeated. Though the repetition throughout is almost incantatory, the grasp of the actual does not weaken; the 'was' of the last line might not have been, without the 'was as' of line 8. It is in some respects a hard-headed poem, however much of mere head it seems to transcend. Or rather, it declares itself as a *Kunstwerk*, which is probably why Tennyson liked it 'as well as anything that I have written'.[17]

Even in the *Prefatory Poem to My Brother's Sonnets* of 1879, written after the death that year of his brother Charles Tennyson Turner, there is still something of life in the tender memories of 'The light of days when life begun, / The days

that seem today'. This elegy has an unusual three-part struc-
ture, with two quatrains in I and II, and three in III. There
may have been a principle of lengthening at work, since there
is a version of the last stanza with an extra line: 'So, brother,
whatsoe'er thou be.' This resembles the 'whate'er he be' of
section CVII of *In Memoriam*, and a cancelled stanza of III is
also suggestive: 'Our brother-days that will not die – / And,
now thou art withdrawn / So far I cannot follow, I cry / To
that first light of dawn.'[18] It is possible that he removed them
because of the resemblance, and it would not be surprising if
even after more than thirty years the measure and purpose of
these elegies could become intrusive.

I

> Midnight – in no midsummer tune
> The breakers lash the shores:
> The cuckoo of a joyless June
> Is calling out of doors . . .

II

> Midnight – and joyless June gone by,
> And from the deluged park
> The cuckoo of a worse July
> Is calling through the dark:
>
> But thou art silent underground,
> And o'er thee streams the rain,
> True poet, surely to be found
> When Truth is found again.

English stoicism before a wretched summer becomes the
vehicle for resignation before the empty years he faces at the
age of seventy. Some of the most poignant English references
to summer are to wet summers, like Hardy's 'wet June' in
Overlooking the River Stour, or like Arnold's *Thyrsis*: 'So
have I heard the cuckoo's parting cry, / From the wet field,
through the vexed garden-trees, / Come with the volleying
rain and tossing breeze . . . ' Tennyson's 'The cuckoo of a

worse July' for a moment resembles a forward look by Housman. But the joylessness, and the feeling of a transition merely from the ill gone by to the ill to come, is tempered first by recognition of the dead man's worth, where 'surely' holds both hope and belief, and then by memories of boyhood and of 'such a day tomorrow as today'.

> Far off a phantom cuckoo cries
> From out a phantom hill;
>
> And through this midnight breaks the sun
> Of sixty years away . . .

The end of it is heartfelt prayer – 'As all thou wert was one with me, / May all thou art be mine!' – in which the 'thou art' of 'thou art silent underground' becomes the 'all thou art' of faith, and yearning.

Perhaps there is no poem in which sadness and a strong sense of life mingle more easily than *Frater Ave atque Vale*, which is of the same period, and alludes to Charles by way of an invocation of Catullus.

> Row us out from Desenzano, to your Sirmione row!
> So they rowed, and there we landed – 'O venusta Sirmio!'
> There to me through all the groves of olive in the summer glow,
> There beneath the Roman ruin where the purple flowers grow,
> Came that 'Ave atque Vale' of the Poet's hopeless woe,
> Tenderest of Roman poets nineteen-hundred years ago,
> 'Frater Ave atque Vale' – as we wandered to and fro
> Gazing at the Lydian laughter of the Garda Lake below
> Sweet Catullus's all-but-island, olive-silvery Sirmio!

It has been described as combining the joy of Catullus' Poem XXXI ('Paene insularum, Sirmio, insularumque / ocelle') with the lament of Poem CI: 'atque in perpetuum, frater, ave atque vale'.[19] The metre is eight-stress trochaics, slowed at the beginning by the Italian names, at the end by the compounds, everywhere by the single long 'o' rhyme, and the sense of time. 'Your Sirmione', and the relaxed chiastic construction of the first line, which delights in the Italian names, and the falling rhythm that accommodates them, establishes the mood at the outset: a gentle indulgence, a love for what is present and continuous, which can contain the 'hopeless woe' that Tennyson echoes. Perhaps Tennyson, or Hallam Tennyson, who was with him, and acting as a kind of courier, as Edward Fitzgerald rather waspishly said, asked the boatmen to row them out to Sirmio, and when the boatmen understood they said, 'Ah, *Sirmione*, signori, *Sirmione?*'[20] 'Your Sirmione' means change, and not change: your Sirmione, my Sirmio and that of Catullus, the ground we all know. There is the whole of Italian travel in the implied exchange: the 'classic ground' of the poem to Lear, and a deep joy in the survival of names and places and feelings. Then with the landing and the breathed 'O venusta Sirmio!' we are in the world of Catullus and his 'salve, o venusta Sirmio'. ('Venusta,' as well as being Catullus' epithet for Sirmio, is appropriate in another sense, since it seems to have had a particular meaning for him.) The ruin and the purple flowers are a common image of decay and life. But it is in the final 'olive-silvery Sirmio!' that the life that breathes in the poem finds its loveliest expression. Tennyson slips it in so that in its context ('Lydian laughter,' 'all-but-island') it looks like a quotation from Catullus, as indeed for one commentator it is. What is so apt in his 'olive-silvery Sirmio' is not so much the assonance and consonance of the phrase, as the wind that blows in it, turning the green of the olive leaves to the silver of their undersides.[21]

Less formally than *To Virgil*, '*Frater Ave atque Vale*' pays glad homage to Roman poetry; it is tempting to think of 'olive-silvery Sirmio' as an addition to Catullus, who does not speak of his olive-trees. The brevity of the 'Experiments in Quantity' of the early 1860s, on the other hand, indicates one attitude to this kind of homage. Much of it is ironic, briefly in *On Translations of Homer: Hexameters and Pentameters* ('These lame hexameters the strong-winged music of Homer! / No – but a most burlesque barbarous experiment'), where the versification is held up to reveal its shame ('Barbarous ex-peri-ment'); at greater length in *Hendecasyllabics*, which has something of the lightness of a fat man performing a slow dance.

> O you chorus of indolent reviewers,
> Irresponsible, indolent reviewers,
> Look, I come to the test, a tiny poem
> All composed in a metre of Catullus,
> All in quantity . . .

>   . . . .
> Hard, hard, hard is it, only not to tumble,
> So fantastical is the dainty metre . . .

Elsewhere he uses this metre privately for contemptuous dismissal of a critic called Friswell: 'Friswell, Pisswell – a liar and a twaddler – / Pisswell, Friswell – a clown beyond redemption, / Brutal, personal, infinitely blackguard' (*The Gentle Life*). Swinburne also wrote correct hendecasyllabics, unlike Coleridge, whose 'Hear, my beloved, an old Milesian story!' was censured by Saintsbury for being dodecasyllabics, with an initial dactyl instead of a dissyllabic foot.[22] Swinburne's near-obsessive interest in form means that he is able to use hendecasyllabics almost as he would use any metre: 'Woven under the eyes of stars and planets / When low light was upon the windy reaches / Where the flower of foam was blown, a lily /Dropt among the sonorous fruitless furrows . . . ' Tennyson's are mockery, even self-mockery. As Saintsbury pointed out in the same context, they are both triumph and criticism: 'As some rare little rose, a piece of inmost / Horticultural art . . . ' (' "*Versi*cultural" rather', Saintsbury comments.) For all the eloquence, something comparable may be at work in *Milton: Alcaics* of the same period. The poem has angered some Miltonists, usually because it is felt that Tennyson did ill to be charmed by bowery loneliness rather than Titan angels, and it is true that Tennyson's vales are not entirely the reflection or delphic abstraction of Keats's description of *Paradise Lost*. His care for the form itself goes farther than the insistence that 'Milton' must be properly disyllabic; he distinguishes between the Horatian Alcaic, and the lighter and freer Greek Alcaic which he was imitating, and when Calverley claimed that in 'God-gifted organ-voice of England' the second syllable of 'organ' was too short, Tennyson pointed out that 'in the few third lines of the stanza left by Alcaeus this syllable is more than once short'.[23]

> Whose Titan angels, Gabriel, Abdiel,
> Starred from Jehovah's gorgeous armouries,
> Tower, as the deep-domed empyrëan
> Rings to the roar of an angel onset.

There is no way, of course, by which this can be seen as 'versicultural'. J.B. Leishman found 'two egregious false quantities' in the second and third lines, arguing that 'from' and 'as', which should be long or stressed, cannot naturally be pronounced so in their contexts.[24] We cannot read that stanza as intelligently as Tennyson, but with the Alcaic pattern to help us we can probably appreciate something of what he is doing. One can have unconvinced quantities in English, but not false quantities, and Leishman rightly adds that what he is looking for is simply Milton's 'fit quantity', or quantity fit for the place where it is required. One context which should be considered is that of the organ-voice which Tennyson is evoking, as distinct from imitating, and to which the effect of the alien pattern contributes. We should also consider the weight that 'from' and 'as' may properly have, from what precedes and follows them. 'From' rises to what follows it ('Jehovah's gorgeous armouries'); 'as', with the pause before and the enjambment after marking even more strongly its linking of 'tower' and 'rings', the poem's delayed first verbs, seems to have a deeper note. This rising or deepening is a personal reading, but both words, in this slow-moving verse, have a weight of confirmation in them for which stress is appropriate.

To Virgil of 1882, written for the Vergilian Academy of Mantua for the nineteenth centenary of Virgil's death, is imitation of another and a finer sort. The poem is in ten stanzas, each of two rhyming trochaic nine-foot lines, with a final catalectic foot, in which the second five feet tend to amplify the statement of the first four.

I

Roman Virgil, thou that singest
    Ilion's lofty temples robed in fire,
Ilion falling, Rome arising,
    wars, and filial faith, and Dido's pyre;

II

Landscape-lover, lord of language
    more than he that sang the Works and Days,
All the chosen coin of fancy
    flashing out from many a golden phrase;

III

Thou that singest wheat and woodland,
    tilth and vineyard, hive and horse and herd;
All the charm of all the Muses
    often flowering in a lonely word.

The opening and Virgilian image, of power that passes from one race to another, comes to rest, with the final salutation, in the new nations, the 'Rome of freemen' and the 'Northern Island', and this commerce between them. After the majestic beginning, Tennyson turns to the mastery of this 'lord of language'. 'All the chosen coin of fancy' suggests the authority of a poet who has the wealth of language at his command. The parallel phrase in the following stanza, 'All the charm of all the Muses', indicates the last effect of such skill, in an achievement which may seem fortuitous, the result of enchantment. The third stanza refers to the *Georgics*, and to an unusual flowering there. But it is likely that Tennyson is also weighing *vers trouvés* and *vers donnés* which are *donnés* only because we do not understand: 'chosen coin' as the conscious artistry, the flowering in a lonely word as the result of a long habit of such artistry, which can indeed seem mysterious to the poet as well as to his readers.[25] Tennyson's own long-practised artistry has produced one of the finest tributes ever paid by one poet to another, and with the simplest of linguis-

tic forms: a single twenty-line period based on 'Roman Virgil,
I salute thee'. The sixth and seventh of the seven stanzas
appositive to the opening 'Roman Virgil' move from direct
evocation of the singer and the song, first to Virgil as most
human of seers, then to a series of laudatory images culminat-
ing in one of the great symbols of the Western world, from
the *Aeneid*.

VI

Thou that seëst Universal
    Nature moved by Universal Mind;
Thou majestic in thy sadness
    at the doubtful doom of human kind;

VII

Light among the vanished ages;
    star that gildest yet this phantom shore;
Golden branch amid the shadows,
    kings and realms that pass to rise no more . . .

Virgil as the golden bough he sings of is more than felicitous,
but it is by another kind of enchantment that the poet of
shores and strands of the upper and lower worlds becomes
'star that gildest yet this phantom shore', with all that 'phan-
tom' indicates of our doubtful realities on earth, and all that
the poem tells us of what passes, and what remains.

With some exceptions (*Balin and Balan, Demeter and
Persephone*), his later successes are in the short poems, more
particularly in short poems which, like '*Frater Ave atque
Vale*', respond to minor occasions. *To Virgil* is a notable
exception; the occasion on which Tennyson acknowledged
in full what the Western world owed to Virgil can hardly be
called minor. Several of the last poems, like *Parnassus*, or, in
its very different way, *Akbar's Dream*, seem to be based on a
principle of large questioning and various reassurances, not
the least of which is the gravity of the utterance. Some of the
largest questioning and gravest utterance is in *The Higher*

Pantheism of the late 1860s, which is a singularly easy poem to dislike, if we overlook its deliberate circling and unobtrusively cyclic structure, around the central stanza on man ('Glory about thee, without thee; and thou fulfillest thy doom . . .'), Tennyson's sadder and milder version of Pope's 'the glory, jest, and riddle of the world'. Its measure is dactylic, like that of several of the later poems, with a challenging rise in the first line, appropriate to the presentation as actuality ('The sun, the moon, the stars, the seas, the hills and the plains') of what the poem knows as God's vision. It is not Tennyson at the height of his powers, but it deserves something better than Swinburne's brilliant but complacent parody: 'Fiddle, we know, is diddle: and diddle, we take it, is dee.' In *'Flower in the crannied wall '* of the same period, on the mystery of created and Creator, the gravity of utterance functions by being in part adroitly concealed.

> Flower in the crannied wall,
> I pluck you out of the crannies,
> I hold you here, root and all, in my hand,
> Little flower – but *if* I could understand
> What you are, root and all, and all in all,
> I should know what God and man is.

The poem turns on 'hold', and 'all', and in the last two lines on the equivalence, mediated by 'all in all', of 'what you are' and 'what God and man is'. 'Root and all, in my hand' works against a 'root and all' which is 'all in all', the hand throughout indicating, obviously enough, the mind which cannot hold. The language aims at a musing simplicity which will pass beyond the expected forms of poetry, but the truth is that it is a sententious little poem which depends for its effect on an evocation of what Tennyson would have liked to say.

'All in all' recurs eleven years later in *De Profundis*, which was begun at Hallam Tennyson's birth in 1852. The cry from the deeps of distress of Psalm CXXX ('De profundis clamavi') becomes praise of a coming to birth and identity – the 'main-miracle, that thou art thou' – from the abyss that in part I is that of space and time, and had contained 'all that was to be, in all that was', and in II is 'that true world within the world we see'. In *Vastness* (1885), on the other hand, it seems at first that nothing has meaning: 'all of us . . . / Swallowed in Vastness, lost in Silence, drowned in the deeps of a meaningless Past?' The poem, in eighteen stanzas, each of a single couplet in eight-foot dactylics, with the usual catalectic final foot, consists of thirty-five lines of full-voiced complaint which are countered by the sudden assertion: 'Peace, let it be! for I loved him, and love him for ever: the dead are not dead but alive.' Tennyson has been blamed not only for using an undemanding form, but also for the human felicity he depicts, admittedly only to reject it: 'Household happiness, gracious children, debtless competence, golden mean'. Household happiness, however, is the desirable opposite of Shakespeare's 'the dark house and the detested wife'; 'gracious children' does not mean epicene moppets with delicate manners, but sons and daughters who will not turn and rend you; and only great souls are free to despise debtless competence and the golden mean which sometimes ensures it. (The couplet of XII is unusual in the poem in that each of its lines has only two dactyls. That the dactylic 'competence' echoes and seems to underwrite the dactylic 'happiness' may be worth indicating to those alert for proofs of bourgeois sentiments.) Nor is it really true that the poem is too much of a complaint, a sustained growling of the sort ('best thing God can do is to squash this planet flat!') that wearied Edward Lear.[26]

> Lies upon this side, lies upon that side, truthless violence
>   mourned by the Wise,
> Thousands of voices drowning his own in a popular
>   torrent of lies upon lies.

There may be various opinions about the bitterness of 'popular', but the weight and pace of this is not the dramatised hysteria of the opening of *Maud*. The poem originally consisted of four stanzas, with the eighteenth stanza countering the pessimism of the first three, and Tennyson later added six lines to the thirty lines of 1885. However memorable the instance, the danger of such an increase is obvious enough. Despite its near single mood, *Vastness* succeeds, not because of its memorable moments (such as the late 'Desolate offing, sailorless harbours, famishing populace, wharves forlorn'), but because of the response of the final challenge and reversal to the pace of the verse throughout. 'What is it all', he says,

What but a murmur of gnats in the gloom,
   or a moment's anger of bees in their hive? –

           ❖   ❖   ❖   ❖

Peace, let it be! for I loved him, and love him for ever:
   the dead are not dead but alive.

The penultimate line is simplified to a formal double analogy; its imagery is classic, and therefore this side of despair. This modulation is followed by a pause which is like a rest in music, and the monosyllables of the last line, which is fully dactylic, seem to lengthen it beyond the eight-foot norm.

In the same year as *Vastness*, Tennyson published that highly formal statement of serenity, *The Ancient Sage*, in which he assumes the mantle of the aged seer, as once in *Armageddon* he had put on that of the young prophet. Often quoted from, and sometimes admired for its form, *The Ancient Sage* is worth looking at in some detail, if only for a comparison with *Demeter and Persephone*, since both are ambitious, and both speak for life. The form of the poem, which contains an impressive statement of his 'Faith beyond the forms of Faith', is that of alternating declarations of faith and scepticism. The sage reads and comments on the poem brought him by a younger sceptic and roué, which is not, as is sometimes supposed, a series of songs, but a single poem of 104 lines, whose burden is that man, alone with time, has overlived his day, and is already in darkness. Longer and less sophisticated than *The Golden Year*, its debate is at the level of ancient wisdom contending with (and formally containing) lyrical despair. But this takes place 'A thousand summers ere the time of Christ', and in the narrative introduction the two actors are presented like figures on a frieze: the Seer; the other 'richly garbed, but worn / From wasteful living'; the ancient city behind; the scroll, the cavern, and the classically 'affluent' fountain that pours from darkness into light. Something of the same stylisation is heard in the song; in 'The passive sailor wrecks at last / In ever-silent seas', 'passive', aided by the abstracting force of 'ever-silent', translates suffering into emblem. What is most characteristic of the song is the hammering insistence of the actual supporting itself, as in *Vastness*, and as it must, by extended instance. Its architecture is sound: the many instances of the ruins of time are succeeded at last by the one death that inspired them. The reductive force, at its sharpest in the image of the rose and lily that mingle at last in dust, not love, is present from the beginning, in

> 'How far through all the bloom and brake
>   That nightingale is heard!
> What power but the bird's could make
>   This music in the bird?'

Language which seems about to celebrate some power beyond the nightingale turns sardonically to the actual, and the single vision. Man is 'fancy's fool', despite the lily 'laughing back the light'; we recognise again Tennyson's fear of a world without meaning. But there is a perceptible creaking. 'And since – from when this earth began – / The nameless never came / Among us, never spake with man . . .': in a pre-Christian context, the dice are heavily loaded.

The sage's language at its best is characterised by a fine limpidity.

> If thou would'st hear the Nameless, and wilt dive
> Into the Temple-cave of thine own self,
> There, brooding by the central altar, thou
> Mayst haply learn the Nameless hath a voice,
> By which thou wilt abide, if thou be wise,
> As if thou knewest, though thou canst not know;
> For Knowledge is the swallow on the lake
> That sees and stirs the surface-shadow there
> But never yet hath dipt into the abysm,

> The Abysm of all Abysms, beneath, within
> The blue of sky and sea, the green of earth,
> And in the million-millionth of a grain
> Which cleft and cleft again for evermore,
> And ever vanishing, never vanishes,
> To me, my son, more mystic than myself,
> Or even than the Nameless is to me.

The diving into the self, and the infinity or abysm of littleness, is later matched by the description of an experience Tennyson knew well: the loosing of 'the mortal limit of the Self', and its passing into the Nameless. Though tinged with the introspection associated with Eastern philosophies, this passage resembles a Victorian equivalent of the passage in *Tintern Abbey* about the presence or 'sense sublime / Of something far more deeply interfused', with a concept of infinity (approached by Tennyson's familiar distinction betwen knowledge and wisdom) overlaying the motion and spirit that rolls through all things. Though passive, it has its own authority: imagery and incantatory repetition are subordinate, even tributary, to the 'within' in 'The Abysm of all Abysms, beneath, within / The blue of sky and sea, the green of earth', which answers the song's clipped 'Behind the green and blue' fifteen lines earlier; to that extent, the blank verse seems to follow a principle of clarity rather than opacity.

   The problem, however, is not with this or that passage, but whether we can accept *The Ancient Sage* at the height of Tennyson's intentions. The famous 'Passion of the Past' lines are intended to act as a living instance of inexplicable experience, to counter the narrow certainties of the song. But its authority – the memory of a dumb yearning, the knowledge of a 'Desolate sweetness – far and far away' – lies outside the poem, which may also be surmised by the device by which the passage is introduced. It comes in by way of comment on the song's 'worms and maggots of today' and 'gleams . . . / Of more than mortal things'; this 'today' looks back over some thirty lines of the song to 'For man has overlived his day', and the mild 'Today? but what of yesterday?' on which the sage turns to his boyhood 'Passion of the Past' is a little disingenuous. The direction at the close to work to be done 'in yon dark city', which may help the penitent on the way to vision, is deeply felt. But there is some plump upholstery of Eastern circumstance just where the poem can least afford it: 'Nor care – for Hunger hath the Evil eye – To vex the noon with fiery gems, or fold / Thy presence in the silk of sumptuous looms . . . ' His memory, so far from stealing fire, as the early *Ode to Memory* has it, is curiously passive. Perhaps the echo in 'If utter darkness closed the day' (line 199) of Scott's 'Till utter darkness closed her wing' in *Marmion* (Canto Sixth, XXXIV) is significant only because it begins one of the weaker passages. And it would be in keeping with some of the intentions of the poem if the world as 'this house of ours, / So beautiful, vast, various' (83–84) were a criticism of Arnold's 'world, which seems . . . / So various, so beautiful, so new' in *Dover Beach.* The blank verse can degenerate badly, and in 'we, the poor earth's dying race, and yet / No phantoms, watching from a phantom shore' (178–9), the 'phantom shore' of *To Virgil* (republished with *The Ancient Sage* in 1885) is dealt out almost like a counter. Since these are days of instant Eastern enlightenment, fewer readers than fifty years ago will reject *The Ancient Sage* for its serenity. There is considerable skill in the interweaving of the song and the passages of blank verse; it is also beyond doubt that the poem contains a good deal, and this is precisely what is wrong with it. We feel that some passages are brilliant, that it recovers well from its weaker moments, that in spite of occasional failures of style Tennyson's dispositions are excellent: in short, we are too conscious of the task, and of the mantle assumed.

From the first line of *Demeter and Persephone*, 'Faint as a climate-changing bird that flies / All night across the dark-ness', we recognise the difference. The quality of 'climate-changing' is both concrete, and curiously abstract, seeming to mix explication and enchantment, and making us linger for a moment, as if over a word whose sources we have just understood. (Persephone's return has changed the climate in another sense, and Demeter will look forward to a final change.)

Faint as a climate-changing bird that flies
All night across the darkness, and at dawn
Falls on the threshold of her native land,
And can no more, thou camest, O my child,
Led upward by the god of ghosts and dreams,
Who laid thee at Eleusis, dazed and dumb
With passing through at once from state to state,
Until I brought thee hither, that the day,
When here thy hands let fall the gathered flower,
Might break through clouded memories once again
On thy lost self.

On the one hand there are the echoing oppositions and distances of the first few lines; on the other, the expository plainness of the seventh line, formally almost on one side, yet central, its 'at once' a different perception from the time and distances of the opening. We can see Tennyson finding his way to weight and plainness through the manuscript changes of the next three lines, arriving at 'the day' by way of 'the flowery gleam / Of Enna', 'thy last bright day', and 'thy last bright hours'.[27] Twenty lines later, in the context of the opposition of the new to the known which is near the heart of the poem, he opposes this to a more habitual music. Demeter has often seen 'the serpent-wanded power / Draw downward into Hades with his drift / Of flickering spectres . . . / But when before have Gods or men beheld / The Life that had descended re-arise . . . ?' One effect of 'draw' fading into 'drift' is familiar to any reader of Tennyson, but the majestic style of the first two lines also indicates the known authority of the serpent-wanded power, and, after the measured lapse of 'The Life that had descended', the opposing 're-arise' – its concentrated repetitions answering that of 'Draw', 'drift', and descended' – distinguishing firmly between the vowels, and forces the event on us. It is a goddess who speaks, however 'human-godlike', and the language is often that of ritual, of what has been ordained, supported by wordplay. The ritual question and answer passage in which Demeter asks her lost Persephone of winds and waves, and of the unnamed Fates (ll.57–86), ends with the laconic 'Nothing knew', which contains a bitter pun reflecting on the unalterable law implicit in the Fates' 'There is a Fate beyond us.' Her fear of the return to Enna of the black team of Hell is also expressed in a pun: the 'deathless heart of motherhood' in her shudders, lest 'all at once their arched necks, midnight-maned, / Jet upward through the mid-day blossom', where 'jet' suggests both fountain, and darkness. In Demeter as 'the Power / That lifts her buried life from gloom to bloom,' the wordplay resembles emblem. This occurs in a central passage, where Demeter recalls the likeness of the rapt Persephone telling her that Bright and Dark have sworn that she shall be the Bride of Darkness. Once again, its sombre strength is that of ritual, from which the poem, so rooted in duality, is never far.

As Earth-Goddess and Earth-Mother, Demeter is closer to helpless man than the high gods she curses after her daugher's rape. She is the corn goddess, who first raised man from his acorn-grubbing state, and grieves for him in the waste places where (in Eastern phrase recalling *The Ancient Sage* and *Akbar's Dream*) he has been supplanted by serpent, scorpion, and tiger. For Tennyson, she is also 'the deathless heart of motherhood', or woman in her noblest role, not less noble for being 'the desolate Mother', 'the *mater dolorosa* of the ancient world', as Pater says. Pater also describes her as the goddess of dark caves, pointing out that she is not quite free from monstrous form.[28] Tennyson's Demeter, however, is wholly beneficent. In the Homeric *Hymn to Demeter* she causes a cruel year of famine, and would have destroyed the race of men. In Tennyson there is no sullen withdrawal, only utter grief, lost in which the goddess fails to send her life through olive and vine and golden grain. The substance of the poem is duality – the duality of bright and dark, life and death, love and fear – but its conscious theme is evolution: Demeter, still ill content after Persephone's return, looks forward to a new race of younger, kindlier gods who will pity man, and destroy hell. (Tennyson's nine months of light and three of dark for Persephone, for the eight and four months of the Homeric *Hymn*, and the equal division of the year in Ovid – a late change after the trial edition, in which he had followed the division of the *Hymn* – suggests that he wanted to play his part in the evolution of the myth, rather as he does with Malory at the end of *Gareth and Lynette*: 'he, that told it later'.) And the conclusion looks forward not only to new gods, but to new men, in 'souls of men, who grew beyond their race, / And made themselves as Gods against the fear/ Of Death and Hell', lines which take up and toss aside the constraint of 'et eritis sicut Dei'. Persephone, once Queen of Death, will join her mother in the work of germination and fruition, and will reap 'the worship which is Love'.

'When I write an antique like this,' Tennyson said, 'I must put it into a frame – something modern about it.'[29] The frame is the moving and eloquent prophecy of Christianity. That the younger, kindlier gods did come must be the answer to the objection that Demeter's interpretation of the Fates' 'There is a Fate beyond us' is too hopeful. Tennyson may have had in mind the version of the legend, mentioned by Lemprière, in which Jupiter sent the Parcae to comfort Demeter, or Ceres. If, as has been suggested, he was countering the fatalism of Swinburne's *Hymn to Proserpine* and *The Garden of Proserpine*, this would help to explain the insistence.[30] (It is possible that he was also responding to the different challenge of Swinburne's *Hertha*, which praises divine humanity (' . . . the morning of manhood is risen, and the shadowless soul is in sight'), and whose title is the name of the Germanic earth-goddess mentioned by Tacitus.) But as many readers feel, the fires of torment and shadowy Elysium in which the poem ends linger beyond their formal negation.

> and see no more
> The Stone, the Wheel, the dimly-glimmering lawns
> Of that Elysium, all the hateful fires
> Of torment, and the shadowy warrior glide
> Along the silent field of Asphodel.

The timeless or infinitive 'glide', the last verb in the poem, weakens the eager futures (shall bless, shall reap, shall see no more), and the preterites within the future ('men, who grew beyond their race, / And made themselves as Gods'), which the will conceives. The final dualism, after bright and dark, life and death, spring and winter, is less the consciously balanced love and fear of Christian and pagan, than the native hope and fear of the human condition, directed to what most gives meaning to life. Of one thing we can be sure, which is that the power of this fabling is far greater than the weight of content in a poem like *The Ancient Sage*.

It is some indication of how a later age has wanted to promote Tennyson, that he is often called either a Symbolist, or a precursor of the French Symbolists. It is probably not too much of a simplification to say that Arthur Hallam's 1831 essay on Tennyson (once discredited, now overpraised) has combined with Yeats's interest in it, and with a mistaken idea that Yeats was a Symbolist, to suggest that Tennyson was a Symbolist too. The most we can say is probably that there is a recognisable tendency in Tennyson towards some of the processes of Symbolism; some of his more Augustan effects, incidentally, may be in part a reaction against his way of letting things melt into each other. Given that for the Symbolists the ideal was a discipline by which the poem becomes a separate object or world, both the product and the instrument of visionary purification, it is hardly surprising that Valéry, rightly described by Marcel Raymond as 'the classic of Symbolism', should have remarked, 'Le Symbolisme a peu existé.'[31] It required from its practitioners devotion to poetry as an instrument of power, no matter how that devotion might hide behind the concept of poetry as only a marginal activity of the mind. And though Tennyson lived for poetry, he does not seem to have had the confidence in it that presupposes the authority of the ideal closed world of some of the Symbolists. The answer of the late poem *Parnassus* to the question of whether the scientific discoveries of the future would make poetry impossible ('Other songs for other worlds!') is courageous rather than convincing. But in *The Voice and the Peak* of 1874 he had shown a different kind of assurance, and the terms of this short meditative poem could deceive us into thinking that here at least Tennyson is on the highroad to *le Symbolisme*. It is true that by the end of the poem the hearing and seeing that it began with are vision, and that we are left with the first and last of knowledge in the inviolate symbol.

The voice and the Peak
   Far into heaven withdrawn,
The lone glow and long roar
   Green-rushing from the rosy thrones of dawn!

It is also true that the structure of the poem can be seen as a process by which the difficulty and the rare authority of poetry make themselves known, and by which it becomes clear that its essence is in symbol. So much at least Tennyson has in common with the Symbolists, but it is no paradox to say that it is little enough. The example of a single poem proves nothing, but *Crossing the Bar* – arguably one of the finest of the late poems, but sometimes criticised for a falling off in the last stanza – is as far from *le Symbolisme* as a poem can be; it is probably the explication, as well as the propriety of the image, which makes some readers unhappy about the Pilot in the last stanza. Stanzas 3 and 4 repeat the basic syntactic and rhythmic pattern of 1 and 2: a musing exclamation, followed by explication and reassurance in which the longer lines that swell from the optatives ('And may there be' . . . 'And may there be') are stayed and kept in hand by the renewed short lines: 'When that which drew from out the boundless deep / Turns again home.' The last line ('When I have crost the bar') repeats the rhythm of 4 ('When I put out to sea'), not 8 ('Turns again home'), and perhaps this interweaving of the two parts helps to make the poem more entire. It is, in its way – it is not everyone's way, of course – a masterly handling of classic imagery, and clear statement. Tennyson may have remembered the last stanza of the fifteenth canto of Byron's *Don Juan* ('the eternal surge / Of time and tide rolls on, and bears afar / Our bubbles'), but since the imagery is classic, such reference is probably pointless.

Crossing the Bar looks forward to death; *Merlin and the Gleam* of the same year (1889) looks back over a life dedicated to poetry, and is therefore an appropriate point at which to take our leave of Tennyson. The gleam, he said, is 'the higher poetic imagination', and in this poem he traces his pursuit of it, singing to the young mariner who will inherit the quest of early summers when the gleam was all around him; of rejection, and a darkening of romantic and pastoral poetry; of the Arthurian poetry, and the loss of Arthur; of how the gleam grew broader and brighter as he grew old, and of the end of it.[32]

> And so to the land's
> Last limit I came –
> And can no longer,
> But die rejoicing . . .

More than half a century before, his Ulysses had spoken of the untravelled world, and the margin which faded as he moved. Now the dying poet's last sight of the gleam is to be understood as fulfilment.

> . . . For through the Magic
> Of Him the Mighty,
> Who taught me in childhood,
> There on the border
> Of boundless Ocean,
> And all but in Heaven
> Hovers The Gleam

Merlin's defeat in *Merlin and Vivien* was the defeat of the imagination, and when Wordsworth speaks in *Elegiac Stanzas Suggested by a Picture of Peele Castle* of 'the gleam, / The light that never was, on sea or land, / The consecration, and the Poet's dream', he is speaking of a power that is gone. There is no defeat in *Merlin and the Gleam*, and that Merlin should die rejoicing is consonant with the spirit of life in so much of Tennyson's later poetry. As for critical mistrust over the gleam as broader and brighter with age, given that the later poetry is inferior to the earlier, the truth is that it has less to do with the value of the poetry than with the pursuit, and the sense of something evermore about to be. What the poem records is greater than the biography that we scratch about in for facts, by which the loss of Arthur Hallam should have appeared not in the seventh but in the third of the nine stanzas. The Romantic quest is firmly stayed on the human action of the poem: a young man looking at an old man, and wondering about the strange fact of age – the insistence of '*I* am Merlin' is both reassurance, and confession – and the passing on of the quest, with the turning to exhortation of the self-definition of the refrain.

Speculation about the identity of the wizard who taught Tennyson is not very useful. What is particularly fitting about this late poem, written 'for those who cared to know about his literary history', is its enigmatic quality, and its air of purity.[33] Like the opening lines of *Demeter and Persephone*, the poetry seems to reach us from a distance (movingly combing this with a certain intimacy), which is in part the result of the verse-form. This is that of two-stress unrhymed dactylic lines: where the line changes to four-stress, it seems to be under the impulse of an old bitterness ('Once at the croak of a Raven who crost it'), or an old sorrow ('The Gleam, that had waned to a wintry glimmer'), and the recovery from it: 'And slowly moving again to a melody . . . ' (The Raven, which is appropriate to the measure, is probably the critic J.W. Croker, and there may also be a hint of the crows in Pindar's Second Olympiad.) The short lines, with their formal parallels and repetitions, are an appropriate form for the distillation of the life that has been lived, which the old alliterative mode translates to something approaching the heroic. Whatever the dilations in the body of the poem ('Griffin and Giant, / And dancing of Fairies / In desolate hollows'), it has a principle of spareness: the only two adjectives in the first and last stanzas are 'young' and 'gray' and 'young'. It is a stubborn faith in humankind which makes Tennyson, so often nearly lost in regret, speak now of his inheritors (with more conviction perhaps than Wordsworth shows when he refers in *Michael* to youthful poets who will be his second self), and turn his own youth to the light of promise. 'Mighty the Wizard / Who found me at sunrise / Sleeping, and woke me / And learned me Magic!': there is something in that 'learned', perhaps of recovered youth, certainly of an older authority. As so often, the nineteenth-century master triumphs with the first and last effect of poetry, the re-creating and renewing of words.

Old and weary,
But eager to follow,
I saw, whenever
In passing it glanced upon
Hamlet or city,
That under the Crosses
The dead man's garden,
The mortal hillock,
Would break into blossom.

Notes

1 Early Experiments

1 Quoted by Hallam Tennyson, ed., *Idylls of the King*, London, 1908, p. 436 (cited by A. Dwight Culler, *The Poetry of Tennyson*, New Haven and London, Yale University Press, 1977, p. 267).

2 'Los mitos crean al mundo, y el mar estaría sordo sin Neptuno y las olas deben la mitad de su gracia a la invención humana de la Venus' (Federico García Lorca, 'Elegy for María Blanchard', in *Deep Song and Other Prose*, edited and translated by Christopher Maurer, London and Boston, Marion Boyars, 1980, p. 6).

3 Culler, *The Poetry of Tennyson*, pp. 24–5.

4 Christopher Ricks, *Tennyson*, New York, Macmillan, 1972, p. 19. W.E. Fredeman draws attention to Tennyson's interest in the moment before an unrevealed end in *St Simeon Stylites*, 'as so often in [his] dramatic monologues and lyrics' (W.E. Fredeman, ' "A Sign Betwixt the Meadow and the Cloud": The Ironic Apotheosis of Tennyson's "St Simeon Stylites" ', *University of Toronto Quarterly*, xxxviii, 1968, p. 72).

5 Christopher Ricks, ed., *The Poems of Tennyson*, London, Longmans, Green, 1969, p. 271. (Hereafter cited as Ricks.)

6 Jacob Bryant, *A New System, or, an Analysis of Ancient Mythology*, 1774–76. W.D. Paden refers to Tennyson's early reading of Bryant (W.D. Paden, *Tennyson in Egypt: A Study of the Imagery in his Earlier Work*, University of Kansas Publications, Humanistic Studies, No. 27, Lawrence, Kansas, 1942).

7 MS first reading, Ricks, p. 66n.

8 Hallam Tennyson, *Alfred Lord Tennyson: A Memoir, by His*

Son, 2 vols, London, Macmillan, 1897 (hereafter cited as *Memoir*), II, pp. 473–4.

9   *Memoir* I, pp. 45–6, cited Ricks, p. 170.

10   Unadopted passage published by Christopher Ricks, 'The Tennyson Manuscripts', *Times Literary Supplement*, 21 August 1969, p. 921.

11   *Memoir* II, p. 355, cited Ricks, p. 171.

12   Ricks, p. 172.

13   The probable source (an article in the *Quarterly Review* by Francis Palgrave) was suggested by W.D. Paden, 'MT. 1352: Jacques de Vitry, The Mensa Philosophica, Hödeken, and Tennyson', *Journal of American Folklore*, lviii, 1945, pp. 35–47 (noted by Ricks, p. 9).

14   Paden, 'MT. 1352', pp. 46–7. Since it is now day, Paden's suggestion of a seventh suitor 'nearing his goal' is perhaps open to improvement.

15   *Memoir* I, p. 23. Jowett saw a number of fragments, including *The Coach of Death*, or part of it, and commented, 'They are most original, and it is wonderful how the whelp could have known such things.' The best of what he saw seems to have been the description of Pandemonium at the end of Act I.

16   The description is in a letter of Tennyson to Sir George Grove of 1872, quoted by Joanna Richardson, *The Pre-Eminent Victorian: A Study of Tennyson*, London, Jonathan Cape, 1962, pp. 17–18.

17   Ricks, p. 156.

II   *Poems, Chiefly Lyrical*

1   Leigh Hunt, unsigned review, *Church of England Quarterly Review*, October 1842, in John D. Jump, ed., *Tennyson: The Critical Heritage*, London, Routledge & Kegan Paul, 1967, p.131.

2   Tennyson, *Works*, ed. Hallam Tennyson, Eversley Edition, 9 vols, London, Macmillan, 1907–8 (hereafter cited as Eversley), I, pp. 358–9. I am indebted to Robert Ussher for guiding me through the Greek origins of Tennyson's compounds.

3   'All these ladies were evolved, like the camel, from my own consciousness' (Eversley I, p. 335).

4   Noted by Ricks, *Tennyson*, p. 45.

5   Edgar Allan Poe, *The Rationale of Verse*, 1848.

6   Since the fluidity of Tennyson's poetry suggests a movement in

the direction of Symbolism, it is of some interest that Stéphane Mallarmé translated most of *Mariana* into French. He omits the third stanza, and (even in prose) can do nothing more with 'the sound / Which to the wooing wind aloof / The poplar made' of the last stanza, than 'le bruit qu'au vent faisait le peuplier' (Mallarmé, '*Mariana* de Tennyson, *Proses diverses*', in *Oeuvres Complètes*, ed. Henri Mondor and G. Jean-Aubry, Paris, Gallimard, Bibliothèque de la Pléiade, 1961, pp. 703–4). Although originally it may have been a hurried translation meant to fill a gap in the journal *La Dernière Mode* which Mallarmé edited, and where the translation first appeared in 1874, it was revised for publication sixteen years later in the *Mercure de France*. The translation of 'weeded and worn the ancient thatch' by 'sarclée et usée, l'ancienne paille' seems to be incorrect.

7   Antoine, Comte de Rivarol, Preface to *L'Enfer, poème de Dante, traduction nouvelle*, Paris, 1785.

III   Poems 1832–1842

1   James Spedding, unsigned review, *Edinburgh Review*, April 1843, in Jump, *The Critical Heritage*, p.142.
2   Ricks, p.400.
3   John Pettigrew, *Tennyson: The Early Poems*, London, Edward Arnold, 1970, pp. 30–2.
4   Howard Jacobson, *Ovid's Heroides*, Princeton University Press, 1974, pp. 176–7n.
5   The second to last line recalls Wordsworth's *Intimations Ode*, 'Turn wheresoe'er I may, / By night or day.' The 'Naked they came' of line 93, incidentally, occurs in the same context in Aphra Behn's paraphrase of the fifth of Ovid's epistles, in Dryden's *Ovid's Epistle's, Translated by Several Hands*, 1680: 'Naked they came, no Veil their Beauty Shrouds.' In Ovid's poem, which is the main source for Tennyson's, it is only Minerva who is naked: 'venit in arbitrium nuda Minerva tuum'.
6   Hallam Tennyson, *Materials for a Life of A.T.*, iv, p. 461; W.M. Rossetti, ed., *Rossetti Papers 1862–1870*, 1903, p. 341: both quoted by Ricks, p. 354.
7   Tennyson is supposed to have said that the Lady's 'new-born love for something, for someone in the wide world from which she has been so long secluded, takes her out of the region of shadows into that of realities' (*Memoir* I, pp. 116–17). A. Dwight Culler

suggests that the explanation is in fact not Tennyson's, but that of Alfred Ainger, author of *Tennyson for the Young* (*The Poetry of Tennyson*, p.44). It hardly seems likely that Tennyson would have reduced the poem to this.

8   Ricks, p. 663.

9   The Archpoet of Cologne, *Confessio*: 'But when Bacchus lords it in / My cerebral story, / Comes Apollo with a rush, / Fills me with his glory' (trans. Helen Waddell, *Mediaeval Latin Lyrics*, London, Constable, 1948).

10   If it was *Childe Harold* as well as the Bible that was in Tennyson's mind in the preceding stanza, perhaps in the vacant 'gentlemen' of this stanza he was unconsciously influenced by the helpless 'gentlemen' throughout *Don Juan* ('Single gentlemen who would be double', 'Thus gentlemen may run upon a shoal').

11   E.C. Stedman, *Victorian Poets*, London, Chatto & Windus, 1876. The best critical discussion is probably still that of J.W. Mackail, *Lectures on Greek Poetry*, London, Longmans, 1910, pp. 220 ff. Robert Pattison's *Tennyson and Tradition*, Cambridge, Mass., Harvard University Press, 1979, is a recent study of considerable interest.

12   Hallam Tennyson, ed., *Tennyson and His Friends*, London, Macmillan, 1911, p. 210 (quoted by Ricks, p. 1633n).

13   Ricks, p. 508.

14   Pattison, *Tennyson and Tradition*, pp. 68, 70.

15   Paul Turner, *Tennyson*, London, Routledge & Kegan Paul, 1976, p. 82; Ricks, p. 705n.

16   Douglas Bush, *Mythology and the Romantic Tradition in English Poetry*, Cambridge, Mass., Harvard University Press, 1969, pp. 224–5.

17   Ricks, p. 537n.

18   This might be taken for additional evidence, if less oblique and so less revealing, for the failure of the narrator to command the poem which Christopher Ricks finds (*Tennyson*, pp. 105–7). Ricks points to several ambiguities, including the use of 'forged' (283). On the face of it, 'forged' confirms the creation of 'inward evidence' opposing that of 'the sense', by which the dead are merely dead, but the connotations of deceit perhaps betray the opposite of the overt intention. W. David Shaw (*Tennyson's Style*, Ithaca and London, Cornell University Press, 1976, pp. 238–40) carries this much farther, and discusses the uses of logic and debate to disqualify themselves. 'Quiet scorn' is too overt to suggest any unconcious mingling of attitudes. Some of the 'arbitrary rhetoric' discussed by

Shaw – 'Of something felt, like something here; / Of something done, I know not where; / Such as no language may declare' – is as likely to be an indeterminacy which validates strong feeling, and given the tone (' "O dull, one-sided voice," said I') of 202–16, its 'I cannot hide that some have striven' and 'And did not dream it was a dream' may not be anything more than unambiguous irony.

19 Carlyle, *Past and Present*, II, ch. 3.

20 Gibbon, *Decline and Fall of the Roman Empire*, ch. xxxvii.

21 Ricks, p. 545n.

22 *Memoir* I, p. 130.

23 John Pettigrew, 'Tennyson's "Ulysses": A Reconciliation of Opposites', *Victorian Poetry*, i, 1963, p. 44.

24 James Knowles, 'Aspects of Tennyson, I & II: A Personal Reminiscence', *Nineteenth Century*, xxxiii, 1893, II, p. 182.

25 Pettigrew notes the biblical echo, *op. cit.*, p. 37.

26 Culler, *The Poetry of Tennyson*, pp. 95–6.

27 This is apparent also in the narrative of the voyage in the *Inferno*, where Ulysses says that although his men, like him, were 'vecchi e tardi', old and slow, he could hardly have held them back from it after he had exhorted them. Incidentally (and perhaps not surprisingly) the words Tennyson gives him resemble the form of a speech of exhortation by Ulysses as given by Pope. Speaking of how Homer adapts a speech of Menelaus to 'the Laconic' in the third book of the *Iliad*, Pope comments: 'Had it been Ulysses who was to make the speech, he would have mentioned a few of their most affecting calamities in a pathetick air; then have undertaken the fight with testifying such a chearful joy, as should have won the hearts of the soldiers to follow him to the field without being desired ... For a conclusion, he would have used some noble sentiment agreeable to a hero, and (it may be) have enforced it with some inspirited action. In all this you would have known that the discourse hung together, but its fire would not always suffer it to be seen in cooler transitions, which (when they are too nicely laid open) may conduct the reader, but never carry him away. The people would hear him with emotion' (Pope's note to his translation of *Iliad* III, Maynard Mack, ed., *The Poems of Alexander Pope*, Vol. VII, London, Methuen, 1967, pp. 196–7).

28 Lucretius, *De Rerum Natura*, I. 3–4.

29 Cleanth Brooks, *The Well Wrought Urn: Studies in the Structure of Poetry*, New York, Harcourt Brace, 1947, p. 143.

30 Malory has ' "Comfort thyself," said King Arthur, "and do as well as thou mayest, for in me is no trust for to trust in, for I will

into the vale of Avilion, for to heal me of my grievous wound. And if thou never hear more of me, pray for my soul" ' (*The Morte Darthur*, xxi: quoted by Ricks, p. 595n).

31 Wendell Clausen, 'An Interpretation of the *Aeneid*', in Steele Commager, ed., *Virgil: A Collection of Critical Essays*, Englewood Cliffs, N.J., Prentice-Hall, 1966, p. 82; Terrot R. Glover, *Studies in Virgil*, London, Edward Arnold, 1904, p. 204. The probable origin of 'revolving many memories' is *Aeneid* I. 305, 'per noctem plurima volvens' (Ricks, p. 597n).

32 'Until near the end of his life, when he finally gave up port because of his gout, his drinking was a recurrent surprise to those who first met him, although he could drink steadily without seeming the worse for it. He said he needed alcohol as a stimulant, to keep him from lethargy, and he took it to overcome shyness when he was with strangers, but even in friendly company he sometimes drank too much' (Robert Bernard Martin, *Tennyson: The Unquiet Heart*, Oxford, The Clarendon Press, 1980, pp. 221–2).

33 Preface to the second edition of *Lyrical Ballads*, 1802. In 1845 Wordsworth changed 'his situation is altogether slavish and mechanical' to 'his employment is in some degree mechanical'.

34 James Spedding, quoted by Martin, *op. cit.*, pp. 221–2.

35 Ricks, p. 736n.

36 For an unqualified celebration, see *The Day-Dream*, 'L'Envoi', and 'all that else the years will show'. Given its theme, *The Poet's Song* is more suggestive.

iv The Princess

1 *Memoir* II, pp. 70–1, quoted by Ricks, p. 743.

2 *Memoir* I, p. 256, quoted by Ricks, p. 743.

3 F.E.L. Priestley, *Language and Structure in Tennyson's Poetry*, London, Deutsch, 1973, p 84. Priestley quotes from the earlier part of the lecture, and suggests that from 124 ('Deep, indeed, / Their debt of thanks to her who first had dared') the reporting changes its mode. I do not think it does: the passages I have quoted are 131–5 and 145–8.

4 'A sight to shake / The midriff of despair with laughter' (I. 197–8) may owe something to *Love's Labours Lost* V. ii. 845: 'To move wild laughter in the throat of death'.

5 In the Epilogue to *In Memoriam* (127–30), the child of Cecilia Tennyson and Edmund Lushington will be 'a closer link / Betwixt

us and the crowning race / Of those that, eye to eye, shall look / On knowledge'. (Speaking of how Balzac thought of the spirit as pervading matter, André Maurois observes '[il] croit confusément que l'évolution qui a conduit du marbre au saint, conduira de l'homme à l'ange' (André Maurois, *Promethée, ou la Vie de Balzac.* Paris, Librairie Hachette, 1965, p. 435).)

6 Ricks, p. 741.

7 A symptom noted by several critics: Hugh I'Anson Fausset, *Tennyson: A Modern Portrait*, London, Jonathan Cape, 1923; J.H. Buckley, *Tennyson: The Growth of a Poet*, Cambridge, Massachusetts, Harvard University Press, 1960; Culler, *The Poetry of Tennyson*, 1977.

8 *Memoir* II, p. 69.

9 Ricks, p. 844n, notes that 111–15 were incorporated verbatim from a MS version of *The Lover's Tale* I. 52–61.

10 'L'objet d'un vrai critique devrait être de découvrir quel problème l'auteur (sans le savoir ou le sachant) s'est posé, et de chercher s'il l'a résolu ou non' (Paul Valéry, 'Littérature', *Tel Quel*, Section I, in *Oeuvres Complètes*, ed. Jean Hytier, II, Paris, Gallimard, Bibliothèque de la Pléiade, 1962, p. 558).

Tennyson's use of Shakespearian comedy and romance is discussed by Gerard Joseph in *Tennysonian Love: The Strange Diagonal*, Minneapolis, University of Minnesota Press, 1969. For some contemporary opinions of the Shakespearian style of *The Princess*, see Deborah Byrd Mantell, '*The Princess*: Tennyson's Eminently Shakespearian Poem', *Texas Studies in Literature and Language*, xx, No. 1, 1978, pp. 48–65.

v *In Memoriam*

1 *Memoir* I, p. 304, quoted by Ricks, p. 859.

2 A.C. Bradley, *A Commentary on 'In Memoriam'*, 3rd edn, London, Macmillan, 1910, pp. 20, 27, 29–30. Although Bradley says his purpose is strictly limited, and that he prefers to abstain from 'aesthetic criticism', his *Commentary* is invaluable. One or two later critics have picked at it rather testily. The divisions recorded by Knowles are I–VIII, IX–XX, XXI–XXVII, XXVIII–XLIX, L–LVIII, LIX–LXXI, LXXII–XCVIII, XCIX–CIII, CIV–CXXXI (Knowles, *Nineteenth Century*, p. 182). The edition, with commentary, by Susan Shatto and Marion Shaw (*Tennyson: 'In Memoriam'*, Oxford, Clarendon Press, 1982) is a notable contribution.

3 *Memoir* I, p. 304; Dante, *Paradiso*, XXXIII. 52–4. 'Because, becoming purified, my view / now more and more was entering the ray / of the deep light that in itself is true' (translated by Melville B. Anderson).

4 Bradley draws attention to Horace, *Odes* I. iii, and Theocritus, *Idylls* viii. 53 *et seq.*, and to the use of some words (e.g. 'ocean-plains', 'favourable speed', 'prosperous', 'perplex') as perhaps due to the associations of Latin poetry.

5 Bradley, *op. cit.*, p. 114.

6 Harry Puckett, 'Subjunctive Imagination in *In Memoriam*', *Victorian Poetry*, xii, 1974, pp. 109–11.

7 Ricks, p. 904n.

8 *Ibid.*; Gordon N. Ray, 'Tennyson Reads "Maud",', Sedgewick Memorial Lecture, University of British Columbia, Vancouver, 1968, Appendix I, p. 39. It is possible that Tennyson had in mind the original meaning of the Latin 'vastus': empty, desolate, deserted.

9 Shatto and Shaw, *Tennyson: 'In Memoriam'*, pp. 13–14, 222.

10 Ray, *op. cit.*, p. 39.

11 *Ibid.*

12 Ricks, p. 917n.

13 The last two lines of XCVI, incidentally ('While Israel made their gods of gold, / Although the trumpet blew so loud'), sound almost as though Tennyson had in his mind the last line of Blake's *Mock on, Mock on Voltaire Rousseau*: 'Where Israel's tents do shine so bright'.

14 Shatto and Shaw note that in T. MS section LXXXVIII is marked by the 'X' which Tennyson used to indicate a section he meant to omit, and that it does not appear in L. MS, though it was reinstated in the trial issue or private printing of March 1850.

15 *Memoir* I, 319. 'Free-will was undoubtedly, he said, the main miracle, apparently an act of self-limitation by the Infinite, and yet a revelation by Himself of Himself' (*Memoir* I, 316–17). Balzac, incidentally, declared that the will was 'la seule chose qui, dans l'homme, ressemble à ce que les savants nomment une âme' (*Jésus-Christ en Flandre*, in *Romans et Contes*).

Bradley refers to Horace, *Odes* I. ix, and the fragment of Alcaeus 'on which that Ode is based' (Alcaeus fr. 135). Charles Calverley, incidentally, used the *In Memoriam* stanza in his translation of Horace's ode into English, and it is not surprising to find him translating Tennyson's CVII (omitting the first stanza) into Horatian Alcaics. Calverley renders the central effect of the *b b* lines of Tennyson's fifth stanza (aptly described by Christopher Ricks, *Tennyson*, p. 229) as 'the solid core of the stanza itself') by the central position in its line of 'cor': 'dic coronant / / Crateras: ignis cor solidum, graves / Repone ramos'.

16 Ricks, p. 971n.

17 John Dixon Hunt, in John Dixon Hunt, ed., *Tennyson: 'In Memoriam': A Casebook*, London, Macmillan, 1970, p. 34.

18 Bradley draws attention to several instances of a failure in the last stanza, which weakens the section. Franklin Lushington would have liked to cut off the last stanza of one or two of the elegies (anonymous review in *Tait's Edinburgh Magazine*, August 1850: quoted Shatto and Shaw, *Tennyson: 'In Memoriam'*, p. 268).

19 Knowles, *Nineteenth Century*, p. 182.

20 Eleanor B. Mattes, *'In Memoriam': The Way of a Soul. A Study of Some Influences That Shaped Tennyson's Poem*, New York, Exposition Press, 1951, p. 105; Christopher Ricks, *Tennyson*, p. 225. Mattes also suggests an attempt to suit the poem to the public, by giving 'an overall impression of compromise and comprehensiveness'.

21 Denis Donoghue, *The Ordinary Universe*, London, Faber & Faber, 1968, p. 241.

22 As perhaps with Isobel Armstrong in her interesting chapter on Tennyson in *Language as Living Form in Nineteenth Century Poetry* (Brighton, Harvester Press, 1982). Since Armstrong argues that *In Memoriam* is a poem about death trying to be a poem about life (a point of view for which there is a good deal to be said), it is natural for her to be concerned with disintegration. But to say that 'should' in the last line of section X 'becomes' an imperative, not a subjunctive (p. 193), or that 'the syntax tangles' to allow Tennyson the opportunity of grasping the hand of the drowned Hallam, is, if one may say so, more picturesque than accurate. The suspensions in *In Memoriam* are probably as important as the disintegrations, and we should be cautious about making every delay an agent of destruction rather than suspension; there are times (particularly in *In Memoriam*) when Tennyson needs almost as much breath as Milton. Her comments on section XV are interesting, but it is one thing to speak of 'ambiguous syntax', another to follow this with 'deranged syntax', and practically a third to conclude that 'the poet and the syntax go mad' (pp. 174–5). Tennyson is playing with ideas of integration and disintegration; it is a serious game, and within the general context of 'play' readers may take some parts of it with all a reader's seriousness. But though 'syntax', like 'psychopath', may

have become a rag-bag term, it is a little on the hectic side to call syntax mad when (as syntax) it is hardly even ambiguous. In the matter of loose syntax and disintegrating mind and language, there are some questionable comments also in W. David Shaw's perceptive *Tennyson's Style* (Cornell University Press, 1976), particularly on *Lucretius*, 157–9: 'And twisted shapes of lust, unspeakable, / Abominable, strangers at my hearth / Not welcome, harpies miring every dish'. Shaw (pp. 282–3) expresses doubts about which word modifies which, and says that 'the loose syntax is exactly right for the disintegrating mind'. There is no difficulty about modification, since everything from 'unspeakable' to 'harpies' describes 'twisted shapes of lust', and there is no loose syntax. (Shaw's interpretation of 'stay' in line 40 of *The Lady of Shalott*, incidentally (p. 64), is even more questionable. To ask whether 'stay' in 'She has heard a whisper say, / A curse is on her if she stay / To look down to Camelot' means 'remain' or 'refrain from', whether or not we feel Tennyson is committed only to hypotheses, is to spirit 'stay' out of all of its contexts ('night and day', 'weaveth steadily'), not least that of the poem; the suggestion that the Lady might remain in her tower looking down to Camelot is not much more strange than the idea that the curse will fall unless she leaves her tower.)
23   Patricia Ball, *The Central Self*, London, Athlone Press, 1968, p. 176.

VI   Maud

1   *Memoir* I, p. 396, quoted by Ricks, p. 1039.
2   Perhaps Geoffrey Tillotson is unfair to Tennyson when, making a comparison with Swinburne, he says that the speaker insulted the power of passion 'when in a famous line he made the fancies of a young man turn to thoughts of love lightly' (Geoffrey and Kathleen Tillotson, *Mid-Victorian Studies*, London University Press, 1965, p. 214). 'Lightly' in 'In the Spring a young man's fancy lightly turns to thoughts of love' means that he took it up lightly, as young men will, not knowing where it would lead; it is histrionically bitter, of course, acting out the interruption of the deep thoughts about mankind.
3   In ' "What is it, that has been done?": the Central Problem of *Maud*' (*Essays in Criticism*, xxiv, October 1974, pp. 356–62), Jonathan Wordsworth argues that Tennyson was probably unaware of the sexual implications of the opening lines about the pit –

the hollow, the bleeding lips, the wood – or of the duel in the pit, and suggests that *Maud* is 'a neurotic poem ... in which the writer's unconscious at important moments dominates the poetry', and that the real story is probably that of the deflowering of Maud, which Tennyson disguises as the killing of her brother, and the narrator's subsequent remorse and madness. He takes account of the difficulties either of taking up 'a straightforwardly intentionalist position', or of supposing that 'a reading that the author could not conceivably have intended *is* the poem'. His arguments are interesting; at the same time, he is a little too severe on what is presented as actuality. The question 'Was it he lay there?' (II. 28) cannot be answered by calling it a seemingly pointless question, and asking 'Who else?' The question, was it the raging dandy-despot who 'lay there with a fading eye', makes very good sense. The story seems sufficiently coherent. The reading proposed adds to our understanding of *Maud*, but it does not transform a muddled and experimental work. The monodrama has its weaknesses, and the probable sources of its power could have made for confusion, but except in the third part there is no muddle.

4   E.D.H. Johnson, 'The Lily and the Rose: Symbolic Meaning in Tennyson's *Maud*', *PMLA*, lxiv, 1949, p. 1226.

5   He told Knowles that the verse of I. XX. iv. 9–13 'should be read here as if it were prose – Nobody can read it naturally enough!' (Ray, *op. cit.* Appendix II, p. 44).

6   *Ibid.*

7   Paull Baum, *Tennyson Sixty Years After*, Chapel Hill, University of North Carolina Press, 1948, p. 138.

8   Ray, *op. cit.*, p. 44.

9   *Ibid.*

10   *Ibid.*

11   R.P. Blackmur, 'The Shorter Poems of Thomas Hardy', in *Language as Gesture: Essays in Poetry*, London, Allen & Unwin, 1961, pp. 59–60.

12   Ray, *op. cit.*, p. 44.

13   Humbert Wolfe pointed out the resemblance (*Tennyson*, London, Faber & Faber, 1930, p. 48).

14   The phrase seems to have been something of a formula: Byron's mother said she thought her son's imprudence with money would ruin him 'unless, indeed, coal mines turn to gold mines' (quoted in André Maurois, *Byron*, 1930, translated by Hamish Miles, 1930, p. 102), and in *La Cousine Bette* of Balzac, Josépha, when announcing to Baron Hulot that she has left him for the rich

Duc d'Hérouville, observes 'il n'y a que les grands seigneurs d'autrefois pour savoir changer du charbon de terre en or.'

15 T.S. Eliot, *'In Memoriam'*, in John Killham, ed., *Critical Essays on the Poetry of Tennyson*, London, Routledge & Kegan Paul, 1960, p. 210; J.H. Buckley, *Tennyson: The Growth of a Poet*, p. 144.

16 Tennyson's shell passage perhaps echoes Byron's lines in *The Island*, I. 133–40: 'The tender nautilus, who steers his prow, / The sea-born sailor of his shell canoe, / The ocean Mab, the fairy of the sea, / Seems far less fragile, and, alas! more free. / He, when the lightning-wing'd tornados sweep / The surge, is safe – his port is in the deep – / And triumphs o'er the armadas of mankind, / Which shake the world, yet crumble in the wind.'

17 *Memoir* I, p. 404, quoted by Ricks, p. 1079n.

18 *Memoir* I, p. 396, quoted by Ricks, p. 1090n.

19 Roy Basler, *Sex, Symbolism, and Psychology in Literature*, New Brunswick, Rutgers University Press, 1948, p. 86.

20 R.J. Mann, 'Tennyson's "Maud" Vindicated: An Explanatory Essay', London, 1856, in Jump, *Tennyson: The Critical Heritage*, p. 199.

21 Culler, *The Poetry of Tennyson*, pp. 194–5. Rader's argument, that *Maud* was 'an act of cathartic recapitulation by which he defined and judged his early life and attempted to put it behind him', is fairly widely accepted (R.W. Rader, *Tennyson's 'Maud': The Biographical Genesis*, Berkeley and Los Angeles, University of California Press, 1963, p. 88). It has much to recommend it; among other things, Tennyson's almost morbid sensitivity to criticism of *Maud* is suggestive. The love affair with Rosa Baring in the 1830s may not have been important in itself, but the evidence for *Maud* as an expression of much that Tennyson had known in himself is strong.

VII *Idylls of the King*

1 *Memoir* II, p. 337.

2 *Ibid.*, p. 123.

3 F.E.L. Priestley, 'Tennyson's *Idylls*', *University of Toronto Quarterly*, xxiii, 1949, and *Language and Structure in Tennyson's Poetry*, London, André Deutsch, 1973.

4 *Memoir* II, p. 62, quoted by Ricks, p. 1465.

5 C.S. Lewis, *The Allegory of Love: A Study in Mediaeval Tra-*

dition, Oxford University Press, 1938, p. 310.

6   The irony of this, of course, is that the decay of the Order begins with peace. The strong enjambment in the closing lines (together with all that has happened since we first heard this voice at the beginning) creates a different movement from that of the parallel passage of 16–19. There is little, incidentally, to support Culler's comment, that 16–19 describe Arthur's conquests before his marriage (*The Poetry of Tennyson*, pp. 218–19); remote as they are, in that context of Aurelius and Uther, and the wastes of time, they include the battles of 514–18, which are nearer and more urgent because of the events of the idyll.

7   The best account of his purpose in *The Coming of Arthur* is probably that of J.M. Gray, in 'A Study in Idyl: Tennyson's *The Coming of Arthur*', *Renaissance and Modern Studies*, xiv, 1970, pp. 111–50, and *Man and Myth in Victorian England: Tennyson's 'The Coming of Arthur'*, Lincoln, Tennyson Research Centre, 1969. The structural proportion of 2:4:1 which Gray finds for the division into 1–146, 147–445, and 446–518 was achieved by the post-1869 additions. Another effect of these additions was to make the taking of the vows central to the 518 lines of the idyll, at 259–61.

8   Tennyson, *Works*, London, Macmillan, 1913, p. 966.

9   Ricks, p. 1516n.

10   Donald Davie, 'T.S. Eliot: The End of an Era', in Hugh Kenner, ed., *T.S. Eliot: A Collection of Critical Essays*, Englewood Cliffs, N.J., Prentice-Hall, 1962, p. 200. Kenner speaks in his introduction of 'the self-sufficiency of the remarkable oeuvre which has cogent uses for its own banalities and gaucheries'. Many readers who admire the oeuvre are unconvinced of this.

11   *Memoir* II, pp. 82–3, quoted by Ricks, p. 1484; *Memoir* II, p. 113n, quoted by Ricks, p. 1484.

12   F.E.L. Priestley, 'Tennyson's Idylls', p. 35.

13   Ricks, pp. 1661, 1463, 1676n, 1680n.

14   *Memoir* II, p. 90, quoted by Ricks, p. 1661.

15   Ricks, p. 1661.

16   *Ibid.*, p. 1709n.

17   Sir Charles Tennyson, *Alfred Tennyson*, London, Macmillan, 1950, p. 484; J.M. Gray, 'Fact, Form, and Fiction in Tennyson's *Balin and Balan*,' *Renaissance and Modern Studies*, xii, 1968, pp. 106–7 (see also his *Tennyson's Doppelgänger: 'Balin and Balan'*, Lincoln, Tennyson Research Centre, 1971); 'I've always said that *Maud* and *Guinevere* were the finest things I've written' (Knowles, *Nineteenth Century*, p. 187).

18   Ricks, p. 1412.
19   Richard Watson Dixon, 'To the Reader', *Mano: A Poetical History*, 1883. Dixon is not contemptible as a poet, but the opening lines give a fair idea of the style of this work.
20   R.W. King, *Review of English Studies*, n.s. xiii, 1962 (quoted by Ricks, p. 1551n).
21   Ricks, p. 1551n.
22   Christopher Ricks, *Tennyson*, p. 270. Many of Ricks's points are well made. *Lancelot and Elaine* 73–6 ('Now for the central diamond and the last / And largest, Arthur, holding then his court / Hard on the river nigh the place which now / Is this world's hugest, let proclaim a joust') are astonishingly weak, and whatever Tennyson's purposes were in *Gareth and Lynette*, 306–9 are a retreat from any kind of reality: 'And out of bower and casement shyly glanced / Eyes of pure women, wholesome stars of love; / And all about a healthful people stept / As in the presence of a gracious king.' This passage (also singled out by Baum) almost achieves the opposite of what it is supposed to mean; it is Tennyson's fault, not ours, if we momentarily read 'slept' for 'stept'. One or two others of Ricks's criticisms are less convincing. 'A walk of roses ran from door to door' is not clumsy, since a walk of roses is striking enough to seem to run, although 'all round it ran a walk / Of shingle' in *Enoch Arden* may take something from this argument. 'He, reverencing king's blood in a bad man' is stilted, perhaps pretentious (it is part of the surface Miltonising of *Guinevere*), but not obscure; if anything, the meaning is rammed home by the complacent crabbedness. ('Who prop, thou ask'st, in these bad days, my mind?') Nor is 'So Sir Lancelot holp / To raise the Prince, who rising twice or thrice / Full sharply smote his knees' a gaucherie, the result of insensibility to rhythm and line-ending; there is little there that a comma would not cure. As for *Gareth and Lynette* 601–6 ('and so besieges her / To break her will, and make her wed with him: / And but delays his purport till thou send / To do the battle with him, thy chief man / Sir Lancelot whom he trusts to overthrow, / Then wed, with glory') – it is clumsy, but there are many commas, and no perilous ambiguity; we are not really held up by any suspicion that the fourth fool proposes to marry Lancelot, after overthrowing him.
23   John Rosenberg, *The Fall of Camelot*, Cambridge, Mass., Harvard University Press, 1973, pp. 122–24.
24   T.S. Eliot, *The Listener*, 12 February 1942: quoted by Christopher Ricks, *Tennyson*, p. 273.
25   David Jones observed that *The Anathemata*, though 'involved

at every point ... with the complex things of Britain and the heritage of the Cymry', aroused more interest and was better understood in America than in Britain (letter to Aneurin Davies, 21 May 1964, in Aneurin Davies, ed., *Letters to a Friend*, Triskele Books, 1980). Speaking of *Idylls of the King*, incidentally, Jones said that Tennyson's trouble was what he left out, and adds that 'all the time we should feel, along with the contemporary twist, application, or what you will, the whole weight of what lies hidden – the many strata of it' ('The Myth of Arthur', in H. Grisewood, ed., *Epoch and Artist*, London, Faber & Faber, 1973, p. 234).

VIII   Later Poems

1   Mackail, *Lectures on Greek Poetry*, pp. 221–2.
2   Martin Dodsworth emphasises the neuroticism ('Patterns of Morbidity: Repetition in Tennyson's Poetry', in Isobel Armstrong, ed., *The Major Victorian Poets: Reconsiderations*, London, Routledge & Kegan Paul, 1969). There is a lot to be said for Enoch's desire to spare his wife, but clearly Tennyson's story has less to do with heroism than with suffering which passes into self-inflicted suffering, and lonely death; the fact that he is made to stay on in the same town is suggestive.
3   Ricks, p. 1152n.
4   Baum, *Tennyson Sixty Years After*, p. 154.
5   Jerome's account of the legend in his additions to the Eusebian Chronicle, on which he based the poem, includes the statement that the unfinished *De Rerum Natura* was written *per intervalla insaniae* (Ricks, p. 1206). Tennyson's friend Hugh Munro, who read and approved *Lucretius*, treats Jerome's account with some scepticism in his edition of Lucretius of 1864.
6   Perhaps this is an indication of Lucretius' deranged state. Although he says (*De Rerum Natura* V. 195–9) that the world is too faulty to have been divinely created, his poetry has something of what Tennyson called in *In Memoriam* (perhaps remembering the 'sic rerum summa novatur / semper' of II. 75–6) 'The glory of the sum of things'. His joy in the shapes and forms of the world is unmistakable, as in II. 502–3, 'aurea pavonum ridenti imbuta lepore / saecla' ('the golden generations of peacocks steeped in laughing grace'), or the instance of the effect of theatre awnings and walls in IV. 75–83: 'haec intus perfusa lepore / omnia conrident correpta

luce diei' ('all within laughs in the flood of beauty when the light of day is thus confined').

7   D.E.W. Wormell, 'The Personal World of Lucretius', in D.R. Dudley, ed., *Lucretius*, London, Routledge & Kegan Paul, 1965, p. 64.

8   W.H. Auden, *Tennyson: An Introduction and a Selection*, London, Phoenix House, 1946, p. x.

9   Although he denied that Drayton's *Ballad of Agincourt* was a source or model, saying that his poem was dactylic (Ricks, p. 1034), the original version published in *The Examiner* is quite close to Drayton's rhythm in at least one passage: 'With many a desperate stroke / The Russian line they broke.'

10   Richardson, *The Pre-Eminent Victorian: A Study of Tennyson*, p. 209.

11   The enlargement and simplicity make it eminently quotable; it was quoted on the death of Churchill, as Christopher Ricks reminds us (*Tennyson*, p. 239), and some years later Mrs Margaret Thatcher applied line 179 to Mr Edward Heath, after refusing him a place in her cabinet.

12   For Tennyson's neglect of old friends like Spedding and Fitzgerald, see Martin, pp. 535–8.

13   J.F.A. Pyre, *The Formation of Tennyson's Style*, Madison, University of Wisconsin, 1921, pp. 218–19.

14   Ricks, p. 1019. Distinguishing between the Horatian and the Greek Alcaic, Tennyson described the first as 'perhaps the stateliest metre in the world except the Virgilian hexameter at its best' (Eversley II, p. 378).

15   Ricks, p. 1123n.

16   Culler, *The Poetry of Tennyson*, p. 247.

17   *Memoir* I, p. 492, quoted by Ricks, p. 1123.

18   Ricks, p. 1261n.

19   Ricks, p. 1284. As Ricks says, the combination of Poems XXXI and CI is characteristic. C.J. Fordyce (*Catullus: A Commentary*, Oxford, 1961, p. 338) suggests that on his journey to Bithynia Catullus had visited his brother's tomb in the Troad, to which Bithynia is adjacent; it is possible that Tennyson remembered that Poem XXXI in praise of Sirmio was written on his return from Bithynia. Harold Nicolson points out Tennyson's use of the two Catullus poems, and goes on to show how the 'o' sounds of the rowing motif contain the 'a' sounds of the Catullan motif, and how they are fused in the last line. The 'o' sounds of the single rhyme throughout may suggest the song of the boatmen which Nicolson

speaks of. (Harold Nicholson, *Tennyson: Aspects of His Life, Character, and Poetry*, London, Constable, 1923, pp. 285–6.) The ruins on Sirmio, incidentally, though known locally as 'The Grottoes of Catullus', are those of a large palace which was probably built after his death. Gilbert Highet, who mentions this, points out that Tennyson, 'with characteristic sensibility . . . did not speak of the imposing ruins at the end of the peninsula as being the home of Catullus' (Gilbert Highet, *Poets in a Landscape*, Harmondsworth, Middlesex, Penguin Books, 1959, pp. 41–3).

20   Edward Fitzgerald to Frederick Tennyson, June 1880, in *Letters of Edward Fitzgerald*, ed. J.M. Cohen, London, 1960, p. 246 (quoted by Martin, p. 430).

21   Fordyce (p. 93), speaking of Poem III, says 'venustus' is 'clearly one of the "fashionable" words of Catullus' society', and goes on to speak of 'how real for him was its connexion with Venus'. Fordyce refers us to Carducci as well as to Tennyson. In *Da Desenzano* (*Odi Barbare*, Libro I), Carducci speaks of 'Sirmio che ancor del suo signore allegrasi'. *Sirmione*, from the same volume, describes 'Sirmio' as 'fiore de le penisole' and 'gemma de le penisole', and contains some rather stiff evocation of Latin usage, as well as a recollection of the scurrility in Poem XI. Nicolson (p. 286) speaks of the 'sighing rustle' of the last line of Tennyson's poem. One of the poem's movements seems to be from the Italian names at the beginning, with the Latin name within Sirmione, to the Latin phrases of Catullus by which his two poems mingle, then to the compounds at the end, where Tennyson's English claims and in a sense renews the Latin of Catullus, and finally to the Latin name. Rachel Trickett ('Tennyson's Craft,' Lincoln, Tennyson Society Occasional Paper No. 4, 1981, p. 15) comments that 'the last descriptions are delighted literal translations of Catullus' own words – Lydian laughter, all-but-island, olive-silvery Sirmio', which is true of the first two of these descriptions.

22   George Saintsbury, *Historical Manual of English Prosody*, London, Macmillan, 1910, p. 124.

23   C.S. Calverley, 'On Metrical Translations', *The Complete Works of C.S. Calverley*, with biographical notice by Walter I. Sendall, London, 1920, pp. 501–2; Eversley II, pp. 378–9.

24   J.B. Leishman, *Translating Horace*, Oxford, Bruno Cassirer, 1956, pp. 55–8.

25   Gilbert Highet draws attention to Tennyson's 'lonely word', in a brief but enlightening comment on individual style in Greek and Roman poetry (*op. cit.*, pp. 157–8).

26 Edward Lear's diary, quoted by Martin, pp. 455–6.
27 Ricks, p. 1374n. See Buckley, *Tennyson: The Growth of a Poet*, pp. 245–6.
28 Walter Pater, 'The Myth of Demeter and Persephone', *Greek Studies*, London, 1910, reprinted 1967, p. 102. This two-part essay was first published in the *Fortnightly Review* for January and February 1876; the similarity with Tennyson's poem was pointed out by James Kissane, 'Victorian Mythology', *Victorian Studies*, vi, 1962, pp. 5–28.
29 Ricks, p. 1373.
30 Curtis Dahl, 'A Double Frame for Tennyson's *Demeter*?', *Victorian Studies*, i, 1958, pp. 356–62.
31 Paul Valéry, letter to Albert Mockel, May 1918, *Lettres à Quelques-uns*, Paris, Gallimard, p. 128; Marcel Raymond, 'Paul Valéry, ou le classique du Symbolisme', *De Baudelaire au Surréalisme*, Paris, Librairie José Corti, 1940, pp. 153–69.
32 Ricks, p. 1412.
33 *Ibid.*

Select Bibliography of
Works Quoted

Armstrong, Isobel, ed., *The Major Victorian Poets: Reconsiderations*, London, Routledge & Kegan Paul, 1969.

Armstrong, Isobel, *Language as Living Form in Nineteenth Century Poetry*, Brighton, Harvester Press, 1982.

Auden, W.H., *Tennyson: An Introduction and a Selection*, London, Phoenix House, 1946.

Ball, Patricia, *The Central Self*, London, Athlone Press, 1968.

Basler, Roy, *Sex, Symbolism, and Psychology in Literature*, New Brunswick, Rutgers University Press, 1948.

Baum, Paull, *Tennyson Sixty Years After*, Chapel Hill, University of North Carolina Press, 1948.

Blackmur, Richard P., *Language as Gesture: Essays in Poetry*, London, Allen & Unwin, 1961.

Bradley, A.C., *A Commentary on 'In Memoriam'*, 3rd edn, London, Macmillan, 1910.

Brooks, Cleanth, *The Well Wrought Urn: Studies in the Structure of Poetry*, New York, Harcourt Brace, 1947.

Buckley, Jerome H., *Tennyson: The Growth of a Poet*, Cambridge, Massachusetts, Harvard University Press, 1960.

Clausen, Wendell, 'An Intepretation of the *Aeneid*', in Commager, ed., *Virgil: A Collection of Critical Essays*.

Commager, Steele, ed., *Virgil: A Collection of Critical Essays*, Englewood Cliffs, N.J., Prentice-Hall, 1966.

Culler, A. Dwight, *The Poetry of Tennyson*, New Haven and London, Yale University Press, 1977.

Dahl, Curtis, 'A Double Frame for Tennyson's *Demeter*?', *Victorian Studies*, i, 1958.

Davie, Donald, 'T.S. Eliot: The End of an Era', in Kenner, ed., *T.S. Eliot: A Collection of Critical Essays*.

Select Bibliography

Dodsworth, Martin, 'Patterns of Morbidity: Repetition in Tennyson's Poetry', in Armstrong, ed., *The Major Victorian Poets: Reconsiderations.*

Dudley, D.R., ed., *Lucretius*, London, Routledge & Kegan Paul, 1965.

Eliot, T.S., *'In Memoriam'*, *Selected Essays*, London, Faber & Faber, 1969.

Fausset, Hugh I'Anson, *Tennyson, A Modern Portrait*, London, Jonathan Cape, 1923.

Fordyce, C.J., *Catullus: A Commentary*, Oxford University Press, 1961.

Fredeman, W.E., ' "A Sign Betwixt the Meadow and the Cloud": The Ironic Apotheosis of Tennyson's "St Simeon Stylites" ', *University of Toronto Quarterly*, xxxviii, 1968.

Glover, Terrot R., *Studies in Virgil*, London, Edward Arnold, 1904.

Gray, J.M., 'Fact, Form, and Fiction in Tennyson's *Balin and Balan*', *Renaissance and Modern Studies*, xii, 1968.

Gray, J.M., *Man and Myth in Victorian England: Tennyson's 'The Coming of Arthur'*, Tennyson Research Centre, Lincoln, 1969.

Gray, J.M., 'A Study in Idyl: Tennyson's *The Coming of Arthur*', *Renaissance and Modern Studies*, xiv, 1970.

Gray, J.M., *Tennyson's Doppelgänger: 'Balin and Balan'*, Lincoln, Tennyson Research Centre, 1971.

Grisewood, H., ed., *Epoch and Artist*, London, Faber & Faber, 1973.

Highet, Gilbert, *Poets in a Landscape*, Harmondsworth, Middlesex, Penguin Books, 1959.

Hunt, John Dixon, ed., *Tennyson: 'In Memoriam': A Casebook*, London, Macmillan, 1970.

Jacobson, Howard, *Ovid's Heroides*, Princeton University Press, 1974.

Johnson, E.D.H., 'The Lily and the Rose: Symbolic Meaning in Tennyson's *Maud*', PMLA, lxiv, 1949.

Johnson, E.D.H., *The Alien Vision of Victorian Poetry*, Princeton University Press, 1952.

Jones, David, 'The Myth of Arthur', in H. Grisewood, ed., *Epoch and Artist*, 1973.

Joseph, Gerard, *Tennysonian Love: The Strange Diagonal*, Minneapolis, University of Minnesota Press, 1969.

Jump, John D., ed., *Tennyson: The Critical Heritage*, London, Routledge & Kegan Paul, 1967.

Select Bibliography

Kenner, Hugh, ed., *T.S. Eliot: A Collection of Critical Essays*, Englewood Cliffs, N.J., Prentice-Hall, 1962.

Killham, John, *Tennyson and 'The Princess': Reflections of an Age*, London, Athlone Press, 1958.

Killham, John, ed., *Critical Essays on the Poetry of Tennyson*, London, Routledge & Kegan Paul, 1960.

Kissane, James, 'Victorian Mythology', *Victorian Studies*, vi, 1962.

Knowles, James, 'Aspects of Tennyson, I & II: A Personal Reminiscence', *Nineteenth Century*, xxxiii, 1893.

Leishman, J.B., *Translating Horace*, Oxford, Bruno Cassirer, 1956.

Lewis, C.S., *The Allegory of Love: A Study in Mediaeval Tradition*, Oxford University Press, 1938.

Lorca, Federico García, 'Elegy for María Blanchard', in *Deep Song and Other Prose*, ed. and trans. Christopher Maurer, London and Boston, Marion Boyars, 1980.

Mackail, J.W., *Lectures on Greek Poetry*, London, Longmans, 1910.

Mallarmé, Stéphane, *Oeuvres Complètes*, ed. Henri Mondor and G. Jean-Aubry, Paris, Gallimard, Bibliothèque de la Pléiade, 1961.

Mann, R.J., 'Tennyson's "Maud" Vindicated: An Explanatory Essay', London, 1856.

Mantell, Deborah Byrd, '*The Princess*: Tennyson's Eminently Shakespearian Poem', *Texas Studies in Literature and Language*, xx, No. 1, 1978.

Martin, Robert Bernard, *Tennyson: The Unquiet Heart*, Oxford, The Clarendon Press, 1980.

Mattes, Eleanor B., '*In Memoriam*': *The Way of a Soul. A Study of Some Influences that Shaped Tennyson's Poem*, New York, Exposition Press, 1951.

Maurois, André, *Promethée, ou la Vie de Balzac*, Paris, Librairie Hachette, 1965.

Munro, H.A.J., *T. Lucreti Cari, De Rerum Natura*, Cambridge, Deighton Bell, 1864.

Nicolson, Harold, *Tennyson: Aspects of His Life, Character, and Poetry*, London, Constable, 1923.

Paden, W.D., *Tennyson in Egypt: A Study of the Imagery in his Earlier Work*, Lawrence, Kansas, 1942.

Paden, W.D., 'MT. 1352: Jacques de Vitry, The Mensa Philosophica, Hödeken, and Tennyson', *Journal of American Folklore*, lviii, 1945.

Pattison, Robert, *Tennyson and Tradition*, Cambridge, Mass., Harvard University Press, 1979.

Pettigrew, John, 'Tennyson's "Ulysses": A Reconciliation of Opposites', *Victorian Poetry*, i, 1963.

Pettigrew, John, *Tennyson: The Early Poems*, London, Edward Arnold, 1970.

Priestley, F.E.L., 'Tennyson's *Idylls*', *University of Toronto Quarterly*, xxiii, 1949.

Priestley, F.E.L., *Language and Structure in Tennyson's Poetry*, London, André Deutsch, 1973.

Puckett, Harry, 'Subjunctive Imagination in *In Memoriam*', *Victorian Poetry*, xii, 1974.

Pyre, J.F.A., *The Formation of Tennyson's Style*, Madison, University of Wisconsin, 1921.

Rader, R.W., *Tennyson's 'Maud': The Biographical Genesis*, Berkeley and Los Angeles, University of California Press, 1963.

Ray, Gordon N., 'Tennyson Reads "Maud" ', Sedgewick Memorial Lecture, University of British Columbia, Vancouver, 1968.

Raymond, Marcel, *De Baudelaire au Surréalisme*, Paris, Librairie José Corti, 1940.

Richardson, Joanna, *The Pre-Eminent Victorian: A Study of Tennyson*, London, Jonathan Cape, 1962.

Ricks, Christopher, ed., *The Poems of Tennyson*, London, Longmans, Green, 1969.

Ricks, Christopher, *Tennyson*, New York, Macmillan, 1972.

Rivarol, Antoine, Comte de, Preface to *L'Enfer, poème de Dante (traduction nouvelle)*, Paris, 1785.

Rosenberg, John, *The Fall of Camelot*, Cambridge, Mass., Harvard University Press, 1973.

Saintsbury, George, *Historical Manual of English Prosody*, London, Macmillan, 1910.

Shatto, Susan, and Shaw, Marion, *Tennyson: 'In Memoriam'*, Oxford, Clarendon Press, 1982.

Shaw, W. David, *Tennyson's Style*, Ithaca and London, Cornell University Press, 1976.

Smalley, Donald, 'A New Look at Tennyson – and especially the Idylls', *Journal of English and Germanic Philology*, lxi, 1962.

Stedman, E.C., *Victorian Poets*, London, Chatto & Windus, 1876.

Tennyson, Alfred, *The Works of Tennyson* (Eversley Edition), ed. Hallam Tennyson, 9 vols, London, Macmillan, 1907–8.

Tennyson, Alfred, *Works*, London, Macmillan, 1913.

Tennyson, Sir Charles, *Alfred Tennyson*, London, Macmillan, 1950.

Select Bibliography

Tennyson, Hallam, *Alfred Lord Tennyson: A Memoir by His Son*, 2 vols, London, Macmillan, 1897.

Tennyson, Hallam (ed.), *Tennyson and His Friends*, London, Macmillan, 1911.

Tillotson, Geoffrey and Kathleen, *Mid-Victorian Studies*, London University Press, 1965.

Trickett, Rachel, 'Tennyson's Craft', Lincoln, Tennyson Society Occasional Paper No. 4, 1981.

Turner, Paul, *Tennyson*, London, Routledge & Kegan Paul, 1976.

Valéry, Paul, *Oeuvres Complètes*, 2 vols, ed. Jean Hytier, Paris, Gallimard, Bibliothèque de la Pléiade, 1962.

Waddell, Helen, *Mediaeval Latin Lyrics*, London, Constable, 1948.

Wolfe, Humbert, *Tennyson*, London, Faber & Faber, 1930.

Wordsworth, Jonathan, ' "What is it, that has been done?": the Central Problem of *Maud*', *Essays in Criticism*, xxiv, October, 1974, pp. 356–62.

Wormell, D.E.W., 'The Personal World of Lucretius', in D.R. Dudley, ed., *Lucretius*, London, Routledge & Kegan Paul, 1965.

Index

Index

Index

Index

Wordsworth, William, 11, 21, 32, 37, 40, 49, 50, 61, 160, 162, 170, 181, 199, 200–1, 203, 204, 221, 240, 247, 248, 252

Wormell, D.E.W., 265

Yeats, W.B., 51, 83, 198, 201, 218, 245